Burn

THE LIFE AND TIMES OF
MICHAEL HUTCHENCE AND INXS

Ed St John

Bantam Books
Sydney • Auckland • Toronto • New York • London

BURN: THE LIFE AND TIMES OF MICHAEL HUTCHENCE AND INXS
A BANTAM BOOK

First published in Australia and New Zealand
in 1998 by Bantam

St. John, Ed.
  Burn: the life and times of Michael Hutchence and INXS

  Includes index.
  ISBN 0 7338 0182 X.

  1. Hutchence, Michael. 2. INXS (Musical group). I. Title.

781.66092

Bantam books are published by

Transworld Publishers (Aust) Pty Limited
15–25 Helles Ave, Moorebank, NSW 2170

Transworld Publishers (NZ) Limited
3 William Pickering Drive, Albany, Auckland

Transworld Publishers (UK) Limited
61–63 Uxbridge Road, Ealing, London W5 5SA

Bantam Doubleday Dell Publishing Group Inc
1540 Broadway, New York, New York 10036

Edited by Rowena Lennox
Index by Keyword Editorial Services
Cover and text design by Liz Seymour
Typeset by Midland Typesetters, Victoria
Printed by McPherson's Printing Group, Victoria

10 9 8 7 6 5 4 3 2 1

Contents

Acknowledgments

The author would like to thank the following people for their invaluable assistance: Phillip Mortlock, Rose Creswell, Richard Clapton, Jude McGee, Katie Stackhouse, Rowena Lennox, Mark Opitz, Nick Launay, David Nicholas, Grant Thomas, Trevor Smith, Richard Wilkins, Gary Grant, Michael Browning, Chrissie Camp, Bruce Butler, Toby Creswell, James Valentine, Robert Young, Susan Chenery, Donald Robertson, Clive Hodson, Katrina Ross and those of you who have elected to remain anonymous.

Special thanks to Katey and all my long-suffering friends and family — and most of all, to my wife, Susan, and our sons, Henry and Thomas, with all my love and gratitude.

In Memoriam: Michael Hutchence

Introduction

E very action, they say, has an equal and opposite reaction. What goes up must come down.

The story you are about to read is about a rock 'n' roll band that put this to the test. INXS began when six very normal suburban teenagers from Sydney, Australia found themselves drawn to the idea of forming a band and taking on the world. What was remarkable was that they possessed the spirit and the verve to pull it off.

Over the first thirteen years of the band's career, they worked tirelessly to attain levels of greatness and heights of fame that most of us can only dream of. Forgoing virtually everything that we take for granted — friends, families and personal interests — the six members of INXS gave every ounce of their emotional and physical energy to take their music to audiences all over the world. For thirteen solid years they maintained a commitment to their music, and to each other, that was unbreakable.

And, in return, the band watched as their fame and their bank balances grew to unimaginable heights. For each and every one of those thirteen years, the band simply grew bigger, and bigger, and bigger. It was, literally, like a fairy-tale. INXS came to inhabit a stratosphere of superstardom that few people in any generation attain — a level that only a handful of Australians have ever experienced. In the context of their country of origin, they were astronauts of fame; stars who burned brightly on the international scene — for a while.

INXS were rock stars in the original sense; they were not negative, shoe-gazing introverts but swashbuckling brigands with a healthy appetite for sex, drugs and rock 'n' roll. They were humble entertainers and yet they were somehow heroic, larger than life.

At the time of their extraordinary global success, INXS were fond of quoting the maxim, 'Be careful of what you want, because you might just get it'. It was an easy thing for these affable and talented young men to think: they had willed a dream into a reality, after all. As they basked in the glow of a thousand spotlights, surrounded by the most beau-tiful and famous people in the world, they were able to indulge themselves in the pursuit of unbridled pleasure. In the parlance of the eighties, they had chosen their reality, and now they were living it.

In so many ways, INXS were emblematic of the decade. They defied the odds to climb the highest peaks — and in their moment of victory, they celebrated lustily. Others might have downplayed their wealth and fame; INXS paraded it. They strutted and swaggered in a bold display of conspicuous consumption. Everything about them upheld the 'greed is good' eighties ethic.

But then, quite unexpectedly, the fuel that had propelled INXS to these heights — luck, talent, sheer determination or a mixture of all three — burned out. The trajectory of success reached its zenith and, from that moment, the band's popularity and annual income went into a steep and inexorable slide. Whatever had changed, whatever they had lost, INXS were unable to get it back.

So this is a story about the price of fame and the nature of the beast. It's about six young men who went out into the world to achieve their dreams — only to find that they would hold those dreams close for barely an instant before they began trickling away between their fingers.

And yes, this is the story of one very charismatic and fascinating man: INXS lead singer Michael Hutchence. Much as Michael started his life with his feet on the same soil as the other five members of the band, it quickly emerged that he was made up of different matter. As INXS grew, and as he developed his skills as a singer, songwriter and performer, it became apparent to everyone around him that Michael Hutchence was incredibly good at what he did. As he was to later say himself, he made a bloody good rock star.

Michael Hutchence had one of the greatest singing voices of the modern era. His languid, sexy voice could lilt softly over a funk groove, or soar into full flight on the updraft of some anthemic, guitar-driven rock 'n' roll. As a songwriter, Michael brought his razor-sharp wit, his love of film and literature, and his wealth of intensely lived personal experience to create lyrics of lasting resonance. Michael was never afraid to expose his inner-most feelings and, over the course of his life as a writer, he expressed himself and his own changing position with honesty and eloquence. If, as time went on, he sometimes threw words at the canvas in an almost random, unstructured way, without an excess of analysis or close examination, this was also a reflection of his free and unrestricted soul.

As a performer, Michael Hutchence was like a bird in flight. A graceful and eminently watchable physical presence on the stage, he expressed an unconcealed sexual energy without ever resorting to stereotypes. Possessed with an onstage confidence that was often in marked contrast to his ironic, self-effacing demeanour offstage, he always appeared to be enjoying himself immensely.

Michael Hutchence knew many people in his life; he was a man who made friends easily, and he certainly had the opportunity to meet many of the most colourful individuals of his age. To this life of a jet-setting rock star, he brought his insouciant charm and his louche sophistication. He wore a smile that said he enjoyed his life and appreciated its ironies. He appeared arrogant to the casual observer, when in truth he was often racked with self-doubt; beneath an exterior of confidence and grace, there lay a troubled soul. Very few people who met or knew Michael had the chance to know him intimately. He was, in a sense, the ultimate chameleon. Everyone knew a side of his personality, but few people in his life had seen the entire picture. None, it turned out, was prepared for the final, rapid disintegration of his ego that left him dead and his band to find a new direction.

If you're a fan of INXS and Michael Hutchence, you know all of this. Over the coming pages, you'll come to relive the extraordinary career of INXS, and appreciate again the extent of their achievement and the magnitude of their ultimate loss. If, on the other hand, you've been drawn to read this book because of the lurid media coverage of Michael Hutchence's death — if for you he seemed to be

nothing more than a fascinating but one-dimensional cari-
cature of a preening rock star — perhaps these pages can
fill in the gaps. Because the fact is that INXS, and Michael
Hutchence, were very human indeed.

Only human, yet superhuman. And now, sadly, no more.

chapter 1 | Australian Music Day

The members of INXS still remember it well: the night the band achieved their ultimate triumph by headlining one of the largest outdoor venues in the world, London's Wembley Stadium. It was July 13, 1991 — a warm English summer evening — when the band played before a sold-out crowd of almost 75,000 fans.

These fans weren't just the loyal expatriates that routinely roll out to support Australian bands making their first tentative forays into the notoriously tough British market (there were only ever a couple of thousand such people anyway). No, this was a representative slice of INXS's enormous British fan-base — tens of thousands of devotees who had come to see these Australian superstars strut their stuff in a spectacular setting. Even on a leg of a tour that saw the band headlining to crowds of 30,000 or 40,000 people across the length and breadth of western Europe, this was a night to savour.

INXS established a reputation as an excellent live band at the very outset of their career. Their dynamic power onstage, combined with singer Michael Hutchence's sensuous, feline grace, made them irresistible. For years, INXS had blown audiences away with performances of conviction and heart-stopping excitement; they'd won over the entire Australian continent before turning their hands to the USA. It took INXS six long, hard years to crack the US — and by the early nineties, they were finally bringing the UK and Europe into their fold.

Timing is everything in pop music. Many talented artists have released the wrong record at the wrong time, and seen their hard work fall on deaf ears. But in Europe and Britain in 1991, INXS's winning combination of supple grooves, streetwise attitude and rock 'n' roll swagger was perfect. For that moment in history, INXS were one of the five biggest bands in the world.

Michael Hutchence was a natural performer — a man who relaxed onstage as if he were in his own living room. Onstage at Wembley, he performed with a loose-limbed self-confidence that wasn't arrogant or self-satisfied. If he was overwhelmed by the crowd's enthusiasm (and let's face it, who wouldn't be?) the experience only gave him strength. 'This is the biggest pub we've ever played,' he announced to the crowd between songs. He was laughing. The whole band was laughing. This was a moment they would cherish forever.

Michael Hutchence was short-sighted. From where he stood on the stage at Wembley, he saw an audience that stretched into the distance, quite literally as far as he could see. In the gathering twilight, the audience appeared to go on forever, a sea of love and adulation that spilled out over the walls of the arena and into the streets of the capital. In this, the second summer of love, when English youth appeared to be floating on a loving cloud of Ecstasy, INXS were in synchronisation with the heartbeat of London. If Michael

Hutchence had spent his life in fear of being left alone, this was his enveloping moment of peace and happiness.

At a pre-ordained moment in the set — just before the opening bars of 'The Stairs' — Michael dropped handfuls of Ecstasy. This was the biggest party they'd ever thrown, and even in this demanding professional environment (the concert was being filmed for a concert video, relayed live to a radio audience of millions and taped for a future live album) the singer was determined to maximise the moment.

There was a lot of love in the house, a lot of chemicals in the system and one genuinely hilarious moment near the end of the set when Tim Farriss forgot to terminate a guitar solo (the problem was only solved when Michael Hutchence, audible to the entire crowd, yelled into his ear, 'Just play the fucking riff, Timmy!'). As the final songs — 'What You Need' and 'Need You Tonight' — erupted in a tightly controlled explosion of pulsating beat and sizzling guitar riffs, and as thousands of fans danced themselves into a joyous frenzy, INXS soaked in the moment like a warm bath.

Fate and circumstance can be unpredictable taskmasters. As INXS played Wembley, they envisaged a life of success that would stretch on into an infinite future. They had certainly worked hard enough to achieve their lifetime goals, and they probably had every right to believe that their lives would now become a little easier. Nobody had told them that maintaining success could be much harder than achieving it. They imagined, as we are all prone to do, that life would continue to get better. They were not to know that in some strange and inexplicable twist, the plug had already been pulled from that all-enveloping bath of love. And as it drained over the ensuing six years, the band were left feeling increasingly stranded and isolated. Until one day in November 1997, when it finally disappeared.

Australian Music Day was to have been one of those grand occasions of which any nation would feel rightly proud. Formulated by a number of companies and government-funded organisations that had a vested interest in such things — including a radio syndication company and the governing body of the major Australian record companies — it was instituted in 1990. On the very first Australian Music Day, decreed as the third Saturday in November, an ambitious series of concerts featuring some of the best bands working in Australia at that time were staged in a number of capital cities and telecast via an ambitious live TV hook-up.

On Australian Music Day, it was proclaimed, pressure would be placed on Australian radio stations — which normally play about 20 per cent domestic content — to play home-grown music all day. All sorts of other events were to be staged around the country in an effort to promote original Australian music. It was a time to celebrate the achievements of the Australian artists who had defied the odds and made a mark on the international recording scene, a time to offer new hope to the hundreds of hopefuls ready to follow in their footsteps. It was one of those worthy, interventionist initiatives that was always bound to fail.

Over time, Australian Music Day came to have less and less meaning. In 1991 and 1992, an ambitious awards ceremony called the Australian Music Awards (the AMAs) had been staged to mark the occasion. The awards were discontinued after 1992 — and yet, strangely, the day continued to hold a certain significance. On the third Saturday in November 1996, for example, Crowded House planned to stage an enormous outdoor concert in the forecourt of the Sydney Opera House to bid a sentimental farewell to their enormous Australian and international audience. Unfortunately for the organisers — and for the legion of hardcore fans who had travelled from all over the country, and from abroad, to see this historic final moment — Australian Music Day was a stinker. Violent storms lashed the city for most of the day, and the concert was postponed to the Sunday.

And so it came to pass that, under clear skies, with a warm breeze blowing in off Sydney Harbour, Neil Finn and his band-mates played their historic and emotion-charged final concert — before a crowd estimated to be well over 100,000 people. The concert was subsequently televised all over the world. A day late, but worth the wait.

Australian Music Day 1997 began innocently enough. Radio stations all over the nation had been playing a steady diet of Australian music all week. In all of the nations' major capital cities and a good many regional centres concert bills featuring Australian music (including the well-attended Push-over Festival in Melbourne) were being staged. As crews went about the business of setting up the stages, another crew belonging to Australia's most successful international rock export, INXS, were preparing the band's gear in an old TV rehearsal studio at the Australian Broadcasting Corporation's (ABC's) Gore Hill complex.

Saturday, November 22, 1997 was to have been the third day of rehearsals for an Australian tour that INXS had jokingly titled Lose Your Head (the name referred to the band's then-current single, 'Don't Lose Your Head', from their tenth album, *Elegantly Wasted*). The band had been playing, on and off, for most of the year, commencing with several months of promotional appearances and TV performances, and culminating in short tours of Europe and the USA. It had been INXS's first proper world tour in six years and the Australian dates were to coincide with the twentieth anniversary of the band's six-man line-up.

It was a strange time for INXS. For members of the band and the 20-odd people included in the INXS inner sanctum, 1997 had been a year in which they were finally clawing back some of the ground that had been lost in recent years. But to other observers, it seemed that the band was playing out the final stages of an elaborate endgame that had been dragging on for years.

INXS were part of a generation of groups that had emerged in the halcyon days of the Australian pub rock boom, flogging their way through the sweaty beer-barns of suburban Australia in the late seventies and early eighties before mounting assaults — like butterflies flying into an electric fan — on the world market. A surprising number of bands overcame the immense odds to make it, including, to a greater or lesser extent, Men At Work, Midnight Oil, The Divinyls, The Birthday Party, The Church, Split Enz, The Hoodoo Gurus, The Black Sorrows, The Angels (or Angel City in the USA) Icehouse and Mental As Anything. Most were, by world standards, mere one-hit wonders (often only in isolated markets in Europe or in Japan). Others burnt brightly for a year or so. Only INXS had truly conquered the world.

From the mid-eighties until the early nineties, INXS strutted the largest stages in the world, playing to massive audiences and selling millions of albums. (Their total sales tally was almost 20 million albums.) But later, the band's fortunes declined and rumours circulated that the band might be contemplating a final split. With the six members of INXS all in their late thirties and early forties, they were reaching a critical moment in their career.

The Australian dates were to be their last official commitment before an extended hiatus. For many people working with INXS, the overriding question was not what to do next, but whether there would be anything to do at all. The band's pride and commitment to one another and to their music remained intact, but their core audience had dwindled to less than a million committed fans. Many bands would kill for a fan-base of this size but it was hard to imagine INXS remaining intact for a small but loyal band of true believers, spread as they were over dozens of countries. Much as they were still playing great shows, there was no escaping the fact that INXS were facing the immutable law of diminishing returns.

By 10.30 am on Saturday, November 22, 1997, most of the band members were awake and making preparations to get to the rehearsal studios by midday. The streets of Sydney were alive with the usual Saturday morning traffic, made worse by the onset of Olympic construction and the imminence of Christmas. In upmarket Double Bay — a suburb of Sydney renowned for its glitzy, Rodeo Drive-style fashion stores and jewellery dealers — the BMWs and Mercedes Benzes jostled for parking spaces while seriously over-dressed women sat drinking coffee in outdoor cafes. The day was warm and the sun was shining on the sparkling blue harbour, a typical Sydney scene.

Five floors above the Double Bay streets, in Room 524 of the Ritz Carlton hotel, something terrible had happened. In the silent, curtained room — trashed from a night of drinking and partying, with sleeping pills and prescription medication strewn all over the floor — INXS frontman Michael Hutchence lay naked on the floor. A leather belt was wrapped around his neck. He was alone.

By the time a hotel staff member discovered this gruesome scene at midday — just as the five other members of INXS were turning up for rehearsal — Michael Hutchence was dead. On Australian Music Day 1997, Australia lost one of its brightest stars — and its biggest band.

In the days and weeks that followed, Sydney police refused to offer a concrete explanation of how Hutchence had died. While the forensic report from nearby Rose Bay police was made available to the singer's family and the band, it asked as many questions as it answered. Prescription drugs were found at the scene, but what about illicit ones? Michael was alone in his room when he died, or so it appeared, but what had happened in that room in the hours before his death? Hutchence had dropped in two letters to the hotel's reception desk approximately one hour before he died. Were they suicide notes? And what was the content of the phone calls to his former girlfriend, Michelle Bennett, his manager, Martha Troup, his partner, Paula Yates, and her ex-husband, Bob Geldof, in the last few desperate hours of his life?

Theories abounded. Some believed that Michael was suffering the effects of ongoing depression, which had started several years before and was only exacerbated by the cocktail of anti-depressants, alcohol and cocaine that was coursing through his body. Others were convinced that the burden of fame, the uncertainty of his career and the pressures of his recent legal battles had finally taken their savage toll. And there were a great many others who saw it in all its tawdry glory, as a kinky sex act gone horribly wrong. Lurid rumours were circulating through the music industry corridors and on the Internet within days, and, as time went by, the rumours seemed to multiply and echo.

Of course, there was the distinct possibility that Michael Hutchence died as a result of any or all of these things. His friends and colleagues knew that he was capable of anything. But, over time, it became apparent that the truth was much simpler — albeit no less poignant or tragic. Contrary to many people's suspicions, Michael Hutchence had hung himself in a deliberate act of suicide. Difficult as it might have been to believe, this was no accident.

In a moment of extreme intoxication and deeply felt frustration and anger, strung out somewhere between the desire for relief, the desire for pleasure and the desire for some kind of resolution, some kind of escape or some kind of *peace*, Michael Hutchence did something that he had no control over. The effects of his action were either obscured, or at least dulled, by years spent on the precipice.

In his hour of desperation, Michael Hutchence — a man who had lived for pleasure, and who had lived his life giving pleasure to others — found himself unable to do either. He had spent 37 years keeping all his loneliness, insecurity and self-doubt at bay and now it all returned with more force than ever before. In that moment, he was sucked into his own vortex.

Michael Hutchence was dead, and INXS as we knew them were no more.

chapter 2 | # Beginnings

I f the line-up of virtually all rock bands is the result of a random series of unrelated events, the circumstances that led to the formation of INXS are probably no stranger than most. Had any one of these events taken a different course, six teenage boys would not have found themselves occupying the same patch of ground on Sydney's north shore in the mid-seventies, and a little slice of pop history would never have happened.

Michael Hutchence was born in Sydney at approximately 5 am on January 22, 1960. He was the first child of Kell Hutchence and his wife Pat — although Pat already had a child, Tina, from a previous marriage. Kell Hutchence was a businessman who had the vision to see the enormous potential in Asia's economies. In 1964 he moved to Hong Kong with his young family and established a business importing Australian wines and spirits. Later, he shifted the focus of his business to fashion.

'Dad was trying to get Hong Kong people into Australian wine,' Michael was to recall of his early life, 'but he soon moved into the fashion business — making expensive clothing for people with too much money, of which there were many in Hong Kong. All I remember was a load of parties full of socialites and some good music — James Brown, Bacharach, a lot of soul music. Mine were hip parents.

'We had a Shanghai maid at home, with a long ponytail to her bum with a little red bow, white top, black patents and slippers,' he recalls fondly. 'There were all these out-there people who passed through our house. It wasn't snobby or colonial. People had a really good time, everyone was creative and very positive. Joss sticks and Pucci clothes. My sister was a go-go dancer. All that stuff.'

For the first eight years of his education, Michael attended Hong Kong's King George V school with other expatriate kids. It was his first taste of an internationalist perspective, playing and learning alongside the children of wealthy diplomats and business people from all over the world, including Natassja Kinski, the now famous daughter of actor Klaus Kinski. Witnessing the electrifying blend of cultures that he found in Hong Kong and the notorious anti-communist riots of the sixties gave Michael a taste for excitement and the exotic that was well beyond the scope of ordinary adolescents growing up in the Australian suburbs.

In 1972, when Michael was 12, the family — which now included younger brother Rhett — returned to Sydney and moved to the north shore suburb of Belrose, where Michael was enrolled at Davidson High School in the suburb of Frenchs Forest. Situated on a ridge of land that lies between the northern beachside suburbs and a vast expanse of suburbia and bushland, this is a part of Sydney that is relentlessly middle class. Large homes set back from leafy streets are reached by long driveways. The north shore — populated by deeply conservative, white, Anglophile families — has always been renowned for its conspicuous lack of nightlife.

On his first day at high school, Michael got himself into a fight. Upon arriving at school he immediately stood out: not only did his accent reflect eight years of life in a British colony, but he had a manner that was soft, effete and somehow aloof. In this bland seventies monoculture that abhorred anything out of the ordinary, Michael was a sitting duck. In the parlance of the day, he was 'up himself'.

'I was dumb enough to pick a fight with the biggest guy in the school,' he was to remark later. 'I had four or five guys whacking me around at lunchtime, throwing fruit at me and shit. I was scared.' He was saved by two boys from the same class. One happened to be very large, which is why Michael walked away unharmed from the fight. The other happened to be Andrew Farriss, the second eldest in a family of four who had lived in Perth for most of their lives. They had settled in Sydney only two years before.

Michael and Andrew became best friends almost overnight. In their way, they were both misfits who had little in common with the sport-obsessed teenagers in their class. Michael was a sensitive soul, a deep thinker with a passion for reading — and writing — poetry. Andrew was an equally intense and complex young man and was already showing a strong interest in music.

But the friendship appeared destined not to last. In 1975, after a period of marital instability and conflict, Kell and Patricia Hutchence parted. When Pat announced that she intended to move to Los Angeles to pursue her career as a make-up artist, Michael decided to follow. For a little less than two years, the teenage Michael was exposed to another formative experience, enrolled in the socio-cultural hotbed that was North Hollywood High. According to Hutchence, he spent most of his time not in school, but playing pool — even going so far as to break into rich people's houses to use their pool tables. He also found the lifestyles of Californian teenagers to his liking. It was in LA that he discovered two of the loves of his life: marijuana and girls.

Much as he was fond of playing up this period in United States as a time of intensive life-education, the fact was that Michael was deeply disturbed by his parents' divorce. Pat Hutchence moved house several times. Michael had no permanent father figure to bond with or to look up to. For this already sensitive teenager, it was a confronting and profoundly disturbing experience that turned him in upon himself. Although his shyness never prevented him from meeting girls (Michael had been attractive to the opposite sex for as long as anyone could remember), he became increasingly immersed in poetry.

'He was taken from a very middle-class set-up into a traumatising, nomadic existence,' comments Gerry Agar, a public relations consultant who worked for both Michael Hutchence and his partner Paula Yates in the mid nineties. 'That was part and parcel of his problems — you take all that crap with you. With those different fathers, different influences, he was a mass of confusion, a collage of identities.'

By 1976, Kell Hutchence was sufficiently worried about Michael that he sought, and was granted, sole custody over his two sons. Within weeks, Michael was on the move again — back to Australia and back to his father's house in Belrose, where he re-enrolled at Davidson High to complete his education.

This period was critical in the history of the Hutchence family and to Michael's development as a person. The break-up of Kell and Patricia's marriage, and the impact it had on their two sons, continued to have repercussions through the years. Even after Michael's death those repercussions continued to resonate. While he found his mother to be often overbearingly possessive and unpredictable, Michael remained a loving and dutiful son. His dealings with his siblings were intense and frequently fraught with drama. Of all the members of his family, it was his father that he was closest to. If Michael had a relationship that provided him with an emotional centre, a constant and undemanding kind of parental love, it was the bond he had with Kell Hutchence. No matter how famous he became, or how crazy his life became, he always found the time to visit his Dad.

Michael was happy to be back in Sydney with his father and brother, and within days, he renewed his friendship with Andrew Farriss, who was already well on his way to choosing a career in music. Before long, Andrew had talked Michael into joining his band, Doctor Dolphin — a group that only ever existed in the rehearsal room. The band contained two other classmates, Kent Kerny and Neil Sanders, and a guy from the year below at nearby Forest High: a bass player by the name of Garry Beers.

'I was a bit of a joke to these guys,' Beers was to remember of these early days. 'But I did have a car — and a licence. It was a real shag-wagon, even though I was a virgin. I was 18 or 19 before I got laid, but there was Michael, already fucking everyone in sight at 15 or 16.'

Michael and Andrew found Garry rather straight. Like all good teenage musicians, they were into pot, while Garry was more of a beer man. Gradually, they converted him and Garry has fond memories of driving all over Sydney with Andrew and Michael, blowing joints and listening to cassettes in the car.

Doctor Dolphin were only ever a bedroom phenomenon and they were never great. But Andrew's two brothers, Tim and Jon, were also budding musicians. One day in 1977, Tim (Andrew's older brother by three years) found a use for Doctor Dolphin: he wanted to take the best elements of the band (Andrew, Garry and Michael) and marry them to his long-standing musical partnership with his schoolmate Kirk Pengilly. Kirk and Tim had been playing together since 1971 as classmates at Forest High, working at various times as either an acoustic duo or as a four-piece band called Guiness. 'We basically had that band going for most of our high school years and about two years after we left,' recalls Kirk. 'It was a band that meant a lot to me because I wrote all the songs and I was the singer as well. We actually auditioned Jon as drummer at one point but he was only nine years old so we kicked him out.'

By the time the best elements of Doctor Dolphin and Guiness were coalescing, Tim and Andrew's younger brother Jon was 16; he had improved immeasurably (indeed he was already working in a covers band called Top Cat) and he was given the job. It only took one jam session for Tim Farriss to know that this was something special. Almost instantly, he recognised that Michael Hutchence was someone who had some amazing qualities as a singer and frontman. And so, after a brief period of rehearsal, the band was ready to appear in public.

On August 16, 1977 (Tim Farriss's twentieth birthday and the night the world learned that Elvis Aaron Presley had passed from one Graceland to another) Michael Hutchence, Kirk Pengilly, Garry Beers and Andrew, Tim and Jon Farriss made their debut as The Farriss Brothers. It was a shocking name, as most band members would come to realise, but it was to stick for a full two years.

The band's early rehearsals were to typify their musical dynamic. With six strong-willed young men, who — even then — had widely divergent musical tastes, the band's song-writing and rehearsals were an exercise in musical exploration, technical development and powerful creative friction.

'Our experimentation with different forms was just incredible,' Jon Farriss remembers. 'We got it all out of our system. We'd do these incredibly complicated suites of music, filled with extraordinary time changes and weird chords. And our poor parents had to listen to it. We were listening to Yes and King Crimson and people like that. And writing original material.'

The late seventies were an exciting time on the Australian music scene. The pub rock boom was in full swing, and on virtually any night of the week, cities such as Sydney and Melbourne had hundreds of pubs (with a capacity for any number from 200 to 2,000 people) featuring live rock 'n' roll. The musical fare was often basic, bluesy rock 'n' roll, and the audience was frequently drunk, violent, belligerent and dom-inated, to a large extent, by men, but it was a fertile envi-ronment that gave Australian music a distinctive flavour.

The pubs themselves varied enormously. Some, like Syd-ney's Civic or Hopetoun or Melbourne's Macy's, were small and relatively intimate, with tiled walls and faded beer posters. Others were enormous, purpose-built meccas of enter-tainment, boasting banks of poker machines and several dif-ferent bars, designed to hold massive numbers of drinkers. Few, if any, had been designed as live music venues but they had all been adapted to accommodate hundreds of sweaty punters most nights of the week.

Sydney especially excelled at this kind of venue. Across the length and breadth of the large, sprawling city lay a network of mega-pubs like Selinas at Coogee Bay, Sweethearts at Cabramatta, The Comb 'n' Cutter at Blacktown, Revesby Workers Club, the cavernous Manly Vale Hotel and, during the halcyon days of the mid to late seventies, that mecca of Oz Rock, The Bondi Lifesaver.

Melbourne had its own network of mega-pubs, including Bombay Rock, the Pier Hotel at Frankston, the Ferntree Gully Hotel and the Chevron.

Overcrowded to the point where it was often impossible to move, the band rooms were an environment of such intense heat and humidity that droplets of moisture would frequently drip from the low ceiling. A dense pall of cigarette smoke would hang in the air, providing graphic proof that the air-conditioning system was not even switched on. Underfoot, the carpet would squelch with wet beer. If you had the misfortune to visit the toilets, it was common to find the facility awash with urine, vomit and water as clogged toilets backed up and spewed their contents all over the floor.

Because of the number and size of the venues, the pub rock scene provided a steady cash flow; bands with a proven ability to pull and entertain an audience could play virtually every night of the week — and those who were willing to work hard were rewarded with something approaching a decent living wage and a wildly decadent lifestyle to match. The pubs were also an incredible proving ground for Australian musicians, an environment in which pretensions and affectations tended to be worn down by the grim reality of entertaining such a tough and demanding audience. In many respects, it was not dissimilar to the atmosphere in the clubs of Liverpool and Germany where so many British bands worked in the late fifties and early sixties, except the rooms were larger, and the beer was colder.

'You get booked into a pub, say in the western suburbs of Sydney,' Midnight Oil vocalist Peter Garrett recalled in a 1985 interview. 'Halfway through your set, two large drunk truckdrivers decide to have a fight. They're beating each other up and careening towards the corner where the band is set up. And meanwhile everyone else is going "Aaah, turn it down, I'm trying to watch TV". Try to contemplate that as an environment to play music.

'The pub audience want rhythm and they want it loud,' he elaborated. 'I think they want to be physically involved in it. They see no value in hanging back, seeing what a band is like and thinking about it, which is what the English audiences do. Australian audiences want to grab a bit of what a band is about and get off on it. In a word, they want to *rage*. That's the word they use.'

In their earliest incarnation, The Farriss Brothers were no match for Sydney's beer barns. Inspired by the new sounds of British punk and new wave — sounds that were unheard of in Australia at that time except in a few small, underground venues — the band were intent on presenting music that was both entertaining and challenging. Much as the band wanted to work the pubs, they saw themselves as representing a new generation, a new way of working, and they were determined to be more than just another Aussie pub band. Michael Hutchence was also a fey and affected lead singer — so much so that early audiences were inclined to dismiss him as homosexual (and in Australia in the seventies, particularly in a pub, being a 'poofter' was one of the worst things to be).

The band were yet to settle on a clear direction, and it would be some time before they would find a way to fit into the pubs. Their influences were many and varied, from The Cars and Steely Dan through to Talking Heads and anything post-punk and British, but they were still a long way from defining their own sound. They were original and different — quite an achievement in those days — but they weren't fully formed. So malleable were they that The Farriss Brothers were even railroaded onto the Christian rock circuit for several months. 'We got involved with the Christian Fellowship thing at that time,' related Jon Farriss years later. 'There was a bearded youth leader who used to organise trips to Wollongong where we'd play.'

The Farriss Brothers would have played virtually anywhere. Most members of the band were supplementing their income with poorly paid part-time jobs. (Garry Beers arranged Michael's first and only 'real' job, in a street light factory. Michael only lasted a week due to his propensity to fall asleep during office hours.) Few, if any, had made the decision to devote themselves to lives as professional musicians. Several band members were still maintaining an involvement with other bands, and Jon was picking up pocket money playing in scratch cabaret bands. According to Michael, Kirk, on the other hand, was sometimes selling pot from the back of his car.

'He had this really straight car like your auntie would drive, with Christian books scattered all over the back seat,' recalled Michael years later in an interview with UK magazine *Q*. 'He had a guitarcase in the back, a good Christian acoustic guitar, and it would just be stuffed full of dope. He'd open it up and do business out of the back of the car. And the cops would never touch him, because they didn't want to get into a conversation about God.'

When the Farriss parents announced that they had decided

to move the family back to Perth with young Jon firmly in tow, as he was still in high school, The Farriss Brothers were faced with their first test. Would they stay in Sydney, and perhaps find another drummer, or would they follow Jon to Perth — an isolated town thousands of kilometres away? Strange as it may have seemed to their friends and families, they decided to go with Jon. As soon as Michael and Andrew finished school at the end of 1977, they headed for Perth.

'The band was loosely formed at that stage,' remembers Tim Farriss. 'In fact Kirk hadn't decided whether he was in or out. It was actually making the decision to go to Perth, which meant signing on the dotted line, which we had to face. We'd made that commitment to quit jobs. It was just on my word that we'd actually have work, but it seemed like a place where you could get things together.'

People join bands for many reasons: to get girls; to get free beer and — if you're lucky — free drugs; to have an instant group of mates and a ready-made social life. But because it is essentially so easy to form a band — and because it is so easy to drift along without a great deal of real hard work, talent or commitment — most bands fold at the first sign of a challenge or a hurdle. For the majority of kids living in Australia in the late seventies, joining a band was something you did for fun, as a pastime. It was a phase to pass through, a highly enjoyable rite of passage. And for most, a few months of poorly paid gigs in the real world of professional rock 'n' roll was enough to get the impulse out of the system. It's in this context that we have to place the decision The Farriss Brothers made to move to Perth together — a journey that is comparable in distance with travelling from London to Moscow.

This was no ordinary act of mateship and camaraderie. It was more than just a good idea. It was the defining moment of the band's career, a decision to stick together through virtually any adversity. And incredible as it may seem, they didn't just decide to remain a band on a trip from Sydney to Perth; they made a decision to remain together forever. Their fate was sealed.

By the beginning of 1978, the six members of The Farriss Brothers had reconvened in Perth. While waiting for his band-mates, Jon had started gigging in a number of different local combos — including a nude band at a nudist resort ('I was scared shitless,' he recalls) — so he was happy to commence writing and rehearsing with his mates. The band (with the exception of Jon) eventually moved into a large house and proceeded to make their presence felt.

In those days, Tim was the undisputed team leader of The Farriss Brothers and, unofficially, their manager. As the oldest member, and the one who had essentially convened the band, he took on most of their business responsibilities. 'Initially it was only Tim who believed we could go somewhere,' Garry Beers recalled in 1992. 'He was always the car salesman, the one pushing us, getting us gigs and talking about us. We all just sat back and thought how good it was that we were living in a house together, playing gigs and getting free beer.'

INXS would later develop to a point where other people were brought in to manage the band's affairs. Other members of the band were to mature into more gifted musicians and songwriters. But there always remained a sense, at least within band ranks, that Tim Farriss was the founding father of INXS. Indeed, as the first member of the band to marry (he wed his teenage sweetheart, Buffy, shortly after the first album was recorded) and the first by some years to have children, he was, literally, the band Dad.

'I think over the years my role has been a sort of team

captain,' he was to recall many years later. 'I basically put the band together in the first place, and very early on I was the manager as well with Kirk, dividing up the money after every gig. I've always been there for everyone, and even as we've matured and things have changed, that role has become an integral part of what we are.'

If, on the whole, the Sydney of 1977 seemed conservative and quiet, it was like downtown Manhattan compared with Perth, a provincial, sleepy backwater. The world's most isolated capital city, Perth is bounded by ocean on one side and an enormous expanse of desert on the other. With little musical or cultural influences from which to gain stimulus other than whatever music they could lay their hands on at the record store, the band were forced in upon themselves as surely as if they had been incarcerated in a concrete bunker. The confinement had a positive effect, and they began to work up a repertoire of strong original material. The only problem was that Perth's live club scene was dominated by a booking agent who insisted that bands play a solid diet of Top 40 covers, no originals.

Faced with a choice of either working up a set of covers (something that many bands had done before them) or sticking with their original material, The Farriss Brothers chose the latter — thus making themselves virtually unemployable. Like cowboys being driven from the Wild West, they were forced to look for work elsewhere. So, finally, in mad, bad mining and fishing communities such as Kalgoorlie, Port Hedland and Bunbury — the band first cut its teeth as a live act.

'The mining centres are like fibreglass towns,' Michael once recalled. 'They'd have the central area, with six pods coming off, and there's red dust everywhere, like Mars. They have wet canteens and dry canteens — one to get pissed in, the other to eat in, which not that many people do. The people there are all escaped convicts ... desperados.'

After ten months based in Perth, it was time to head back to civilisation — and to the more promising prospects of the Sydney pub scene. To finance the trip east, The Farriss Brothers travelled to Port Hedland (a staggering 1,760 km north of Perth) in two rented Hi-Ace vans to play gigs. 'It's a big prefab town,' recalls Garry Beers, 'where they've got a mess hall, four major meals a day and everyone wants to make you happy and make sure you have a good time so you're never short of pot. And there's girls all over the place. You just sit by the pool and read *Fear and Loathing in Las Vegas*.'

The band then headed off across the desert to Sydney, wrecking the vans in the process. It was a tough trip, and it was to be the first of many long road trips that The Farriss Brothers would take, the beginning of a journey that would take them across every continent on the planet many times over. As successful as they eventually became, they never forgot the hardship of the road.

'We started out our life as a band living together, travelling together with all our gear in a cramped van ... sleeping by the side of the road, whatever,' recalled Tim Farriss years later. 'Once you've been through all those experiences, you tend to have a different bond. The shit we used to go through was unbelievable.'

Back in Sydney in early 1979, with Tim still holding down the job of The Farriss Brothers' team captain and manager, the band began picking up gigs on the vibrant Sydney pub circuit. At the outset, the band's stamping ground was confined to the affluent suburbs north of Sydney Harbour. Their turf stretched from the lower north shore venues like

Cammeray's San Miguel up the long coastal spur of the northern beaches — replete with surf clubs and large rock pubs like the Manly Vale, Avalon RSL and The Narrabeen Antler. Eventually, The Farriss Brothers were regarded as entertaining enough to be given shows in the hipper inner-city suburbs — and then the sprawling south and west of the city. Later still, they started making forays into towns and cities all over the country.

Offstage, the band were no different to any other. Much as they were constrained by a lack of income, they were already being tempted by the pitfalls and pleasures of the road: drugs, girls and drinking. They'd moved into a large beach-house together (a former mental asylum, as it happens) and already knew how to party hard.

Onstage, they were relentlessly experimental — working up different sounds, textures and looks. For a brief time, Tim wore yellow plastic see-through trousers and jacket — he was naked underneath. ('That was an interesting look,' recalled Michael.) At one gig, the band turned up wearing white overalls; at another, bandanas and straw hats. Whatever else you could say for The Farriss Brothers, they were never afraid to look completely ridiculous. If pub rock bands were defined by a strict dress code of jeans, cowboy boots and T-shirts, The Farriss Brothers were intent on breaking the mould.

'We were pretty wild, pretty out-there at that stage and really pushing to see how far we could go with the audiences,' Michael Hutchence remembered. 'We were one of the first Australian bands playing funk music, and that was pretty tricky, 'cause Australian audiences were used to AC/DC, Cold Chisel, Midnight Oil — very heavy guitar music — and we were up there with congas ... We were searching for an identity, basically.'

While the band's internal dynamic had not yet found its natural balance, The Farriss Brothers were a complex and volatile blend of individual characters. The three Farriss siblings were all very different from one another, for a start: Tim already had a somewhat wild, hedonistic character with a true rock 'n' roll spirit and a generous, gregarious nature. Andrew was an intense and highly creative young man who took himself terribly seriously and often had trouble communicating verbally. Jon was also intense — and primarily interested in becoming the finest drummer in the world, applying himself to his task with a methodical attention to detail. Perhaps because he had youth on his side, good-looking Jon would also soon emerge as the band's most eligible member.

Michael was a law unto himself — a free spirit who found it difficult to commit to anyone or anything — and that left Garry and Kirk to provide some much-needed balance. With no sibling rivalries to contend with, and none of the insecurities of a singer, both were renowned for their quiet professionalism and ironic take on all that happened around them. If Garry was the solid, practical guy and the most ostensibly 'normal' member of the ensemble, the bespectacled Kirk had a nerdy, bookish manner that belied an impish sense of humour and an incorrigible party animal. It was a combination of characters that worked curiously well onstage.

Upon arriving from Perth, the band had recorded a set of demos of songs they'd been working on during their year away. It wasn't these tapes that held the secret of their success, however, but a chance meeting later in the year in the carpark of a legendary Sydney watering hole, the Narrabeen Antler. Positioned just metres from one of Sydney's great surfing beaches, North Narrabeen, The Antler was the unofficial home of another northern beaches band, Midnight Oil, and it had a well-deserved reputation for its wild, tequilla-guzzling surfie crowd. One day, while sticking leaflets under windscreen wipers outside the pub, Tim Farriss was approached by the charismatic manager of Midnight Oil, Gary Morris.

'I remember him coming up to me and saying, "Who are you working for, mate?" and I kind of went, "Oh, we have this band and we're called The Farriss Brothers",' laughed Tim. 'He offered to give us some work supporting Midnight Oil on the spot.'

Gary Morris was to become the band's first manager, and The Farriss Brothers began supporting Midnight Oil and other local bands regularly. One day, Morris came to The Farriss Brothers with some great news: a member of the Oils crew had come up with a new name (the band had already been thinking about an alternative name, and briefly called themselves The Vegetables). He suggested the band change their name to INXS. 'He had a slightly different concept,' explains Tim. 'He wanted us to be inaccessible, so for the first couple of years we would play behind these bars made out of lights and we'd never talk to anybody. We thought that would be a bit much — but it was a good name.'

Funnily enough, it *was* a good name. The Farriss Brothers had already established a reputation as inveterate party boys — and the name INXS managed to capture the band's penchant for excessive behaviour. It was also remarkably apt for the decade that was looming. The band's first performance as INXS was on September 1, 1979 at the Oceanview Hotel, Toukley. Before long, they were gathering pace as bookings and audiences increased. Slowly but surely, INXS were gaining recognition from booking agents and punters alike for their improving stage performance. However, Morris was already busy with Midnight Oil's rapidly escalating career. 'He kept disappearing from the tour for days at a time, then coming back to tell us he had a vision that we should turn Christian and then we'd be the biggest band in the world,' says Kirk. 'We couldn't see it, surprisingly, so we dropped him.'

A young man by the name of Chris Murphy had already become involved with the band's career, securing them gigs through the talent booking agency he co-owned, Nucleus. He was the son of a hotshot independent agent, Mark Murphy, who had died of a heart attack at the age of just 34. Chris Murphy was young, aggressive and extremely ambitious. He was also acutely conscious of his family heritage, maintaining the name of his father's company (Mark Murphy and Associates, or MMA) rather than creating a new company in his own name. Murphy was as persuasive as he was passionate — a brilliant and tenacious negotiator who was a perfect match for the newly named INXS. By the end of 1979, Chris Murphy had become the manager of INXS.

Richard Clapton — hailed in the late seventies as Australia's finest singer–songwriter, a tag he wore until well into the late eighties — had been managed by Chris Murphy some years before. He was ultimately to produce INXS and become a lifelong friend of the band. 'Mark Murphy faced a lot of battles with the people who ran the Australian music business in the sixties and seventies, and there are certainly some people who will tell you that the stress killed him,' says Clapton. 'In some sense, the Australian music business, as it existed then, contributed to his death. So, depending on what kind of mood he was in at the time, Chris would mutter about avenging his father's death. And what he created was always very family based and loyalty-conscious. That sense of looking after your own. Blood Brothers.'

Chris Murphy was a good-looking, suave young man with prematurely greying hair and penetrating blue eyes. Murphy's driving ambition and creative approach immediately gelled with the band; they had finally found someone who shared their vision and was prepared to take them as far as they could go. Murphy also provided a new, objective voice — he was someone who could give the band direction and encouragement. He was also an adept businessman and negotiator and by early 1980 he had signed them to a five-album record deal with Sydney independent label Deluxe. Run by Michael Browning, a former manager of AC/DC, Deluxe also boasted two other successful local pop bands at the time, The Numbers and The Dugites.

'When I first ran into Chris Murphy, I'd just done a distribution deal with RCA for Deluxe,' recalls Browning. 'Murphy played me a rough demo of a band that was still called The Farriss Brothers — and then he dragged me down to this funny old theatre in Maroubra to see them play. There weren't many people there, but there was something about the band — particularly Michael. They had no direction, they were trying a bit of everything, and they played everything ridiculously fast.

'They became INXS shortly after that, and they started developing the songs that you hear on the first album. The band was never cutting-edge — or, should I say, they were never perceived that way. They were always seen as being on the pop end of the spectrum — but also very hard working, a band that could cut it in the pubs. They had the potential to be a really good band from the outset. They had spirit and they had a vibe.'

From the late seventies, Chris Murphy had been making a name for himself in the fledgling Australian music business. At a time when Australian record companies were largely devoted to the task of distributing international product and releasing little of the local music that was going down so well on the live circuit, Murphy cut a swathe. Like Gary Morris, from whom he had clearly learned so much, he was sharp and ambitious. The live scene had traditionally been run by thugs and standover agents. Murphy was determined to operate outside the prevailing systems, and brought a new sense of professionalism to the business. And, importantly, he had a vision for his act that went well beyond the week's commission cheque.

Chris Murphy had plans for INXS but he knew that no band could attempt an assault on the world without a thorough knowledge of the international pop scene. It was apparent to him that Australian acts were disadvantaged by their isolation from the day-to-day development of international rock 'n' roll. He could see that a band in London or New York — with the greatest acts in the world on their doorstep, able to hear the hottest new records on the radio and inspired by a vibrant music media — were clearly better positioned to succeed. So although it wasn't practical to give the band a taste of the world just yet, Murphy himself made an exploratory trip to the UK — before INXS had even commenced work on their debut album — to soak up the prevailing trends. He brought back with him news about the late-seventies post-punk British scene, including the ska resurgence.

The first INXS single 'Simple Simon' was released in May 1980. An over-complicated slice of jumpy, ska-influenced pop, the song achieved little on the charts, but it did give the band its first national media exposure. Their performance on the national TV chart show *Countdown* was charmingly naïve as the band and the show's producers strove for a 'modern' look. But even then, there was something in Michael Hutchence's performance that was assured and striking.

As soon as 'Simple Simon' was released, the band started work in earnest on their first album. Working five or six nights per week on the live circuit, INXS recorded the album after gigs, between the hours of midnight and dawn.

Their self-titled debut album was recorded at Trafalgar Studios and co-produced by the band and Duncan McGuire, with all songs attributed to the entire band. A session musician who was already in declining health (he died in the late eighties), McGuire also had a drug problem, and the band were given an early introduction to the pitfalls of rock 'n' roll as they watched their producer regularly pass out at the recording console. 'He used to take Mandrax all the time,' recalls Andrew Farriss. 'One night he had a glass of scotch and he knocked it all over the console and we had to pull it apart and try to clean it out. I think it was the same day the multi-track caught fire.'

As Michael Browning observes, 'There weren't too many choices for a producer in Sydney in those days. Duncan was a very good musician — and I think he had a pretty solid impact on the band's playing.'

The first album was typical of young bands of the era — tentative, played too fast, and full of artistic pretensions and ambitions that they didn't have the skill to realise. Musically, the band owed a clear debt to English bands active at the time — from XTC to The Specials. The parallel musical tendencies that were to later define INXS's sound — rock guitar,

British synth-pop and slightly funky settings — were all in evidence, but unresolved. Many of the lyrics reflected a youthful mixture of poorly articulated angst, raw ambition, pretentiousness, and a vague, undirected disdain for suburban life and normality that was *de rigueur* in the modern world of post-punk rock.

The album's anthem was a slice of raw attitude called 'Just Keep Walking'. The single received a modicum of airplay on Sydney radio stations, but was only able to reach number 38 on the national hit parade. It's difficult to say what the song is actually about, but it drips with arrogance, defiance and disdain for polite society. Chillingly, it contains the faint suggestion that, despite their current position as underdogs, the band might just have the last laugh. Even then, when very few people were listening, the message of 'Just Keep Walking' was perfectly clear: just watch us go.

The first INXS album was eventually to go gold (sales in excess of 35,000) but it took several years of escalating popularity to achieve this figure. At the time of its release, however, the album was largely passed over in the rush to praise new albums by the reigning heroes of Australian music such as Cold Chisel, Split Enz and Australian Crawl. In an era where such bands could comfortably sell more than 200,000 copies of an album, the few thousand units that *INXS* sold were encouraging, but insignificant. Speaking about the album in 1990, Hutchence said, 'I'm not a great fan of the first album. It's naïve and kinda cute, almost. It's these young guys struggling for a sound. All I can hear is what was going to happen later and it's probably an interesting album because of that. 'Just Keep Walking' was the first time we thought we'd written a song. And that became an anthem around town. It's funny, I remember kids in pubs saying it and hearing it on the radio for the first time. We'd never heard that before.'

Between 1979 and 1981, INXS toured Australia virtually non-stop, racking up some 300 gigs a year. It was touring at its most frugal and unglamorous, with the band, their two-man crew and all their equipment crammed into two vans for long hauls on highway. When the band did get to sleep, there were two or three people in a room in some of the worst hotels the country could offer. On their earliest visits to Melbourne, they actually managed to fit the entire band and crew — eight people — into a single, cockroach-infested room of a cheap hotel.

'We played every nook and cranny,' recalls Gary Grant, who signed on as tour manager in 1981 before becoming the band's co-manager a year later. 'Three thousand dollars was a big night and $5,000 was phenomenal on a $7 ticket — which was the top rate. But that was in the days before fire restrictions. Making money was only possible if you could overcrowd the venues. You'd play the Manly Vale and get 1,800 kids in there. It's legal now for 265. It was all cash in those days. In the country towns you'd go and get the key to the hall from some old guy in the pub. There was no tax man there to know how much money you'd taken. The crew would wire up the lights from a power point in the kitchen, set the till up and away you go. We had three or four of us in a hotel room. In the old days we were so poor it was like, whoever had a filling, "Here, chew the Alfoil, you drive", because we couldn't afford speed.'

It was already apparent that INXS had the talent and deter-mination to take their music a long way. The band also revealed a capacity for hard work that was almost unsurpassed at that time. They were, quite literally, slaves to their own destiny — and doing hard time. Also, Chris Murphy was blossoming as an entrepreneur, living up to all of his father's promise. 'The band's success was directly proportionate to Murphy's ambition,' says Michael Browning. 'Chris had a burning desire to achieve success, and I don't think anything was going to stop him. INXS was his vehicle, and they went out there and did it together.'

Browning also paid tribute to the band's work ethic — a quality that was to prove INXS's international trump card. 'There are a few ingredients that can make a huge difference in this business. Talent is obviously one of them, but so is a band's ability to work hard. If you don't have that, you just won't get over the hurdles. INXS always had this incredible work ethic. It was always like, "Let's fucking work", you know. I can remember once some members of the band driving to Newcastle — which in those days was at least a three-hour drive — just to put up some posters. Two days later, they drove up there again to play the gig.'

The tours became bigger and bigger — and the Australian pub circuit was able to accommodate the band as it moved from playing supports to headlining shows in smaller pubs, to playing major tours of the largest rooms in the country. The touring was near-constant, but with typical Murphy savvy, blocks of time were given names: the Fear and Loathing Tour, the Campus Tour, Stay Young Tour, Tour with No Name. Regular Friday night gigs at the Manly Vale were held under the rather romantic and memorable title of The Moon Tan Dance. In the process of doing this immense amount of work, INXS acquired a road-hardened toughness, and an inherent ability to entertain a crowd under even the most trying circumstances, that would stand them in good stead for many years to come.

Although INXS were not yet stars in the charts, they were stars in the pubs. In over-crowded sweatboxes, the band pumped out loud, adrenaline-charged party music. Michael strutted the stage, his chest poked out and his head held high, tossing his mane of hair. In this peculiar universe, he was a superstar.

'It was so weird at that point, because they weren't famous,' remembers Richard Clapton, who toured regularly with INXS during this period, 'but as soon as Michael walked onto a stage, everyone just went crazy. Backstage it was like they were the Rolling Stones, with all these people hanging around and this entourage. They were stars before they were stars. I remember Michael's favourite stage trick was to shake up cans of beer and then spray them all over the girls down the front. It was like having your own wet T-shirt competition.'

'Being thrown onto the sticky carpets of pub stages all over the country was do or die,' remembered Michael. 'That's where we developed our mix of styles. I was quite a fey bloke — writing lyrics and poetry and the rest — and then you'd be up on stage with people screaming right in your face. Everything was a real mixture of arty stuff and real hard attitude, which definitely affected the music. It took us a long time to get our shit together.'

As early as 1981, the frenetic pace was taking its toll. Most of the band members were already in their early twenties, yet they had never experienced life as normal people. On the road almost constantly, they never had the opportunity to establish the most basic social contacts or personal lives. In one of his earliest interviews, Michael Hutchence — then only 21 years old — revealed how much this lifestyle was affecting him.

'Last year, we almost played too much. When you're working six nights a week, getting down to that constant touring, you hypnotise yourself, you get numb to the fact of what you're doing. Your subconscious takes over and when you walk out there you're not really quite aware. Your automatic nervous system takes over. You start doing the same things every night and you're not even aware of it.'

But there was no time to dwell on such things. By early 1981, Richard Clapton was in Chris Murphy's sights as the producer of INXS's second album. Murphy dragged the singer along to a show at the Paddington Green Hotel — a small pub on Sydney's Oxford Street with a popular upstairs band room — which on this occasion, ironically, was attended by approximately nine drunks. Clapton was immediately convinced. 'The very first time I saw them play they had the same passion and musicianship as they displayed all those years later,' says Clapton. 'I mean there was just Chris, me and eight or nine drunks, but the band was playing this incredible set like the room was packed. Without a word of a lie, it was the most amazing band I'd seen since The Rolling Stones. The material wasn't great, they were basically playing the songs from the first album and they're not good, but I've never seen a young band like it.

'And the really weird thing about them is that even then, at that first gig, they already had this incredible charisma. They were absolute stars. And they didn't even have fans then. They just had something special.'

Although Clapton's primary musical influence was the US west coast folk rock sound, he was also an avowed fan of bands like Steely Dan. It was in this musical area that the band and their future producer found an element of common ground. But the going was tough. 'At our first pre-production meeting, at Michael's flat, I'd come armed with a whole lot of albums so we could discuss drum sounds, things like that.

I remember I had a Roxy Music album for the drum sound. And they had a few albums they wanted to play me, things like [David Byrne and Brian Eno's] *My Life in the Bush of Ghosts*, XTC, Magazine and really left-of-centre British stuff. I remember thinking, "Oh shit, I can't do this. I hate that kind of shit." '

At first, Clapton and INXS entered Studios 301 in Sydney and recorded a cover of the Australian rock classic 'The Loved One' (by a band called, coincidentally, The Loved Ones). When the song received a positive response at radio, the producer was sent back into 301 (and later Paradise) to create an entire album, between July and August 1981. Prompted by Clapton, it was to be an album that explored and defined the musical turf the band would subsequently inhabit. Because the band had been on the road constantly, the songs for their second album were written quickly.

'Most of the songs on *Underneath the Colours* were written in a relatively short space of time,' said Michael. 'Most bands shudder at the prospect of having 20 years to write their first album and four days to write their second. For us, though, it was good. It left less room for us to go off on all sorts of tangents.'

INXS were learning some hard lessons about studio discipline. From the outset, their biggest musical challenge was taming the six creative impulses in the band, focusing the work of at least four songwriters and six very opinionated musicians into something that could be defined as INXS. They were beginning to learn about the subtleties of record production, about achieving feels and moods that could enhance a song.

Although the writing credits on *Underneath the Colours* were well distributed between the various members of the band (four songs were attributed to the whole outfit, three to the songwriting team of Andrew Farriss and Michael Hutchence, and the remainder to other combinations), Andrew was already emerging as the band's driving force in the studio. Working closely with Clapton, Farriss was already taking a keen interest in arrangement and production. He already felt comfortable directing his band-mates and even dictating what parts they should play. This was a source of tension, as Kirk and Tim were still inclined to see themselves as the band's leaders, but there was no denying Andrew's creativity.

'You could see that Andrew was just going to get better and better,' says Clapton, 'but I was also blown away by the band. Even on the songs that didn't bear a band credit, the other guys were incredibly instrumental in creating the sound of the song. There are some amazing players in INXS, all with a very distinctive sound ... Obviously Jon is just amazing.'

Even though the six members of INXS had been playing together for only four years, they recognised the need to escape the confines of the group. No sooner had sessions for *Underneath the Colours* finished than a number of members were busy working on outside projects. Garry Beers, Jon Farriss and Andrew Farriss had been enlisted to play (alongside members of Australia's most popular rock band of the day, Cold Chisel) on Richard Clapton's new solo album, *The Great Escape*.

Meanwhile, Don Walker, songwriter for Cold Chisel, wanted Michael to sing a song he had written for a soundtrack album. The film was called *Freedom*. It was an obscure road flick that made little impact but the director was a very young Scott Hicks, the Adelaide-based film-maker who was to enjoy international acclaim many years later for his film on the life of David Helfgott, *Shine*. Few could say they own a copy today, but Michael Hutchence's first solo single — a song called 'Speed Kills' — was released through Australia's WEA Records in early 1982.

Although the single failed to graze even the bottom of the charts, it was perhaps the first development to challenge INXS's impregnable armour: despite the best efforts of INXS to present themselves as six equals against the world, the fact remained that Michael Hutchence was a natural star. Even in conversation he was charismatic. On a stage or in front of a microphone, he had a powerful and undeniable presence. Don Walker recognised that difference — and soon enough, so did plenty of other people.

Although it boasted no hit singles, and few songs that could be played on the radio, *Underneath the Colours* was well received by the music press. With the band's profile building steadily thanks to their live work, the album succeeded in cementing INXS's reputation as a musically adventurous outfit with a distinctive original sound.

Playing the pub circuit constantly through the second half of 1981, INXS just kept getting bigger and bigger. As they garnered support spots with some of the biggest Australian rock 'n' roll bands of their era, they started to gain some experience of playing to large crowds. If the audiences were frequently less than welcoming, that only made INXS work harder.

Although the pubs toughened INXS and carved away their pretensions, the pub circuit never entirely contained or eliminated the qualities that made INXS special: their love of funk, their instinctive rhythms and their soaring, inspired melodies. Nor could it tame Michael Hutchence, who stood out from the reigning pack of Australian male singers with his agile, feline grace. In a country — and an industry —

where men were very definitely men, Hutchence possessed a sensuality and a sexuality that crossed gender lines.

Unfortunately, Deluxe Records was having little success attracting interest in the band internationally. Browning and Murphy both made trips to the US and the UK to shop the band's tapes but, despite gold sales for both albums (a highly credible achievement for a new band in those days, albeit hardly spectacular), there were no takers other than a degree of interest from France.

'We tried shopping the band internationally a couple of times,' recalls Michael Browning, 'but there was really no interest. For most of the overseas markets, the music just fell between the cracks. It was hard to pigeonhole the band. I mean, at that time you had the American market into a lot of heavy metal while the British were really into punk and the stuff that came after it. INXS didn't really add up, but hey, there's nothing unusual in that. There are plenty of good bands, particularly ones who are doing something a bit different, that don't react instantly with people.'

chapter 3

To America

In January 1982, INXS toured New Zealand for the first time as guests of Australia's then-biggest rock 'n' roll band, Cold Chisel. INXS were clearly no strangers to life on the road, but they were undeniably excited about playing shows in another country — and even more excited about the experience of hanging out with Australia's most notorious rock 'n' roll outlaws.

After five years of multi-platinum record sales and sold-out tours Cold Chisel seemed to be sliding slowly into an unworkable chaos. By the time they toured New Zealand with INXS, tensions had reached breaking point within the group, who were well known for their wild behaviour. Backstage arguments were sometimes ending in fist-fights. It was an eye-opening experience for INXS, but one that helped strengthen their resolve to remain focused on their goals.

INXS were impatient to start cracking international markets — even though they had barely cracked their own country to any significant degree — and Murphy had become convinced that their future didn't lie with Deluxe Records.

The band members were evolving at a dramatic pace now as writers and musicians, and they were keen to prove that they had the qualities to be signed to a good deal with a major label. INXS were now pulling thousands of punters a week to shows all over the country and they knew that this enormous fanbase was ready to transfer its immense loyalty from ticket stubs to albums and singles. So, at their own expense, they entered Paradise Studios and recorded a new song called 'The One Thing' with Australian producer Mark Opitz.

The choice of producer and studio were far from coincidental; Opitz had produced several landmark albums for Cold Chisel in the same studios and he had also seen what the INXS rhythm section was capable of when he produced Richard Clapton's *The Great Escape*. In Australian terms, it was like doing a session with George Martin at Abbey Road — and it said plenty for Chris Murphy's ambition, and the band's self-confidence, that they would attempt such an audacious move. 'The One Thing' proved that Murphy and INXS had what was needed on their side. It was an amazing, breakthrough track — and it was only when the young manager had the master tapes for the song tucked firmly under his arm that he finally approached WEA Records Australia (not coincidentally Cold Chisel's and Richard Clapton's label) with a view to putting together a new deal.

'The band were looking towards world domination even then,' recalls Phillip Mortlock, then creative services manager at WEA and a participant in this historic meeting. 'He was basically tired of the indie label thing. He wanted big record companies that would make big moves so he could get the band out to a larger audience. We were offering him the standard deal, but Chris said that wasn't good enough. And he was right to say that. He was basically saying that he wanted commitment from all the territories he was signing for — and without that, no deal. It was a very smart way to operate.'

There were good reasons for Murphy's approach to recording deals. When INXS had originally been contracted to Deluxe two years earlier, Murphy had allowed the band to sign contracts that effectively ensured that Browning owned the band's master tapes and songwriting copyrights. The deals were stock-standard fare for new acts in the seventies, but the implications appalled Murphy — indeed he was so incensed by the idea of someone else owning a part of INXS that he eventually paid out several hundred thousand dollars to buy the masters back in the mid-eighties. His attempt to buy back the bands's publishing was less successful — he was gazumped by MCA — but the experience of being shackled to an old-fashioned recording contract left deep scars. He would never allow himself to be placed in a position of weakness again.

In those early days. Murphy's audacity raised plenty of record company eyebrows — but it also had to be admitted that in INXS, Murphy had one very special young band.

To Mortlock, the band's appeal was their ability to combine elements of the music emerging from Britain at that time with the tough, road-hardened rock sound of an Australian pub band. But, at that time, it was a blend that had not been perfected. 'They were a pop band first and a rock band second. They knew all the elements that had to go into the package — and Michael and Andrew had the songs. But, at that point, they hadn't really achieved a sound that was truly awesome. At a time when *really* tough-sounding bands like Cold Chisel and Midnight Oil reigned supreme, I found their sound a little thin and lacking in punch. They didn't do guitar solos, you know. They were a much more keyboard-based thing, more of a pop band. And this was an era when rock bands played pubs and pop bands appeared on *Countdown*. INXS wanted to be able to do both.'

In July, in a deal brokered by Warner's managing director Paul Turner and Artists and Repertoire (A&R) manager Gibson Kemp, INXS signed to WEA Australia for Australia, South East Asia, Japan and New Zealand. Attempts to get affiliates of WEA to pick up the band in either Europe or North America were unsuccessful, but in the US Doug Morris's Atco Records, a subsidiary of Atlantic Records (like WEA, part of the Warner group of companies), showed interest. Eventually, the company sent Atco managing director Reen Nalli to check out the band live on their home turf (Nalli attended a number of pub gigs in the Sydney area) and INXS were signed almost immediately for the US and Canada. Through his contacts with his previous label, Gibson Kemp set up a deal for the band with Polygram for Europe and the UK.

'INXS got signed not because some A&R guy thought we'd sell a lot of records, but because we sold out so many venues,' Andrew Farriss was to claim with typical arrogance — and a grain of truth — some years later. 'No journalist picked us as the next big thing, but there were thousands of punters coming to see us.'

While contracts were being finalised, Chris Murphy decided that what the band needed — prior to recording their first truly international album — was some time abroad absorbing new cultural influences. So he packed off Kirk, Michael and Andrew to the UK and the USA for exploratory visits. The band members took a tape of 'The One Thing' with a view to selecting a producer for the new album.

However, no-one they wanted was available, and a number of people told them that Mark Opitz's work on the single was as good as they could wish for.

Mark Opitz had had INXS in his sights for some time. When he had been appointed WEA's A&R manager in 1980, they were the first band he had wanted to sign. He arrived at an INXS show to offer them a recording deal the day after they had signed with Deluxe. Now, two years later, the band were proving themselves worthy of his initial hunches. Opitz had ceased working for WEA as A&R manager, but he was still highly active as a producer for the label — and he couldn't wait to get them into the studio.

Thanks to his experience producing hard-rocking guitar bands such as The Angels and Cold Chisel, Opitz was well prepared for INXS. Recording at the recently opened Rhinoceros Studios — a facility co-owned by Opitz — INXS put down their third album (eventually to be titled *Shabooh Shoobah*) in the winter of 1982. Whereas their previous producers had been keen to nurture the band and help them develop as musicians and writers, and to learn the basic disciplines of the recording studio, Opitz was a professional producer with an ear for hooks and a sound working knowledge of tough, uncompromising rock 'n' roll. It showed.

'We never stopped playing and playing, right through that year, and that turned out to be a great asset for recording,' says Tim Farriss, whose first child, Jake, was born during the period the album was recorded. 'Mark was the first producer that was able to capture some glimmer of what the band felt it was like live. Prior to us, Mark had done bands like AC/DC, Cold Chisel, The Angels. Big guitar sounds, mighty drum beats.'

Opitz found INXS to be a challenging proposition in the

studio. The band were certainly developing their rock 'n' roll chops but they were still prone to reach beyond their abilities as composers and musicians. There was a tendency — common among many young bands — to over-complicate their work.

'They had all these really strict rules about their music,' recalls Opitz. 'They were very determined to be different from all those four-on-the-floor pub bands, and they'd always be saying things like, "We don't do guitar solos" . . . They were like wide-eyed boys in the lolly shop, they were looking at a whole world of musical possibilities, but they were also very conscious of what they didn't want to be.

'I distinctly remember that "The One Thing" was great from the first moment they played it to me — but it had about three really quirky bridges in the middle of the song that just wrecked it. It was a pretty typical scenario of my work with this band; you'd say, "Pull all those bits out", and when they had, the song sounded amazing.'

Although the songwriting team of Michael Hutchence and Andrew Farriss was emerging as the dominant creative force in the band, the pair only wrote two of the album's stand-out tracks: 'The One Thing' and the ska-influenced 'Black and White'. The band's first truly great ballad, 'To Look at You', was in fact written solely by Andrew Farriss, while the album's rousing closer, 'Don't Change' — a song that was to become one of the band's most distinctive anthems and their traditional set closer for many years — was credited to the entire band.

'Andrew and Michael hadn't emerged yet as the band leaders,' recalls Opitz. 'If anything, people still acted like it was Tim and Kirk's band because that had been the original dynamic. They were the older guys with steady girlfriends and cars. It still felt like the songs came from all sorts of different places, too, rather than just two guys. One song on the album came from a jam that Tim instigated and we just cut it up to make a song. But after all that, I don't think *Shabooh Shoobah* was a patchy album. I think it sounds like what we wanted it to sound like: a complete work. It's like a woven tapestry.'

In the very year in which another Australian band, Men At Work, were already conquering charts all over the world, INXS had recorded an excellent third album and were quietly biding their time. Their constant live work was already generating enough income to keep them in relatively comfortable circumstances, but it was still not much more than a basic living. The best was yet to come.

'Even by that stage, they didn't strike me as a bunch of guys who were struggling,' remembers one colleague. 'By that stage Chris already had an infrastructure going, with staff, financial structures and so on. The band were all renting flats in nice North Shore suburbs like Neutral Bay and Kirribilli, nothing flash but not exactly squats either. Most of them had cars. They weren't wealthy, but there was income coming in.'

INXS travelled to Adelaide to shoot three videos with director Scott Hicks. It was originally planned that the band would travel with Hicks into the desert north of the city to shoot — but bad weather forced them to revise their plans. The videos — for the songs 'Don't Change', 'To Look at You' and 'Black and White' — were ultimately made in an aircraft hangar.

Following the release of *Shabooh Shoobah*, INXS embarked on their longest Australian tour: a mammoth 78-date run that took them across the length and breadth of the country, including many small towns that few bands ever reach. With typical Murphy flair, the tour was given the improbable title

Una Brilliante Banda De Musica Amenizara Espectaculo.

On and off the road, band members' free time was frequently gobbled up with promotional chores designed to help break INXS in foreign markets. Many a night was spent by Michael and other band members doing hour upon hour of 'phoners' — back-to-back telephone interviews, 20 minutes each — with some foreign territory. To amuse himself and maintain some vestige of sanity, Michael wore the national dress of the country he was talking to. For the German phoners he wore lederhosen. For the French phoners, he wore a beret and a striped T-shirt.

By February 1983, with the American Atco deal complete, INXS had their first stateside release with 'The One Thing' and, remarkably, the impact was virtually instant. Because the most powerful hit-making tool in Australia in this period was *Countdown* (hosted by well-known industry identity Ian 'Molly' Meldrum), Australian bands were accustomed to making strong videos. Regular video play on *Countdown* was a sure-fire recipe for home-town success, and INXS had already lashed out and made an expensive and eye-catching video for 'The One Thing'. Seated at a long banquet table groaning with food and wine, the band and an assortment of beautiful models proceeded to demolish the feast — and each other — with Bacchanalian lust. The video had a vaguely New Romantic treatment with big hair and flamboyant costuming, but more than anything else, 'The One Thing' was simply excessive. The message came through loud and clear.

Just as the fledgling American cable television channel MTV had warmed instantly to Men At Work because of their striking, humorous videos, it responded instantly to INXS. MTV, the channel that came to represent the aspirations of an entire generation and create a global culture, was right on the cusp of becoming arguably the most significant and powerful medium in the history of American music — and it had found itself an Australian band it liked. They had the look, they had the sound, and they had an eminently watchable video. It was the beginning of a love affair that would continue unabated for eight years.

By the time INXS jetted into Los Angeles in March 1983 for their first US dates, they had an American record deal, 'The One Thing' had delivered a credible national profile and a Top 30 hit, and *Shabooh Shoobah* was in the stores. It was a great way to start an American career, and even though the band's first American gig (in San Diego) attracted just 24 people, it was clear that the cards were stacked in their favour.

The elements that made INXS different — the elements that had made their climb to the top in their homeland less than meteoric — were what the Americans found appealing. In an era when American music was still divided along racial lines (rock music for white folks, soul music for black), INXS stood out as fresh and different. Unlike many British bands, this was new music that still had recognisable and easily digestible elements.

'We were a band that came out of the suburbs of Australia,' Michael Hutchence recalled. 'We were just white, middle-class boys, but we were funky. We were, in retrospect, very tuned in to what was happening all over the world musically at a time when Australian musical tastes were very conservative, very straight. We were listening to things like War and Bootsy Collins, and that all came out in the music.'

The fact that INXS had one song on MTV did not mean they had conquered the country, however. As previous generations of international rock 'n' roll bands had found, the USA can only be broken properly by long, arduous months of touring. To connect with the American heartlands, bands have to visit every city and every town. Audiences *need* to put a face to a name.

Chris Murphy also recognised one of the principal reasons why most other Australian attempts to crack the USA had essentially failed: the bands, and their managers, had no presence in the country. As soon as a band and their manager returned home after a tour, the record company quickly took them off the priority list. Only AC/DC had fully grasped the need to locate themselves, and their management, in the northern hemisphere on an almost permanent basis. Now Murphy was to hit upon an expensive but undeniably inspired strategy: he would position Gary Grant — by then co-manager of the band — in New York permanently. Better still, he would persuade Atco to give Grant an office in their New York headquarters. With Grant's infectious enthusiasm and Reen Nalli's dogged support for her young antipodean signing, INXS began the task of cracking America.

In the USA, all but the biggest bands tour by bus. While the road crew travel by van with the gear, bands and their support staff travel in large, purpose-built coaches (with varying degrees of comfort), complete with bunks, lounges, TVs, stereos, bathrooms and kitchens. The coaches are designed to keep a band on the move and are guaranteed to encourage a semi-nocturnal lifestyle. They also ensure that bands see little or nothing of the country they're travelling through.

On bus tours, a band will typically board the bus straight after a show and travel immediately to the next town while remaining awake. (This part of the process at least makes sense — most bands enjoy a few hours of relaxation after a show, and it's just as easy to party on a bus as it is in a dressing room.) Depending on the destination, the town might be reached three hours later or the next morning. Bands then check into a hotel room, where they sleep through at least part of the day before going to their next soundcheck and show. Needless to say, after several weeks living in such conditions, most people are lucky not to go insane.

But when INXS boarded their first US tour bus and joined a tour as support for Adam and the Ants (whose insignificant career was already in decline), they were in no position to manage even this level of luxury. Touring is expensive for any band and INXS were a large act that had to pay for at least six international airfares before they could play a note. As a result, they had to do it tougher than most.

To save money, INXS decided to take their crew and equipment with them, on the one bus. This meant that the band were unable to leave a venue until all their gear was packed up. It also meant that eleven people had to share the confined spaces of the tour bus. As a further money-saving measure, hotels were rarely checked into. The band would typically sleep in the bus — if and when they could — and then use the backstage showers at the venue, when it opened, some time after arriving in the next town. It was an alienating, dehumanising existence — one that can, and does, force lesser mortals to pack up and leave — but INXS steeled themselves to endure it.

Much as INXS were adapting to the American way of running a rock band, they were also bringing some Australian ideas about promotion to the US. Handbills and illegal street posters — a part of the Australian live music circuit — were far less commonplace in the US. The more the band were told that such methods were unworkable, the more they persisted — and the results were undeniably effective.

After the Adam and the Ants dates, INXS went on to play supports for The Kinks and a string of dates with The Go-Gos. Riding high on the US charts with a series of hits, The Go-Gos were notorious LA party girls — and more than a match for the members of INXS.

'Six boys, five girls — you can work it out,' laughs Gary Grant, who was on the road with the band for long stretches in this period. 'I'd ring up their road manager and say, "I'm missing a couple of guys" and he'd say, "I think they're travelling on our bus today". The next thing he'd call up and say, "Have you seen Belinda?".'

Luckily the members of INXS were well suited to touring. They made a virtue of their affable party-heartiness to win friends wherever they went. They were already exhausted by years on the road — and they certainly hadn't achieved any financial security to soften the workload — but they fell in love with America instantly. Just as importantly, America fell in love with them.

'They were such nice guys,' remembers one Atco staffer who was regularly assigned to work with the band. 'They were always very polite, very gentlemanly, and I think we all felt sorry for them because they didn't have their friends or families with them. The girls in the office were always being sent out to help members of the band buy new stage clothes, stuff like that. You couldn't help but like them.'

INXS were acutely aware of the absurdities of life on the road; they were doing it so tough they had little choice but to make light of their situation. They developed a complex language of nicknames, codes, rituals and in-jokes to keep themselves amused and everyone else baffled. They also took great delight in making up silly names to hide behind when booking hotel rooms.

During the mid-eighties, for example, Michael preferred to be known as Michael Gentley ('as in "Michael, gently",' he explained to me once, using a woman's voice for emphasis), while the eternally optimistic Garry Beers (who had recently proved his wacky sense of the absurd by giving himself a second name, Gary) opted for G.W. Fuller-Love. Kirk Pengilly showed extraordinary prescience by going under the name Rock Melon (he was to marry the former singer of a band called The Rockmelons years later).

'I think one of the other factors that has helped us get through some of the tough times is that we're all pretty funny guys,' Garry Gary Beers observed years later. 'We kind of use humour to help each other along. We don't take ourselves too seriously, and we always tend to see the funny side of what's going on — and hey, there are a lot of funny things to look at when you're in a rock band.'

But in between the nude load-outs and devising a system for scoring aeroplane landings, most of INXS's life on the road was just sheer hard work. When the fatigue wasn't killing them, other factors conspired to: in the middle of the night on one of their earliest tours, the bus in which they were travelling flew off the road and careened into a ditch after the driver fell asleep. For the next six tours, Andrew sat bolt upright in the front seat, diligently watching the driver for the first signs of fatigue.

INXS kept working their way through America. They were a long way off making money or becoming household names, but their first visit Stateside was going well and new dates kept getting added. In May 1983, INXS played the massive US Festival in Silicon Valley, California, which was heralded as the largest rock concert ever. They were featured on the 'New Wave' bill alongside such British luminaries as U2 (at that time still a relatively new act) and The Clash (who were in fact playing their last-ever show). INXS were second on the all-day bill, but the experience of playing before 150,000 people stuck with them — and they were chuffed to earn themselves an encore from the crowd.

The band remained on the road in the US for most of the year, picking up supports for Men At Work and returning infrequently to Australia for brief visits. If their touring in Australia had been essentially a financial exercise, following well-worn trails to well-paid gig after well-paid gig, INXS's earliest foray into America was far more strategic. More often than not, the band were actually losing money hand over fist — remaining afloat thanks to their carefully preserved savings and substantial cash support from their American label — but Chris Murphy and Gary Grant knew that INXS would only break America by playing there constantly. Every time a US radio station put an INXS song on high rotation, Grant made a mental note to add that city to their next itinerary.

By mid-1983, INXS were headlining venues such as The Ritz in New York, and there was a clear sense that progress was being made. In Toronto, following a support show for Men At Work, INXS met someone who was to give them their next big hit.

By the time he walked into their dressing room, guitarist Nile Rodgers was something of a legend in black American music. He was the guitarist and leading creative force of seventies disco band Chic — a band that defined the funky, string-laden sound of the era as much as anyone. Rodgers had also emerged as a producer of distinction, having helped a number of acts to create music that combined elements of white rock and black funk while retaining credibility. (David

Bowie's Nile Rodgers-produced album, *Let's Dance*, was the biggest commercial hit of the singer's career, and Rodgers was later to do the same for Madonna with her album, *Like a Virgin*.) He was an important person to have on side in the American music scene in the early eighties, and he had an interesting proposition: he wanted to record INXS.

By September 1983, an awestruck INXS were in the main live room at New York's legendary Power Station Studios playing a song Andrew and Michael had written on the road several weeks earlier. The song was called 'Original Sin' (it was originally titled 'Brand New Day') and its subject matter addressed the issue of black/white relations — personal, sexual or professional. It was tough subject matter, particularly for Americans, and it was interesting ground for a band already addressing the black/white divide in their own music. The session was run along unconventional lines, by the band's standards, but there was no arguing with the result.

After insisting that the band members eat some fried chicken to put themselves in a funky frame of mind, Rodgers asked them to start running through the song in the studio. 'We were fresh off the road,' recalls Andrew Farriss, 'so we had the basic song completed and we'd been playing it live in the set. He was talking to us through the headphones, kind of saying things that were meant to encourage us, and we figured he was just getting levels and stuff on the whole band playing together, but after we'd run it down a couple of times he said, "OK, come in and have a listen". We went in and the control room was sort of full of people dancing. Apart from adding backing vocals and the sax solo, we were finished. We didn't even know he was recording.'

The session with Rodgers gave the band an injection of

confidence that was to prove critical. Although INXS were already committed to recording their next album with English producer Nick Launay, the session with Rodgers was graphic proof of just how far they'd come. 'It was a real milestone for us simply to be working with someone of that calibre,' recalls Andrew. 'It made us feel very proud and made us realise what we were achieving. Whether or not the single was successful, we felt we'd stepped into a whole new world. And of course it was successful at radio, it went to Number One in France, Argentina, Australia, New Zealand and it was a radio hit in the US.'

Apart from one brief visit INXS had been away from home, friends and family since March — but their work wasn't over yet. After hopping on a flight to London, they headed up to Oxford to meet Launay for sessions at the residential Manor Studios. Launay was regarded as a cutting-edge hotshot and he had already recorded the extraordinary *10,9,8,7,6,5,4,3,2,1* for another Australian band, Midnight Oil. He had come up through the British scene in the early eighties, and his work with the likes of the Gang of Four and Public Image Limited ensured his credibility. He had an implicit understanding of the new sophisticated sounds being pulled by British produc- ers such as Trevor Horn and, just as importantly, he knew more about state-of-the-art studio gadgetry than virtually any producer around.

'Nick was always going to be the major production force behind *The Swing*,' says Andrew Farriss. 'We had a really genuine interest in the stuff he had done and we knew he was the right guy for us at that time. It was funny, actually, because we arrived at the Manor, which is up in Oxford, and we basically walked in and said, "Nick, we've already recorded one song for the album". And he was like, "Oh yeah, where did you do that?" And we said, "New York." "Who'd you do that with?" "Nile Rodgers." And his face just went white because he was a major Nile Rodgers fan himself. So he said, "Well, 'spose we'd better listen to it", and we put it on and he was just blown away. I think that started poor old Nick off on a bit of a — he wasn't as secure and confident as he probably would have been.'

In INXS, Nick Launay encountered a young band who were more than ready for all manner of adventurous sonic experimentation. They might have been ambitious and commercially minded, but the members of INXS were still music fans with a love of new technology and cutting-edge sounds. Andrew Farriss was an early and enthusiastic user of synthesizers, while Jon Farriss had been quick to seize the possibilities of drum machines, and sampling, looping and other rhythmic concepts that were to become popular in the nineties. Together, INXS and Launay took to their task with gusto — cutting up tape, experimenting with sound and pushing the edges of the envelope.

'They were really tired,' remembers Launay today. 'They'd been on the road in America all year, and they arrived at the studio with very little material ready to go. The other negative I remember from that period was just the really unwieldy nature of the band; with a lot of groups you've got one, maybe two, songwriters and everyone else just does what they're told. With INXS, you had six very strong personalities who all want to be involved in the process — and that makes it very hard to get creative work done.'

Launay was also concerned about 'Original Sin' and the implications it had for the album's sound. 'I was a great fan of Chic,' he says, 'but it wasn't the kind of album I had in mind, and I felt a bit uneasy because I wasn't sure whether I really had the ability to create something that slick and polished.'

As it turned out, Launay need not have been worried. Launay and INXS hit if off immediately, and once they made it clear that they were up for precisely the kind of sonic experimentation that Launay was pioneering, the sessions relaxed immeasurably. 'We ended up having a fantastic time,' he remembers. 'The Manor is a beautiful place, a lovely old house with its own grounds and a lake, all that stuff, and a few members of the band flew out their partners to be with them. Tim's wife Buffy was there, so was Michelle [Bennett], and I remember the whole period there being like this really nice family outing. One day it started to snow, so we set up the speakers outside and everyone was dancing around to the rough mixes and throwing snowballs at each other. Tim decided to walk across the lake, which was iced over. We all told him it was an incredibly dangerous thing to do, but he did it anyway.'

Nick Launay was presiding over the flowering of INXS as a creative force — and he was hugely impressed with what he saw and heard. 'I loved the band's musicianship and the sound of Michael's voice; he had this incredible ability to walk into the studio and make a track sound so . . . *exciting*. But it was Andrew who really stood out, even then. To this very day, I firmly believe that there is no-one else in the world like him, and apart from Michael himself, he was the reason for all their success. He was only young, but he had such a vision of how INXS should sound. As a producer, it didn't take me long to realise that this guy knew what he wanted and what he was doing, and that I should spend a lot of time getting to know him and understand him.

'I mean, wow, he's a very odd person. When he talks to

you, his eyes fix on this place above your head. He's one of those people who has an opinion about everything, a theory to explain everything. But I also think that he's incredibly gifted and one of the most remarkable people I've ever worked with.'

If *Shabooh Shoobah* was the first album to really indicate INXS's scope as songwriters and musicians, *The Swing* was the album that delivered on the promise. Songs such as 'Melting in the Sun', 'Dancing on the Jetty' (with the immortal lines, 'Watch the world argue/Argue with itself'), 'I Send a Message', 'Johnson's Aeroplane' and 'Burn for You' sounded magnificent. The sound bore little relation to the way INXS sounded live — it was very programmed, very studio based — but it managed to be tough, edgy and danceable at the same time.

Launay had managed to deconstruct INXS and rebuild their sound from the ground up, using the band's essential elements to create something very new and also wildly commercial. The album represented a coming of age for the band as songwriters. Though they had just spent a year on the road, *The Swing* overflowed with strong material. And although the album had five tracks featuring contributions from other band members, there was no denying the fact that the best songs on *The Swing* were the product of the writing partnership of Michael Hutchence and Andrew Farriss. Much as the whole band had developed a sophisticated understanding of songwriting and production techniques over three previous albums, it was Michael and Andrew who were emerging as the dominant creative force. If Andrew was the consummate tunesmith and arranger, Michael had developed an upbeat and inspirational lyric style that seemed to be improving with the confidence brought about by hundreds of live performances.

Together with the band's exceptional tightness, it was an explosive package.

'I think what happened sonically, with *The Swing*, is that Nick Launay realised that the band's biggest musical asset was Jon Farriss,' says Phillip Mortlock. 'He identified this rhythmic, bottom-heavy sound, which had been missing from all the other albums and he really brought Jon into focus. Suddenly, the band had this massive bottom end. Plus this sharper, more experimental sound. And at the same time, Andrew was getting into some very sophisticated arrangements.'

After INXS had completed the album, they called Mark Opitz and asked him for a favour. 'They basically wanted to know whether I'd mind sitting with them in a studio for a day to listen to *The Swing*. I really think that it was so different to anything they'd ever done before — and they just wanted someone outside the band, someone objective I guess, to tell them it was OK. I was already a fan of Nick's work — I'd thought that *10,9,8* was amazing and I knew he'd be perfect for INXS. So anyway, they played me the album, and I remember standing up and saying, "This sounds fucking amazing". There was no question.'

No sooner had *The Swing* been completed than INXS were on a plane again — this time to Japan where they promoted the album and made a video for 'Original Sin'. With its overt Japanese references, the video was another masterstroke in terms of marketing the band to an international audience. Instead of defining INXS as an Australian outfit, Chris Murphy was ensuring that INXS would be viewed as an international phenomenon.

Chris Murphy was quick to recognise the potential of Japan and other parts of Asia — both as markets for the band's music, and as future sources of repertoire. While INXS was in Japan doing their extensive promotional chores, Murphy was busy forging links with some of the more promising local acts. Before long, he began releasing records and promoting tours by Japanese rockers Sandii and the Sunsetz — adding yet another dimension to what was already becoming a diverse business empire.

As Phillip Mortlock observes, 'As all of this was happening, you have to remember that this was the heyday of Men At Work, who were huge all over the world but really as a kind of novelty act. I mean, they were touring with a big backdrop of a kangaroo, it was really dinky. INXS went the opposite way and kind of buried their Australian-ness. Not that they weren't proud of it or tried to hide it, but they wanted to look like they'd come from . . . anywhere.'

chapter 4 | # The Swing

B y early 1984, INXS had been a unit for seven years but they had little to show for all their hard work. They might have been stars at home. Having toured the USA and recorded in the UK, they might have achieved more than most Australian bands could ever hope for, but INXS were yet to achieve international fame or any kind of fortune. Their touring and recording activities had done little more than keep their operation on the road and maintain the band's lifestyles at a subsistence level.

On a personal level, members of INXS were beginning to resent the time spent away from their friends and loved ones. Three members of the band had regular partners. Michael was maintaining a steady relationship — between flings at least — with Michelle Bennett; Kirk was dating Karen Hutchinson, with whom he was to later have a child; and Tim was married to Buffy and struggling to support a young family. Although Michael and Kirk could now afford to bring their girlfriends along for occasional stretches of the road (Buffy Farriss was a less frequent touring companion due to the logistical challenge of small children), on the whole the band members were seeing little of their partners and finding it difficult to maintain relationships at all.

In retrospect, it was Michael who suffered most from this self-imposed lifestyle. If his early childhood had left him yearning stability, he was also inclined to reject anything that smacked of suburban normality. Michael's relationship with Michelle had the potential to be a life-long partnership: the pair were incredibly well-suited and many commented at their uncanny similarity. A part-time model who was to later develop a career as a video director, Michelle was far more grounded than Michael, but no less intelligent or adventurous. Together they made a glamorous and exciting couple — and one that stood out at the hippest parties in Sydney.

If Michael's fame with INXS had reached a plateau at this point, Michael and Michelle might well have settled into long-term wedded bliss; as early as 1983 they were living together and thinking of themselves as a permanent couple. They were, indeed, to remain together for three more years. But perfect as they were together, they were no match for what lay ahead.

What most people outside the band didn't realise was that the INXS story was only just beginning. In *The Swing*, they had a monster commercial album full of great songs, stone-cold grooves and progressive production — and for the duration of 1984, INXS took their music to the world. In January, 'Original Sin' was released in Australia and went immediately to Number One (the song was to top the charts in a number of other territories, including France and Argentina). The band embarked on a sold-out Australian tour that took them through the month of January — and when *The Swing* was released in February, it entered the Australian charts at Number

One. They embarked for the UK, where they spent two months doing promotional chores, playing low-key club dates and shooting videos.

Like the video for 'Burn for You' (shot in the north Queensland cane town of Mackay during the January Australian tour), 'Dancing on the Jetty' was directed by a gifted young Australian film-maker by the name of Richard Lowenstein. One of the leading lights of Melbourne's experimental film-making community, Lowenstein came to the band's attention after Hutchence happened to see the director's seminal low-budget video for the Hunters and Collectors' single 'Talking to a Stranger'. Hutchence sought out Lowenstein for an initial meeting, thus triggering a tight working relationship and an enduring friendship that were to prove pivotal in Hutchence's life.

While he was in London to shoot 'Dancing on the Jetty' (a typically edgy visual treatment, shot in black and white, with plenty of leather and urban street scenes), Lowenstein introduced Michael to another leading figure of the Melbourne underground: Nick Cave. In the early eighties, Cave fronted a noisome, agitated proto-punk art band called The Birthday Party and by his own admission was heavily involved in heroin at the time. In those dark, post-punk times, Cave symbolised the essence of dangerous cool. Like a number of other alternative Australian bands of the era (including The Go-Betweens, The Saints and The Triffids), The Birthday Party found London a more sympathetic and stimulating environment than the Australian pubs — and smack was notoriously cheap there. Hutchence and Cave barely spoke the night Lowenstein introduced them backstage, but the director will always remember Hutchence's enthusiastic reaction to meeting Cave and some years later, when they were both resident in London in the mid-nineties, the two singers struck up an indelible friendship.

Cave and Lowenstein already represented something that Hutchence didn't have. Despite the wonderful friendships and bonds of loyalty that held INXS together, the outfit never challenged Hutchence musically or creatively. They were never more or less than a pop band. Although their musical tastes often leant towards the interesting edge of pop — and while the band's music was far from bubblegum — they were never truly experimental and rarely, if ever, dangerous. Somewhere inside Hutchence was an artist who wanted more than INXS could give. Michael had always been well-read, with a passion for challenging ideas and confrontational art forms, and he yearned to take his own work into darker and more ambitious areas. But it was another year before he'd have time to explore that side of his personality.

During 1984, INXS were on the road non-stop. When they weren't in London attempting to crack the tough British market — something they took years to successfully accomplish — they managed to crisscross the UK and Europe three times, playing small clubs and theatres. They then mounted a three-month US club tour and they finished the year, as they'd begun it, playing another sold-out Australian tour. While *The Swing* was too sonically challenging to ever give INXS the international breakthrough they needed, it was a credible fillip that kept the band in the public eye. In Australia, with three albums to precede it and years of touring providing the audience base, it was a different story. By Christmas 1984, *The Swing* was double platinum, making it — at that time — one of the five biggest domestic albums in the history of Australian music.

Life on the road — and life with a modest hit record —

was beginning to have its rewards for some members of INXS. While Garry Beers and Jon Farriss languished on minimal wages, the key songwriters in the band could now afford their own homes, and in late 1984 Michael bought himself a pleasant two-bedroom terrace house in Wentworth Street, Paddington (an affluent inner-Sydney suburb), which he moved into with Michelle Bennett.

The fact that someone as young and unconventional as Michael Hutchence was investing in real estate — at the tender age of 24 — said much for Chris Murphy's management style. He had always been fixed on the notion that the members of INXS, and their families, deserved some kind of long-term financial security and stability in return for their heroic personal sacrifices. As the band began earning money, he was always careful to channel as much of their income as possible into canny investments that would continue to guarantee their financial security well into the next millennium.

Having seen how difficult it was to extract the band from traditional recording and publishing deals, Murphy also developed a personal philosophy that he instilled into the band and MMA employees: never allow anyone else to own anything that might allow them to make money from INXS. More than any other manager in Australia — with the possible exception of Midnight Oil's Gary Morris — Murphy went about ensuring that all relevant copyrights, whether they be songs, recordings, photographs or videos, were owned by the band. Flying in the face of practices that had governed the music industry for decades, he even refused to allow the band's own record companies to own recorded masters of INXS albums. The recordings were always owned by one of several INXS holding companies, and were only ever leased to the releasing labels. It was an approach that earned Murphy plenty of enemies in the early days of the band because it made it impossible for labels to exploit INXS. Ultimately, it earned Murphy grudging respect from the music industry and turned him into something of a hero for a generation of young bands and managers.

Having spent most of 1984 offshore, INXS were well aware that they needed a monster hit record that would help them to break America in the coming year. While their previous albums had yielded plenty of songs that received airplay around the world, and while the touring had helped to build up their familiarity in a number of key markets, they were yet to score a really bankable hit. At this stage of their careers, such a hit was becoming mandatory. The band had been thinking about producers throughout their year of touring, and though they had one in their sights, there was a question of whether he would agree to work with them.

Chris Thomas was highly experienced, incredibly well regarded and — due to demand — astronomically expensive. In choosing a producer of his status, INXS were acknowledging that the stakes had risen very high indeed. A traditional British producer who had worked on dozens of hit records — including The Sex Pistols' *Never Mind the Bollocks*, Pink Floyd's *Dark Side of the Moon* and albums by artists such as The Pretenders and Elton John — Thomas was renowned for running a tight ship in the studio and was only in the habit of producing two or three albums a year. He was not particularly interested in experimental music or alternative sounds: he was a pop producer par excellence, and the band courted him religiously for several months. Thomas saw INXS in three cities — Los Angeles, Tokyo and Sydney — before he committed to working with them.

'Chris has a great instinct for crafting pop songs,' says David 'Chipper' Nicholas, an Australian engineer who has worked closely with Thomas for many years and engineered two of the three albums Thomas produced for INXS. 'He's a great arranger, and he also takes a big interest in the song-writing. He basically isn't interested in recording a song until the structure is there, and he was someone who had the authority to override Andrew. He was probably the first person to try and override Andrew, and to be honest, that's something that Andrew has always needed.'

'Chris was one of the most talented, most eccentric and demanding people you'd ever want to meet,' says Richard Clapton, who remained close friends with the band after producing *Underneath the Colours* and was a frequent studio visitor. 'I mean, what an eccentric guy — but from the moment you walked into the control room, there was no doubt you were in the presence of greatness. INXS met their match with Chris Thomas. He was the only producer they've ever had who told them what they needed to hear.'

Where *The Swing* had sounded like the edgy, electronically progressive albums being made in the UK around this time, *Listen Like Thieves* — the album Thomas produced with the band at Sydney's Rhinoceros Studios in March 1985 — was far more conservative. Based around live takes that showcased the band's ensemble strengths, it featured guitar-driven rock songs (including the anthemic title track, the majestic splendour of 'Kiss the Dirt' and the beautifully constructed 'This Time') along with doses of funk and a lovely country ballad, 'Shine Like It Does'. It was, in a phrase, tailor-made for the USA, particularly US rock radio (which recoiled in horror at anything that sounded vaguely arty, progressive or funky and, at the time, was in the thrall of big, guitar-driven rock albums like Bruce Springsteen's *Born in the USA*). It was also an album to play live.

'This is what we've been trying to do one way or another for a few years now, and that is to make an album that is purely just the form and function of the songs,' Michael Hutchence said that year. 'We haven't spent hours on countless overdubs — it's a rock 'n' roll album. It's really our first turn-it-up-loud album, you know. Just have a good time with it. It has no great artistic pretensions.'

'All the tracks on this album are primarily live, because of the way we recorded them,' said Tim Farriss at the same time. 'With our other albums, we had to go into a rehearsal studio before a tour and sort of learn to play the material as a band. With this one, nothing like that was needed. Although I do think there's more sweat, blood and tears gone into this album than any of the others. Instead of working ridiculously late hours, it was more or less recorded from nine to five, with weekends off. It gave everyone a chance to think about songs still needed for the record, what kind of songs they should be. The different ideas people had blossomed into all kinds of different songs.'

As the sessions were drawing to a close, Chris Thomas told the kind of difficult home truth INXS were not accustomed to hearing: the album wasn't good enough. Producers of Chris Thomas's calibre are not paid to be yes-men, and Thomas laid it on the line to the band, explaining that the album still didn't have the killer track it needed. Although the sessions had already exhausted their repertoire of finished works — with Thomas discarding anything that didn't appeal — he told INXS to look for anything that might fit.

Typically, it was Andrew who rifled around in his bag of colour-coded demo tapes and pulled out a cassette of a funk song he had been working on with his Portastudio (a primitive multi-track home-recording unit). The song — called 'Funk Song No. 13' — evolved into something that would capture the attention of the world: 'What You Need'. A career-defining slice of rock 'n' funk, 'What You Need' was fuelled by a desperate sexual energy and a smouldering band groove. This was pop music at its most urgent and kinetic. INXS had arrived.

'Even though we had our weekends off when we were recording, we decided that we needed this one track,' Hutchence said at the time. 'What we needed was "What You Need." We wrote it on Saturday, rehearsed it on Sunday and recorded it on Monday.'

While the band was recording, WEA released *Dekadance*, a limited-edition cassette-only EP of INXS remixes. It was a savvy marketing move designed to keep the band's loyal Australian fan-base happy while they were recording, and the cassette sold its run without difficulty. While WEA worried about the band's local audience, Chris Murphy was working to another agenda. Like any good rock manager, he knew that one of the biggest challenges for any band is to master the politics of their own record label.

It's now well documented that the international music business of the seventies and eighties was often ruthless, corrupt and morally bankrupt. The success of an act had as much to do with who you knew, and what relationship you had with them, as it did with talent. The internal politics of international record companies can be complex and Byzantine — not to mention constantly changing — and it has often been observed that band managers who are not resident in the US or the UK always risk being out-manoeuvred by competitors closer to the seat of power. Murphy had foreseen this pitfall and was reaping the benefit of having Gary Grant on the ground in New York to handle a myriad of day-to-day crises.

'Chris went at it with a vengeance,' says Grant Thomas, himself the manager of highly successful antipodean rock export Crowded House. 'He did a bloody amazing job — but let's never forget that he had a great band to work with. Chris was always big on spotting trends, trying to be one step ahead of what was happening everywhere else. He was very conscious that an Australian band needs to be constantly setting the agenda.'

Says Thomas, 'People probably don't realise just how difficult it is to run an international music career from here. People like [U2 Manager] Paul McGuiness — or for that matter any manager based in LA, New York or London — have it so much easier because they're only ever an hour or two away from any major meeting. For us, we're looking at a 24-hour flight just to attend a meeting — and I know Chris did that dozens of times.'

Changes were afoot at Atlantic. A series of internal coups had seen Atco president Doug Morris elevated to more senior positions within Atlantic — and the Atco imprint, originally set up as a boutique label for a number of British acts, was no longer needed. Atco acts were folded into the much larger Atlantic roster, and while this might have been a disaster for INXS, Murphy had put in plenty of hard work massaging his relationship with Doug Morris. As the band began to show signs of having real sales potential, Doug Morris took INXS under his wing as a personal project. Months later, when Morris started showing up at shows with Atlantic founders Ahmet and Nesuhi Ertegun, Chris Murphy knew that the Holy Grail was in sight.

While INXS worked on the new album with Chris Thomas at Rhinoceros, a number of interesting things happened. Firstly, their standing with their adoring Australian audience, and the strength of feeling in Australia towards *The Swing* were proved when they won an unprecedented seven awards at the (popularly-voted) Countdown Awards. Sales of both *Shabooh Shoobah* and *The Swing* had now eclipsed 300,000 domestically, and INXS were widely regarded to be the biggest act in the country. In July, that status was confirmed to a worldwide audience of billions when INXS were selected to be the only Australian representatives for the international charity event Live Aid. The performance — beamed live from the Sydney Entertainment Centre — took place in July.

Not surprisingly, *Listen Like Thieves* was an instant hit at home. However, if INXS were hoping for a rapturous response from the world's media, they would have been disappointed. The British music media delight in putting down all sorts of music as part of a bizarre ritual that has been played out for decades. Australians have generally received short shrift from the British music hacks and the *NME* (*New Musical Express*) made INXS no exception. Calling the band 'INX-cusable', and the album 'INX-plicable', the reviewer declared *Listen Like Thieves* to be a 'complete and utter turkey' and noted the band were 'horrendously named'.

The album was more warmly received by the US media. It was clearly exactly the right sound for that market. As American *Rolling Stone* stated with typical hyperbole: 'INXS rocks with passion and seals the deal with a backbeat that'll blackmail your feet'. Most importantly, American radio embraced the album with open arms. *Listen Like Thieves* was the album that broke the band in America.

Virtually as soon as *Listen Like Thieves* was complete, the touring began again in earnest. Kicking off with a massive Australian run in August ahead of the album's October release, INXS moved on into South America before making a brief return home to appear in Melbourne at a royal command performance for Prince Charles and Lady Diana (presented on Australian TV, rather endearingly, as *Rockin' the Royals*).

The band showed both that they were capable of being dutiful sons and how their wallets had swelled by ensuring that their parents were flown in for the show. Their parents were even invited to sit with the Prince and Princess in the royal box, thus ensuring a consensus of parental approval that had not always been forthcoming. In November, December, January and February, INXS toured solidly through North America, Europe and New Zealand — not so much reaping the benefits of their international success (which was, realistically, still only building) but rather working as a commando unit, going into territories that could benefit from their presence in an effort to build their profile.

Between Chris Murphy, who remained based in Sydney, and Gary Grant, who was now bouncing between offices in New York and London, INXS were being strategically managed as no Australian band before them had been. While the two managers are essentially very different people — Murphy has a certain suave, laid-back demeanour that hides a core of steel, while Grant's edgy, aggressive style obscures a surprisingly co-operative human being — the chemistry was magic. During countless meetings and innumerable international calls, the pair looked at every scenario, and strategised every move.

Part of this plotting involved investing time in markets that were yet to show any interest in the band. To this end, INXS put a concerted effort into cracking the UK, basing themselves in London and playing as often as they could. Although the band found it difficult to achieve airplay or record sales (their sound, at that time, was markedly out of step with British pop), they were able to build up a considerable live following and the British media recognised Michael as a potential star. 'People tended to be big fans of Michael, not necessarily fans of INXS,' the band's UK press officer at the time, Linda Valentine, recalled. 'He was cool and confident and quite arty for an Australian. He was cosmopolitan and interesting to talk to.'

As *Listen Like Thieves* was still building in the US, Chris Murphy decided to give the band a two-month break before embarking on one more American tour to break the album. But what the creative nucleus of INXS needed more than time off was time to work on something else: anything but INXS.

For Andrew Farriss, this work took the form of writing and producing a song called 'You're Gonna Get Hurt' for New Zealand singer Jenny Morris. She had worked as a backing vocalist with the band and had once shared a flat with Michael Hutchence. For Michael's part, the break was the opportunity he'd been waiting for to flex his creative muscle; he flew to Melbourne to act in *Dogs in Space*, Richard Lowenstein's second feature film.

For Michael Hutchence, the making of *Dogs in Space* was risky. As a pop star, he might have had something to gain from the increased profile of a feature film role but, equally, he was an unproven acting talent and Lowenstein's screenplay was full of the kinds of things — casual sex, hard drugs and anti-establishment attitudes — that can cause all sorts of bad press. INXS were nonplussed about his interest in the film, and some members of the band — as well as Chris Murphy — advised against it, believing that it ran the risk of offending both the parents of the band's substantial teenage audience, and the conservative US media. Among the conditions placed on Hutchence's involvement was final cut approval of the film's sex and drug scenes.

However, showing a steely determination that was to become more pronounced as his fame and its pressure grew, and revelling a little in the controversy that his perverse career move had caused within the band camp, Hutchence dived into the project with gusto. *Dogs in Space* was set in a semi-derelict shared household in Melbourne and revolved around the lives of the house's inhabitants. Michael's character, Sam, was based on a friend of Lowenstein's, singer Sam Sejavka. The character is listless, drug-addled and going nowhere fast. Like Mick Jagger's starring role in Nicholas Roeg's unsettling psychodrama *Performance*, it was precisely what Michael needed to toughen up his image.

Despite Michael's tough look with the long hair and leather jackets, he remained conscious that he was still perceived as a pop star with little genuine street cred and even less artistic legitimacy. Lowenstein, for his part, was under no illusions about Michael's motivation for making the film. 'It's part of his endless search for credibility,' he joked in 1989. 'He still has got a strong desire to be an actor and he feels that he has some connections to that world. I think that he also felt close to that Melbourne underground scene and it was a way of developing that contact and also keeping himself fresh.'

It was true that Michael Hutchence saw the film as important from a career-development point of view. He was increasingly self-conscious about INXS's image as shallow pop stars, and longed for the kind of bohemian, underground creative environment he found in Melbourne. He was also serious in his intention to pursue acting as a career. In publicising the film, he made no attempt to hide his interest in expanding his involvement in the medium.

'This is not a whim,' he declared. 'Acting is what I've always wanted to do.' As for the film's perceived glorification of drugs, Hutchence was at pains to defend Lowenstein's vision. 'You can't just say no, no, no to drugs. It's better to present a balanced account and give the facts. The film shows people taking drugs and having a good time, but it also shows the consequences.'

While a song from the movie — an Ollie Olsen composition called 'Rooms for the Memory' featuring a powerful lead vocal from Hutchence — fared well in the charts, the film wasn't so lucky. Released into Australian cinemas under an avalanche of hype, it received very positive reviews but was ultimately not a massive commercial success. Restricted to over-18 audiences because of its explicit scenes of drug use, the film was denied the principal audience it might have attracted, and for which it was apparently intended: teenagers.

By May 1986, with the shooting of Michael's scenes complete, it was time to head back to the States. *Listen Like Thieves* was climbing the US charts (the album ultimately peaked at Number 11) and receiving strong airplay in Europe. It was time to kick the touring into overdrive. Over six months, the band rattled through 32 European shows, 42 US shows and 12 Australian shows on a tour that was titled, appropriately enough, If You've Got It, Shake It. And shake it they did.

By now, INXS were turning into a six-headed touring monster. If Michael Hutchence had shown promise as a young vocalist in the Australian pubs, he had blossomed into a remarkable stage performer in the ensuing decade. Many critics seeing him for the first time compared his stage moves to both Mick Jagger and Jim Morrison, but he was neither as camp and mannered as Jagger, nor as pretentious and self-absorbed as Morrison. With his magnetism and instinct for entertaining and seducing an audience, Michael was ideally suited to larger stages and bigger crowds. He learned to use every available inch of stage: tirelessly running, kicking and skipping from one end to the other. From the lip of the stage or from the catwalk, he reached out to the audience in an electric exchange of energy. As audiences and venues grew, so, in a sense, did he.

The onstage dynamic of INXS, worked out in the pubs and bars of Western Australia, was firmly based in logic and it had its own inherent power. In the frontline, to either side of Michael, stood Kirk Pengilly and Tim Farriss. The pair traded the sharp, melodic guitar breaks that defined INXS songs, with Kirk swapping constantly between guitars and saxes. The pair always looked the part, with Kirk taking a slightly nerdy role in his rimmed spectacles while Tim played the rock-star role for all it was worth. In theatrical terms, the pair represented opposite sides of the same coin. Tim signified rock's past, while Kirk signified its future. Tim was about the physical, visceral experience; Kirk was about the cerebral. Together, they provided Michael with a complex musical and visual foil, a frontline of attack and showmanship that gave audiences a feast of visual entertainment.

At the rear of the stage lay the work team: Andrew Farriss behind a bank of keyboards and samplers (from which he would regularly emerge with a guitar) and the band's watertight rhythm section: Garry Gary Beers and Jon Farriss. Rarely straying from their allotted positions, Jon, Andrew and Garry were the engine room of INXS, generating a formidable bottom end that was notable for its economy as much as for its force. But what set them apart from most bands was their absolute commitment to the performance. This was a band that worked for a living.

'We assumed our natural positions onstage years ago,' Tim noted in 1992, 'with Michael in the middle and Kirk and I on either side. Kirk and I have been playing for such a long time, and we've always had the attitude that whatever we did in music, it should entertain people.'

Kirk Pengilly believes it was INXS's professionalism and discipline that led to their prowess and consistency as a live band. 'After all those gigs, you'd like to think that you'd never put on a bad show,' he noted at the peak of the band's touring years. 'We've learnt how to pace ourselves and enjoy being there, every night. Even if one of us isn't feeling that great, I think we all still do a pretty good show that the audience will enjoy. With a band in our position, every gig is important, every gig has to be professionally presented and as good as it can possibly be. We all have that common goal.'

INXS were finally starting to make money from the American touring, particularly from the lucrative merchandising concessions that sell everything from T-shirts to belt buckles. Instead of pocketing the profits, the band put their money back into their stage show, pushing their dollars hard to create the most impressive show they could afford.

To their credit, INXS *were* impressing people. America's influential *Musician* magazine called them 'the best live band in the world'. But intriguingly, even as far back as the mid-eighties, some critics were already wary of the band's please-everyone-at-any-price ambition — and not all of them were in Britain. Critics observed that the band appeared to be trying too hard to entertain. In a review of a gig in November 1985, the *LA Times* raised some fascinating questions about

INXS (whom they referred to as the 'most shamelessly commercial rock outfit since Queen') and their fatal flaws.

'INXS doesn't convince you it has any driving originality or vision,' read the review. 'To be sure, lead singer Michael Hutchence is an effective front man. He keeps the momentum going as he races about the stage and he's enough of a sex symbol to keep the teen-queen hearts pumping. The band also laid down an infectious beat that kept the eager, enthusiastic crowd dancing through the evening.

'At the end, however, you are left only with appreciation for INXS's game plan. In the hit-conscious mood of seventies rock, there was almost something exciting in Queen's climb to the top. But times have changed. There is a renewed sense of integrity and purpose in rock today that makes INXS' struggle for success seem irrelevant.'

Nevertheless, 14 months after they started to promote it, *Listen Like Thieves* was clearly the band's biggest album. With worldwide sales of some 1.4 million, it wasn't an unqualified monster but it was a massive hit by Australian standards. And slowly, subtly, it dawned on Chris Murphy and the members of INXS that something strange was happening to their lead singer. Before their eyes, Michael was transforming into a superstar.

The feyness of his youth had been toughened by years on the road. His early aloofness had been replaced with a knowing, self-mocking confidence that seduced women and made men feel like his friend. He was singing and performing like a demon, and as his face aged and his hair matted, he started to *look* terrific. But Michael was not a star in the traditional sense: where most famous singers are loud, outspoken and extremely self-confident, he was in fact rather softly-spoken and somehow shy. Articulate and amusing as he was in private conversation, he often became a stammering, mumbling mess in public. Talk show fodder he was not — but he *was* a star.

'The thing about Michael is that he had this incredible charisma, far more than most singers in pop, but he was also very self-effacing about it,' recalls Phillip Mortlock. 'And that was maybe because he was a very sensitive and intelligent person, and he didn't believe his own crap. He didn't take himself seriously as a pop star. He was the first person to acknowledge how funny it all was, how ridiculous it was — and yet, through all that, he took the work very seriously.

'You see that image of Michael looking like the ultimate up-himself pop star. But the split second afterwards, he probably would have burst out laughing: laughing at himself, basically.'

Michael responded positively to fame. Instead of running from it, or denying it existed, he lapped it up. But in doing so, he was always at pains to ensure that his own ego remained closely in check.

'I love being famous,' he declared later. 'It's like a totally Freudian thing — it makes me feel wanted and loved and noticed. Anyone would want that, wouldn't they? It would be stupid of me to pretend that singing in INXS isn't exciting — because it's an unbelievable thing. It's so good, it's beyond words; it's ridiculous to even attempt to quantify it. But perhaps just to deal with it I find myself saying, "It's no big deal, this is just what I do".'

'I don't really believe I'm there, to be honest. I find it very, very weird that I'm onstage in front of thousands of people. On one level I'm completely involved with what's happening, but on another level I'm completely cut off from it, like I'm in a bubble.'

chapter 5

Sometimes You Kick

Although INXS were supposed to be taking an eight-month break before commencing work on a new album, it was too tempting not to capitalise on their ongoing status as the biggest band in Australia. Chris Murphy was canny enough to know that, having toured the country several times in the past few years, INXS would need to stage something a little special — something that would signal that the band had reached a new level as a touring act. He also wanted a vehicle to showcase the growing stable of acts he was handling via his management company, MMA.

Thus the Australian Made concert tour was born: it was a series of major outdoor shows featuring INXS, Jimmy Barnes, The Models, The Divinyls, Mental As Anything and I'm Talking. To promote the tour, INXS and Barnes entered Rhinoceros Studios with Mark Opitz and recorded a barnstorming version of an Australian rock 'n' roll classic, the Easybeats' 'Good Times'. The debauched sessions were captured for perpetuity in the high-octane video for the song. The song proved to be something of a harbinger: over the handful of mammoth outdoor dates they played in early January 1987, the Australian Made entourage partied like there was no tomorrow — and played to over 200,000 people.

It was another successful chapter for INXS and the band's financial worth was beginning to grow. Murphy urged the band members to invest their jointly held funds in real estate, with the result that members still own whole blocks of flats in smart harbourside suburbs of Sydney, such as Kirribilli, to this very day. He also urged them to put some of their money into a new Australian film called *Crocodile Dundee*. This was, in retrospect, one of the best pieces of advice he ever gave them.

The band's involvement in the film project had followed a circuitous course. INXS had originally been asked to contribute a song for the film soundtrack — and after being flown to Queensland to visit the film set and meet the movie's star, Paul Hogan, Andrew and Michael sat down to pen a song called 'Different Worlds'. The exercise was not particularly fruitful for any of the parties — the song was buried in the soundmix and eventually surfaced as an INXS B-side — but it did lead to their investment in the film.

But it was also clear that life in the spotlight was taking its toll. Much as INXS had begun to achieve the international recognition that most musicians only dream of, they were paying an extremely high price. For Tim Farriss, the greatest compromise was the enormous amounts of time he'd been forced to spend away from his young family. His brother Andrew had never been particularly fond of the hedonistic party atmosphere of the tours and the way it took him away from favoured pursuits such as writing and producing. (It's a complaint that has dogged the creative members of many bands, including Brian Wilson and John Lennon.) As the years went by, Andrew was coming to resent touring more and more.

And while other members of INXS, particularly Michael, appeared to be embracing life on the road warmly, there was a feeling within the band that it was a lifestyle with the capacity to destroy him. The availability of cocaine on the road — particularly in America — was proving a temptation for most of the band. As good-looking party boys and emerging stars, INXS were offered coke and other drugs in all sorts of situations. Along with pot and alcohol, it was becoming a nightly phenomenon, and, with it, Michael's behaviour was becoming more erratic and unpredictable, his attitude more arrogant.

Beautiful women were also in plentiful supply on the road. After seven years, Michael's relationship with Michelle Bennett came to a halt. While the relationship had never been monogamous, it had at least provided him with a strong emotional centre. Suddenly he was free to lead the life of a swinging bachelor. 'The first years INXS toured America, I slept with a lot of women,' he recalled later. 'I was in a hotel room with someone, and the bedhead was making too much noise on the wall, so I put a pillow behind it. Then that girl left and another girl came in and asked "What's that pillow for?" and I thought "You'll find out in a second."'

'All of a sudden you get famous and the combination of money, attention and travelling gives you an artificial feeling of power. You start to think that you can do whatever you want without being judged. You think that everything is automatically meant for you. The scary thing is that this feeling is being created, daily, by waiters, cabdrivers, slimy people from the record company and too many fanatic fans. You're being pulled into this world without noticing it. At the same time you have this constant feeling that it could all end tomorrow, so being unfaithful becomes a virtue, something which is justified.

'You'd think, "I'm on the road now for a year", so you just take what you can get. I've done a few stupid things in my time, but it's just frustration and boredom. That's the same reason anybody does stupid things, though it's good fun too. But after a while you just get smart. You've got to have respect for yourself, otherwise *you* end up getting used.'

In the months after Australian Made, Andrew Farriss ventured further into the world of freelance writing and production, creating a new album for Jenny Morris. Jon Farriss, meanwhile, took on the somewhat daunting task of producing Richard Clapton's new album. Bankrolled by millionaire entrepreneur Rod Muir (a former radio man who had made a fortune from his stake in Sydney's Triple M radio network), Clapton's *Glory Road* was one of the most technically brilliant albums ever recorded in Australia.

'I think it was very good for Jonnie that he came and did that album,' says Clapton. The album also featured cameo performances from most other members of the band. 'I think they've all needed, at various times, to get their minds off INXS. And that's why I've often encouraged them to come away and work with me.'

'We'd been close friends for a long time,' Jon said, speaking of the *Glory Road* project. 'We'd been talking about the songs as he was writing them and talking about how they should be recorded. I wanted to play on the album — and when [original producer] Mark Opitz had to leave to do the Hoodoo Gurus album, I just kept with it. I just saw my role as helping Richard — who I think is a great poetic genius of his generation — to record his songs to their level of excellence.'

Michael Hutchence was one of several members of INXS to turn up on *Glory Road* as a guest artist. He also found time to produce a single called 'Motorcycle Baby' by a group called Ecco Homo. The creation of music-business stylist Troy Davies — a close associate of Richard Lowenstein's — Ecco Homo was notable more for an uncredited (and unacknowledged) performance by U2 on 'New York New York' than for any commercial success.

The upward mobility of INXS was subtle, but noticeable. Andrew Farriss bought a house on the north shore of Sydney, just a few streets from where he had grown up; Kirk Pengilly bought himself a duplex in Cammeray, a suburb of Sydney, with a view to extensive renovations; and, on the advice of his financial adviser Gordon Fisher, Michael Hutchence decided to put his Hong Kong passport to good use and make the city his permanent place of residence. In taking advantage of the Hong Kong's favourable tax regime and in placing himself in a convenient position geographically, half-way between Australia and the rest of the world, Hutchence was also losing something very precious. From that point on, he would be unable to spend more than six months of the year in Australia. He bought an apartment in Hong Kong and invited Jon Farriss to move in as his flatmate.

'For eight months we've all been as far away from each other as possible,' Tim Farriss told Australian *Rolling Stone* as the band reconvened to record their new album halfway through 1987. 'It feels really good. I think we're a lot closer as friends after the last ten years. We've grown up together, lived in houses together, the whole thing. These days, though, the little arguments that would never have bothered us before can really hurt people. A little tiff that would have been shrugged off three years ago now seems to last that much longer. Travelling together for months on end is not easy — it's never easy — but, on the other side of the coin, when you're onstage there's that much more emotion.'

'The group has become more intense as the years have gone by,' he continued. 'These days the energy and emotional level are just brilliant. The expectations tend to be so high that it's like a whole different attitude, going into something that's going to be better than anything we've done before.'

As Farriss pointed out, INXS had become a hotbed of emotion — and not all of it was positive. As well as individual resentments about the size of their workload, the undeniable damage that ongoing self-abuse was wreaking on some members of the band and doubts about the band's prospects of finally breaking through, there were simmering jealousies about what other members were contributing — and what they were gaining financially. Some members of the band were frustrated because they weren't adequately represented as writers (consequently missing out on massive royalties) and there was a continuing dispute over the band's musical direction. To a significant extent, Andrew was beginning to dominate the band's studio sessions, often playing guitar or bass — or even programming drums — in addition to his keyboard duties.

Although INXS remained committed to each other and their common goal, and each member recognised that no resentment or dispute would be large enough to jeopardise the long-term stability of the band, there was no denying the undercurrents.

For Michael, at least, the band's profile in Australia was creating problems of its own, as the demands of fame and the loss of personal privacy began to take their toll. At times, the pressure appeared to be getting too great.

'The days before *Kick* were hard for the band,' Gary Grant observed later. 'The band hadn't yet cracked the mega-album and everyone was pretty frazzled. I know that there had been well over a million dollars spent in advances for tour support.'

The sessions for *Kick* — which commenced in June 1987, again at Rhinoceros with Chris Thomas producing — started badly. While INXS had been well prepared for *Listen Like Thieves*, and had worked intensively on the songs prior to commencing recording, they were nowhere near as well prepared this time. Despite the lengthy lay-off — or perhaps because of it — band members had simply not been inclined to get together for songwriting. The relationship between Andrew and Michael was becoming strained, too, as the differences in their tastes and lifestyles became more dramatic by the day.

'The way Andrew and I write now has completely changed,' Michael observed at the time. 'We used to write everything together but that's not as easy any more and Andrew's style has got more eccentric. He'll send me tapes and he'll look at my lyrics and then we try to squash the two together. I just write stuff down all the time and throw it in a laundry bag. When I start writing songs, I empty out the bag and go through what's there for a long burst. I just immerse myself in the process of it. I ain't no Shakespeare and it's hard work not to write filler, but sometimes there's nothing better than just shutting off and writing.'

Much as members of the band had become adept writers, arrangers, producers and musicians with a sophisticated understanding of pop structure, they were also at loggerheads with each other. In addition, the relationship with Chris Thomas was becoming tense.

'When we first went into the studio, the band really didn't have enough material,' recalls David Nicholas, who engineered *Kick*. 'We recorded about six tracks, and then Chris called a halt to the sessions and sort of banished Michael and Andrew to Hong Kong to do some writing. When they came back, they were really firing — and one of the songs to come out of that second set of sessions was "Need You Tonight".

'I don't think you can say that the break in the middle was any kind of negative thing — in fact, after *Kick*, I worked with Chris Thomas for eight years straight and that became one of our standard working methods with lots of other artists. You just focus on the tracks that are working, abandon the ones that aren't coming up to scratch and then take some time out to reassess what you've done. It's a luxury that many artists couldn't afford, but at this point INXS definitely could.'

Listening to *Kick* with the benefit of hindsight, it's easy to hear it as a pop masterpiece. It is, in many respects, the definitive INXS album — and it was to become one of the most successful albums of the decade. But as it was being made, most of the participants were unaware that they'd just created a little piece of pop history. They were relieved that the album had turned out so well, perhaps. They were possibly even excited by a number of tracks. But they didn't yet realise exactly what they had created.

'*Kick* was the album where everything came together,' says Nicholas. 'We'd been searching for a sound for some time, this sort of hard-edged funk sound, but really clean and precise, but we never quite got it on tape. As soon as we put down "Need You Tonight", we knew we had it. I wouldn't say there was any particularly special feeling in the studio —

I mean, we were usually happy with what we'd done — but I remember everyone feeling very satisfied.'

'The sessions were really a bit slack,' says Richard Clapton, who was frequently present during recording as he was still producing *Glory Road* — with Jon Farriss and David Nicholas — in the studio next door. 'The band already had a lot of external distractions because they were reaching the point in their careers where it was all about to break wide open. With *Listen Like Thieves*, they had put a lot of pre-production work into the songs. They were structured; they'd worked on them. With *Kick*, they didn't really have the songs down in the same way, but they'd reached a point where they were such great players that they were very casual and confident in the studio. They didn't feel so pressured. I think at that point they really did sound amazing — and Chris's genius was that he was able to capture those grooves.'

Although Andrew had already emerged as the band's most musically creative member, INXS had a long history of creating music as a unit. Many of their best songs resulted from band jam sessions, and the six members all exercised their rights to be involved in the making of the band's music, writing and producing all manner of album tracks and B-sides. While Chris Thomas was keen to contain the band's tendency to run off at tangents, he and Nicholas could only stand back and admire the ensemble sound in the studio.

'Like all great bands, the whole is greater than the sum of the parts — but having said that, there's an incredible amount of musical talent in the band,' says Nicholas. 'I mean, take Tim. He doesn't write a note, but nobody plays guitar like him; he's one of the most underrated musicians I've ever worked with. Jon is . . . technically very capable . . . but I must say he has a tendency towards the flamboyant. But when you put him together with Garry Gary, who has a very simple, basic style — and is also a very good player — the effect is just awesome.'

Nicholas says his albums with the band were marked by a tremendous work ethic: 'They're very, very disciplined people,' he says. 'I mean, nobody really wants to be in a studio for weeks and weeks on end, it's a place to work so you can get out of there. But on all three albums, all the band members were always there, working at it together.'

Even though INXS were under-prepared for recording *Kick*, they had managed to create a magnificent pop album — and nobody could take that away from them. 'Need You Tonight' sizzled with frightening sexual energy, and songs such as 'New Sensation' and 'Devil Inside' were paradigms of pop songwriting: they were tough, they were memorable and they were laden with hooklines. And as strong as the album was, it was capped perfectly by the band's truly masterful ballad, 'Never Tear Us Apart'. By the time they recorded *Kick*, INXS implicitly understood their individual roles; to a highly sophisticated degree, they had come to understand their strengths and weaknesses. In short, they knew what worked.

'With this album we've definitely done exactly what we wanted to do,' Michael Hutchence explained upon its release. 'Songs like "Mediate" we never would have considered once. Andrew's had that around for a couple of years and we both felt, "Let's go for it, indulge ourselves". This album has a lot more bubbling underneath. The last album was very white guitar music and this is funkier. I hate, more than anything, sexless music.'

Phillip Mortlock (by then promoted to managing director of EastWest, thanks in large part to his work with INXS) says, '*Kick* was the album where it all came together musically.

But it came together in every other way as well. The package was brilliant. The videos were sensational, and you can't underestimate the impact that had in the US. The record sounded amazing on the radio. And finally, the band had evolved into this incredible live act and they were just covering the globe with great shows. In every conceivable way, they got it right.'

After wrapping up album sessions in August with final overdubs at Studio De Le Grande Armee in Paris (the album was mixed later at London's Air Studios by the legendary Bob Clearmountain, creating a finished product that the band regarded as 'too slick'), INXS moved immediately into the longest tour of their career. It was a tour that would take up a staggering 15 months of their lives. Within the band's inner circle of friends, advisors and aides, there were concerns that the band were in no fit state to undertake such an emotionally and physically draining exercise. They were already drained beyond exhaustion, although their partying lifestyle was probably masking the impact. Michael, particularly, was becoming increasingly disconnected from his band-mates. He found success both empowering and deeply disturbing — and those close to him began to feel a sense of impending doom as the tour approached. Even before the first note was played, the other band members had private fears about Michael's ability to handle the pressure.

'I think the press is a major reason Michael stays out of Australia,' Tim Farriss told a reporter in 1987. 'He couldn't handle it any more. He likes going out a hell of a lot and everywhere he goes he gets treated as *Michael Hutchence* rather than someone just hanging out at a club. There were a couple of days during the recording of *Kick* when Michael just didn't turn up and we knew he was off somewhere feeling really depressed about all of that. I just wonder how this tour is going to be for him. He seems to be a little homeless at the moment, but that's what he wants. He doesn't want to be tied to anyone or anything, so we'll see how it goes. It's important that we all remain close, because it's hard to do this kind of touring without some kind of centre.'

Hutchence had his own take on fame: 'I think it's really hard to keep a sense of yourself because everybody takes a little piece of you. Sometimes, if too many pieces get taken, you end up with nothing. So in the end you just go, "OK, fuck you, have it all! I'm not going to be a person any more, I'm just going to be this item". And you start to think callous, you start to think heavy, you start manipulating.'

As the band prepared for the *Kick* world tour, Michael predicted that he wouldn't be back in Australia for at least a year — and his reasons included criminal charges which had been brought against him in Queensland and the Northern Territory arising from his dispensing of condoms from the stage on their last national tour. Typically, he seemed to be dramatising these events for his own ends, as the charges were never particularly serious and he had no intention of being in Australia anyway. The tax avoidance measures he had put in place effectively prevented him from remaining in the country.

'Apparently I'm going to be arrested for "Irresponsibility in a Public Place",' he told reporters at the time, clearly enjoying the role of rock outlaw. 'Joh Bjelke-Petersen [then premier of Queensland] has got taxpayers' money to spend on things like prosecuting me and he's got the bucks to spend months in court pushing it through.'

The Calling All Nations tour kicked off in the US and Canada and rocked on for a solid 15 months. Although four short breaks of approximately a month were built into the schedule (including one for compassionate leave when Kirk Pengilly and Karen Hutchinson's first baby, April, was born in April 1988) these were often interrupted with promotional chores of one sort or another. The *Kick* album was turning into a monster throughout the world, and the demands on the band's time were escalating daily. All up, the band played 170 shows across Europe, the UK, the USA, Canada, Japan and Australia. Originally budgeted to gross $3.5 million, Calling All Nations took some A$6 million.

INXS had never been a particularly loose, improvisational kind of rock band. They had always favoured a show that was big on well-rehearsed dynamics and low on indulgent solos — or moments of genuine inspiration. But as they went to mount the *Kick* tour, the band began to develop a stunning stage show that managed to blend a very rigid sense of structure and form with moments of real warmth and excitement. Working on a clean, uncluttered stage that gave full impact to the band's co-ordinated stagewear and dramatic lighting plots, INXS laid down grooves that were crisp and economical.

Andrew Farriss had not yet gained the confidence to move out from behind his bank of keyboards and by necessity Garry Gary Beers remained close to Jon Farriss's drum riser. That left only Kirk and Tim to prowl the stage, inserting angular stabs of melody into the sound while Michael commanded the stage and delivered his vocals. Like all large-scale rock bands of the era, INXS in concert were highly structured — possibly even to the point of predictability. But in an element they knew so well, live performance, the band succeeded in transcending the impressive technology to deliver a riveting spectacle of sound and vision. It was little wonder that the band was able to fill venues night after night.

Around this time the INXS management partnership of Gary Grant and Chris Murphy was dissolved and Gary Grant became managing director of MMA Management as well as INXS's Australasian manager. For Grant it turned out to be bad timing, as he missed out on a large slice of the fortune generated by the band's international success.

Well before the tour reached its final days, INXS were becoming one of the biggest bands in the world. With sales for *Kick* exceeding five million units and a US chart peak for the album of Number Three, the band swept the pool at the MTV Video Awards, taking home five statuettes. When INXS returned to Australia in October 1988, they did so as conquering heroes. In a legendary six-night stand at the Sydney Entertainment Centre, they played to over 75,000 fans.

As their fame increased, the gap between Michael and the rest of the band widened. Whereas once the members of INXS had seen themselves as six equals united against the world, it now felt like one singer, his songwriting partner and The Rest. Internationally, the media made no secret of the fact that they were only interested in speaking with Hutchence (although they were frequently given other members of the band to talk to anyway). While this is far from unusual in rock bands, it's rare for so *much* focus to be placed on a front-man, and so *little* on his band.

When, mid-way through the Calling All Nations tour, American *Rolling Stone* wanted to feature INXS on its cover — undeniably one of the greatest honours a band can receive — it was clear that only Michael was wanted. (Like many magazines, *Rolling Stone* takes the view that bands simply don't work graphically, and generally pushes for a maximum of two heads.) Chris Murphy insisted that the magazine should run a shot of the full band, or none at all. The magazine called his bluff and declined the offer.

Michael Hutchence was being singled out for practical reasons: the media and even the fans found it difficult to get their heads around six different names and faces; it was a lot easier to deal with one. Also the band's other core creative member, Andrew Farriss, was less charismatic and an awkward interview subject (a few journalists became so exasperated with Andrew that they specifically requested to never interview him again). But it was mainly because Michael had that indefinable quality of stardom. It was a quality which was already beginning to isolate Michael from his band-mates, friends and family; a quality that placed a strange, existentialist distance between himself and everyone else.

'We tried to fight it for a while when it first started to happen,' remembers Garry Gary Beers. 'We'd refuse to do magazine covers unless the whole band was photographed, but finally it got to a point that no matter what we did it just got out of control anyway. If they couldn't get Michael for the cover, the magazine would find an unauthorised shot of Michael and work it onto the cover anyway. Not only did we lose control, there'd be all these crappy shots of Michael appearing on all these covers! So we decided to go along with it for a while.

'Ultimately, I think the rest of us in the band are pretty happy that Michael gets the attention because it's not that glamorous. It's a lot of work. For me, it's great because I can walk around just about anywhere in the world and not get recognised — which is an essential part of life. I like to have a really good time at being a bit of a rock star onstage, but when I walk off, I'm off stage.

'With Michael, he's basically always in the focus and grabbing attention, but he handles it really well — I'd say a million times better than the rest of the band. It's fine with him, so he has no problem with it, which allows the rest of us to just be the band.'

Kick continued to ride high in charts all over the world — and things kept getting stranger. At one stage, INXS were offered the support slot on The Rolling Stones' mammoth Steel Wheels tour. The band knocked it back (arguably to their detriment as it was the tour that broke Guns 'N' Roses). Hutchence was quoted as saying: 'We're too big for that. I mean, come on. I love Mick and everything, but we sell a lot more records. They're legends but we've been at this for too long to support them.'

Calling All Nations was not a tour that began and ended at the same level. At the outset, INXS's agents had booked them into theatres and college auditoriums befitting a band with a platinum album. The Grant/Murphy idea was that it was preferable to sell out multiple small shows (in the 3,000 to 5,000 capacity range) rather than testing INXS's pulling power by attempting one large arena. But as the hit singles, 'Need You Tonight', 'New Sensation' and 'Devil Inside', rocketed up the charts, and as *Kick* lodged itself firmly in the US Top Five, INXS began filling larger and larger venues. By the mid-way point, they were comfortably selling out 12,000-seat rooms. By the final stages of the tour, they were headlining venues such as Madison Square Garden with a capacity of between 15,000 and 30,000 people.

As one of the band's agents at ICM was fond of saying, bands who play the US market should ideally see themselves as prostitutes. INXS had spent several years wandering the block, touting for business. Now, said the agent, it was time to 'Open your legs *real wide*'.

Richard Wilkins was one of several Australian media representatives who travelled to the US to witness the extent of the band's success. A former singer whose band Wilde and Reckless had supported INXS on more than one occasion, Wilkins was appointed host of MTV when it was launched in Australia in 1987. The following year, he found himself watching INXS headline the LA Forum and marvelling at the sheer size of the crowd.

'I know plenty of people have said this,' says Wilkins, 'but when I saw them that night I was simply blown away. I had no idea that they were that huge, you know. When you were confronted with this huge auditorium full of screaming kids, you realised that these guys had really made it. And I also remember the backstage scene being a real blast — because you'd make your way back to say hi to the band, and you needed three different laminates [security passes] just to get back there. And when you finally reached the inner sanctum, there were all these incredibly famous people standing around. The night I was there it was John McEnroe, Julian Lennon, Belinda Carlisle ... but it would have been different the next night and the one after that. Michael was being invited to parties at Andy Warhol's place. I don't think most Australians had any idea this was even happening.'

For all the delirium of success, the tour was taking an immense physical toll. The band members were still able to connect with each other for the two joyous hours they spent together onstage, but offstage their health was deteriorating. Jon had contracted a bacterial parasite that affected his legs, inflicting intense pain every time he played. Tim's legs were becoming increasingly affected by an painful arthritic condition known as Reiter's syndrome. The band had been forced to cancel some European dates and were barely able to play the Australian ones.

'I had the worst experience of my life, on a physical level, on that tour,' Jon revealed soon afterwards. 'The whole process really took a lot out of me, including the mental stress of having to cancel those dates. When I hit the last crash cymbal at the end of "Don't Change" at that last gig in Sydney, I had tears running down my face. I was literally weeping. It was like "I can't believe I did it. I made it".'

Emotionally, the band were all so drained that they were unable to see beyond the next show. Particularly for Tim and Kirk, who had forsaken months of precious time with their growing families, the stress was become unbearable. 'Towards the end of the *Kick* [Calling All Nations] tour, I guess we started to feel a little bitter because we were tired and we'd had enough,' Garry Gary Beers observed. 'We were probably stupid to feel that way, because the whole world was going nuts for the album, but we were just feeling the pressure.'

The impact on Michael was even more severe. As the tour grew in size, and Michael's profile as one of the best known rock stars in the world increased, he seemed to be picking up and dropping girlfriends as quickly as he changed towns. Some — including Australian actor Virginia Hey and American model Jonnie — lasted for some months. Others lasted two or three nights. Michael could still be a hell of a lot of fun to be around, but he was distancing himself from the band and his management; he was surrounded by an inner sanctum of friends, staff and drug buddies and had a ready supply of Ecstasy, coke and Halcyon tablets for the come-downs. He took to disappearing for days on end, only turning up at a venue in time for the show.

The other members of INXS had experienced Michael's tardiness and general unreliability for years; it had become a running joke within the band. But now, with the band under immense stress — and with INXS finding themselves playing to tens of thousands of people each night — it was disturbing. Much as Michael would invariably turn up and dispel every-one's tension by making profuse apologies, it was a little like the drunken groom who turns up late for his own wedding: funny, but not that funny.

Friends and associates started relating stories of an increas-ingly erratic Michael swanning through hotel lobbies at 3 am, his long hair limp and greasy after nights without sleep, wearing nothing but a bathrobe. Some band members were drawn into Michael's world for sections of the the tour and then found themselves outside the circle again. Others simply felt they hardly knew him any more.

This was not the way it was supposed to be. INXS had always prided themselves on their ability to take care of each other. Just like a sporting team, they had covered for each other in numerous times of difficulty. The band's dynamics had always been founded on a series of powerful allegiances that went deeper than friendship or mutual interest: the familial bond between the Farriss brothers; the alliance between the two main writers in the band, Andrew and Michael; and the invisible ties that still bound Tim and Kirk (the band's oldest members and the two players who had been working together for longest).

'We've always looked after each other, looked out for each other,' says Jon Farriss. 'There have been times when certain people have been going through a bad patch, where they're not as motivated or happy within themselves, but we all work through it.'

No-one, however, was able to reach out to Michael. For some weeks, he even took the step of making separate travelling arrangements from the rest of the band. Privately, many members of the touring party started to worry whether the day would come when there'd be an audience, five band members and no singer. One night in 1988, at a time when manager Chris Murphy was valiantly trying to reign in the excessive behaviour that was becoming rife in the entourage — Michael's drug use in particular — Richard Clapton witnessed a show in Paris that will stick in his mind forever.

'I was standing in the wings with Murphy and Michael,' remembers Clapton, 'and the band had already walked onstage and had laid into the groove for the first song. Chris said something like, "Have a good show, Michael", and Michael just looked at Chris, looked at me, then opened his hand to reveal several Es. He popped them into his mouth and said, "Thanks, I will", then walked out in front of 25,000 people.

'I went to the mixing desk to see what would happen, because I was seriously wondering whether he'd get through the gig. And the funny thing was, the band was so good and so popular that I really don't think anyone noticed. At one point Michael just stood there on the edge of the stage, high as a kite, saying, *"Je T'aime* Paris! I want to fuck you!" and the audience was just going nuts.'

Michael had a licence to be — and do — whatever he wanted. Without losing his sly sense of humour or his charming, loving nature, he was pushing that licence to its outer limits.

'When you're in a band at that level,' says a friend, 'you can be almost anything you want to be. You're in a fantasy world. Famous stars and beautiful models who you've never even met are coming backstage to party with you. If you have a nature to indulge yourself in drugs or drinking or sex, you tend to do that because it's all laid out for you on a platter. You want a gram of coke at 2 o'clock in the morning? There are people in the entourage who can organise it for you. There's a party on literally every night, and people are going out of their way to offer you *everything*. It can be very seductive, but obviously it's also very dangerous because there are just no limits.'

Michael Hutchence had little to say about this period of his life — at the time or later. (He did offer this writer a delightful *bon mot*: 'The band worries about me too much, which is, you know ... charming.') In 1990 he told *Q* magazine that: 'At the end of the *Kick* tour there were so many demands on me as a human being that I just stopped relating. The hysteria that surrounded that album meant that I couldn't see where I fitted in any more. I started disconnecting and flipping out into my own world that revolved around nothing else but acid house and a boom box. I couldn't cope, so I retreated.'

After the last Australian show, the band members scattered in six directions, taking little time for fond or emotional farewells. Like long distance runners, they had maintained their focus on the finishing line for what had seemed like an eternity. They went their separate ways with little thought for the immediate future. 'In a sense, INXS split up after the *Kick* tour,' Jon Farriss observed a few years later. 'We all sort of went, "Goodbye, I don't know when I'll see you again", and walked away from it. It was a wonderful break because it was the first taste any of us had ever had of real personal freedom. So when we got back together it was a very conscious decision. We weren't fulfilling an obligation, we were doing it because we wanted to.'

Few band members were idle for long, however. After the tour, Andrew Farriss produced another album for Jenny Morris, titled *Shiver*. (The album was to become a major hit in its own right, achieving triple platinum sales and earning Andrew a prestigious Australian Record Industry Association (ARIA) Award for Producer of the Year.) Garry Gary Beers formed a band with Sean Kelly, singer/guitarist with another well-known Australian band The Models. Their band, Absent Friends, proved to be a surprise commercial success, and will always be remembered as the band that launched the career of singer Wendy Matthews.

With some help from Kirk, Tim Farriss found time to do some production work with Sydney band Crash Politics and he commenced work on a documentary about his favourite leisure activity, fishing. Entitled *Fish in Space*, the documentary was self-funded and remained in a state of perpetual production for many years. One of the most expensive documentaries ever made in Australia, at the time of writing the film has not been completed and it's unclear whether it will ever be given a commercial release. Kirk Pengilly invested in a state-of-the-art computer and spent much of his holiday learning to use it as a songwriting and studio production tool.

For Chris Murphy, who had been collecting an estimated 15–20 per cent of the band's gross earnings for more than a decade, the time had come to expand his own business empire. The company's artist management division, MMA Management, boasted a large and diverse stable of acts, including The

Models, Jenny Morris and a slew of others. MMA Music, the music publishing division, didn't have INXS's songs to generate millions, but they were accumulating a healthy catalogue of talented songwriters nonetheless. And, meanwhile, Murphy had opened a whole new branch of his business with rooArt, an independent label that would go on to become one of the most successful on the local scene.

Chris Murphy's efforts with INXS had earned him enough to build, at just 35, a multi-faceted business empire. After years spent running MMA from small and relatively unassuming offices — first in Mosman and Neutral Bay in Sydney's north and later in Kings Cross — Murphy was soon upgrading to a massive heritage building that had previously housed the Sydney Women's Hospital in inner city Darlinghurst. Murphy's office in this building was so large it was almost comical — bigger than most residential apartments. His father would have been proud of him.

The band were also showing the signs of their new-found wealth. While Tim bought a fishing boat, *King Kong*, and extensively renovated his house in Frenchs Forest, Garry Gary purchased a large farm near Somersby, NSW, and set about renovating the house and building a 24-track home studio. Kirk commissioned respected Australian architect Luigi Roselli to draw up designs for his Cammeray Road duplex. Michael barely paused for breath.

There's an old adage in the music business that rock stars who develop bad habits on the road normally develop *really* bad habits off the road. Once the discipline of touring is removed, and there's no longer any reason to keep upright and sober — and once the boredom and chronic lack of attention and excitement set in — the wheels generally fall off in spectacular fashion.

However, Michael had never been a self-destructive drug-user. 'The thing about Michael and drugs was the same as Michael and sex — he was just someone who wanted to explore the whole experience,' says a close friend. 'He wanted to submit his body and his mind to whatever states he could find. He didn't do drugs to kill the pain or kill himself, he did them because he wanted to learn, he wanted to experience, he wanted to have more fun.'

To the surprise of his friends — and perhaps even himself — Michael Hutchence had a strong sense of control. In the pantheon of rock behaviour, Hutchence was never a Keith Moon, a Jim Morrison or a Keith Richards. As much as he loved drugs and was capable of sustaining days or weeks of near-constant intake, he was also deft at pulling back from the brink. He was more than capable of drying himself out, and indeed there were many periods when Michael was very health-conscious, working out in a gym or practising kick-boxing. He was too smart and too ambitious to be something as tacky as a rock casualty.

So, just when it was least expected, Michael cleaned up his act as he dived headlong into a busy schedule of activity. Between adventure holidays to outback Australia (on his beloved Harley Davidson), Morocco, northern Thailand and southern France, he purchased a grand new two-level apartment in the upmarket Hong Kong suburb of Stanley, overlooking Repulse Bay and the South China Sea. The singer also found time to work — maintaining his public profile by appearing at a number of international awards shows to either present or receive awards. At the 1989 Grammy Awards, he created a major controversy by attending the show with a radically shorn haircut. For a star whose familiar face had been framed by a lanky mane of curls, this was a staggering change.

'That's hilarious, isn't it?' Michael said at the time. 'I wanted to cut my hair short — it was as simple as that. I saw all these guys in heavy metal bands like Cinderella, who I don't like, with long-hair perms, and I was afraid I'd get associated with that. I just like short hair. But people went nuts.'

Most importantly, Hutchence used the break for two vitally important creative projects. The first was *Frankenstein Unbound*, a film by legendary Hollywood B-grade director Roger Corman (his films include *The Trip* and *The Wild Angels*). Shot in Italy with John Hurt and Bridget Fonda, with Michael playing little more than a walk-on part as the Romantic poet Percy Bysshe Shelley, it was a performance that generated as little interest as the film itself. Yet, for Hutchence, it was a wonderful experience. He took to the role with great studiousness, reading up on the lives of the Romantic poets. He found his time at Lake Como during the shoot highly stimulating, and often recounted the night that he sat with John Hurt reading poetry by candlelight in a old ballroom overlooking the lake, the curtains billowing in the vast windows while a thunderstorm raged outside. For Michael, this was a creative liberation.

'I think it turned out OK,' Hutchence observed at the time. 'It was a strange kind of thing to be plunged into. Roger is in his sixties but he's still very young, he's got a very wild eye. This is the first time he's had a lot of money for a film and he was like a kid with a lot of new toys. I think it's going to look fantastic. There was a serious amount of method acting going on when the cameras weren't running. The thing I learnt was that there are no rules. You just have to get out and do it.'

The main creative project Michael undertook in his year off was to form a band called Max Q with Melbourne experimental musician Ollie Olsen. Michael had met Ollie when they worked together on *Dogs in Space* (Ollie was the film's music director, and he was also a close friend of Richard Lowenstein's and a lifetime member of the Melbourne underground), and they had spoken several times about working together. Early in 1989, Michael booked ten days of studio time at Rhinoceros (which was by then co-owned by INXS) so that he and Ollie could work on some possible tracks.

Both Michael and Ollie were pleased with the results. Later in the year, while he was holed up in Los Angeles sitting out some time between awards show appearances, Michael had an urge to record an album. Immediately. As only rich rock stars can do, he summoned Olsen and had staff arrange his ticket and passport. Within days Olsen was in LA, ready to work. If Olsen was eccentric, difficult and unreliable, these were all qualities that Michael found refreshing and exciting.

'I think he is crazy,' Michael noted in 1989. 'I think he's one of the few people I can say that about without being flippant. I think his lyrics are great and he lives like a super-hero. His approach to life and his values are so high and noble it's inspiring. He's definitely the master of another universe. In LA the Americans didn't know what to make of him. He's telling them what he thinks and they're going "Oh yes, Ollie, I really love your anger. I appreciate that".'

It was clear that Hutchence saw the album, simply titled *Max Q*, as a golden opportunity to stretch himself creatively. While he made less of a contribution to lyrics than he had ever made with INXS (most of the songs were largely complete Olsen originals), he played a far more active role as an arranger and producer. Importantly, the music Hutchence made with his collaborators in Max Q was among the most powerful and exciting of his career. Completed in Sydney at Rhinoceros before being mixed in New York by Todd Terry, the album was edgy and demanding, yet undeniably commercial and accessible. It was an album that was years ahead of its time.

'It was born out of enthusiasm,' Michael said. 'I've learnt how to produce. It's painful. I went through a lot to do it but it's very satisfying when you make your own decisions; you stick by them and you learn something. Whether or not the record does well doesn't really matter at this point because I think it will stand the test of time.'

Hutchence was also convinced that Max Q could adopt a far more radical position, politically, than INXS would ever dare to do. He was coming to view the world of mainstream rock 'n' roll as somehow distasteful, possibly even evil.

'There is a Reagan mentality, even in music, that is almost right wing,' he observed. 'It's somewhere between heavy metal and a lot of the older rap that's getting above the crotch — the sort of, "It's money I want, and a Porsche", and it's vaguely homophobic and misogynist. The Guns 'N' Roses ideology, which is basically let's make some money, let's bash some fags. And the weird thing is that there's all these kids who are saying to their parents, "Mum, I don't want to be a doctor, I'm going to join a heavy metal band". And their parents think that's fine, it's basically the same thing to them, only you'll probably make more money with metal. Max Q is the opposite to all of that. It's very political, it borders on the anarchistic. It's a subtle thing but it's in there.'

The Max Q project created substantial divisions in the INXS camp. The band members were horrified to learn that Michael was taking his talents and lending them to a project over which they had no control. Bizarre as it may sound, Andrew Farriss later claimed that he knew nothing of the project until he turned on his TV one day to find Michael fronting another band. INXS were terrified that Max Q would actually have a hit, because they saw in that possibility the danger that Michael might take this as his cue to leave INXS or attempt to maintain parallel careers.

Chris Murphy was in a slightly different position. As Michael's manager, he brokered the Max Q recording deal (the band remained on Atlantic in the US and with Polygram in Europe, but switched to CBS for the Australian market). But as the manager of INXS, he had to be extremely careful not to undermine the band's chances for future success. He also had five furious band members insisting that Murphy contain Max Q to a manageable size.

Murphy ensured that the project would be lucrative by doing a favourable deal with Australian distributor CBS. But he insisted that Michael's name and likeness be kept from all advertisements and publicity materials, a decision which may have adversely affected Max Q's commercial success. This was probably compounded by the fact that Michael's availability to do interviews or perform live to promote the album was also limited because INXS were back in the studio working on their next album.

While Max Q never attained a fraction of the success that INXS were enjoying, Michael remained proud of the achievement, and seemed determined to maintain the same sense of creative control and daring adventure when he returned to INXS.

'Prior to Max Q, I don't think I'd really been my own person in a creative sense,' he said in 1991. 'I'd never been able to pick and choose what I wanted to do or where I wanted to go, but in that 12-month period I took control of all that. I wrote and recorded an album with Max Q, and made a film as well. I found it incredibly liberating. The whole exercise gave me faith in myself as an artist, it gave me confidence that I was capable of doing something outside INXS.

'I had so much life and spirit in me after that year. I felt it [Max Q] was the best thing I'd ever done, not just for me but for INXS. I'd never really thought of myself as a musician before that. My contribution to INXS had been quite naïve in a lot of ways, but through my other experiences I found I was capable of so much more.'

In the final months of 1989, the six members of INXS began talking regularly again — partly because the time was coming to make plans for a new album and partly because they were in the midst of renegotiating their contract with Chris Murphy. Like many bands who become very successful, they were beginning to resent the amount of money that Murphy had made in commissions. In the early days, Murphy had worked 18-hour days for his cut of the band's meagre earnings but now he was CEO of a rather large and unwieldy business empire that included artist management, a record company, a publishing company and other interests. The band felt that they no longer had their manager's undivided attention; indeed they noted that they sometimes experienced difficulty in getting him to take their calls.

Even though the band was surrounded by a large inner sanctum of permanent staff — including Gary Grant, publicist Niki Turner, tour manager Michael Long and MMA staffers like Sam Evans, Paul Craig, Martha Troup and Kim Frankiewicz — they had every reason to expect a full-time manager. Given the money Murphy was now earning from the band, they felt it was no longer acceptable to be fobbed off onto mere support staff.

'The band dragged it on for as long as possible — partly just to give Chris the shits,' relates a close friend. 'They had their own lawyer and accountant, and I think they all enjoyed the game of it, the sport of it, and the sense that they had something that Chris wanted desperately.'

At that time Michael Hutchence might have thought that he had become as famous as anyone would ever hope to be. But, in November 1989, he began a relationship with a 22-year-old Melbourne woman, which who would ensure that he would enter a whole new phase of his life — a period of intense public attention — that would not even end with his death in 1997. Her name, of course, was Kylie Minogue.

chapter 6

The Kylie Thing

U p until the end of 1989, Michael Hutchence's love-life had generally taken place behind closed doors. Like any rock star, he'd had more than his fair share of groupies, celebrity flings and short-terms romances. While he had generally maintained a steady relationship throughout most periods of his life, he found monogamy difficult and his eye was always wandering. But even after his long-term relationship with Michelle Bennett disintegrated, there had been shorter relationships with others.

'Michael loved women,' his friend Richard Lowenstein observed recently. 'It's not so much that he messed around a lot. I don't know that he did, but he loved women and he loved flirting. It wasn't just about women, he would flirt with anything and everything. He would flirt with a rock if he could.

'The normal rites of sexual possession broke down around Michael. I remember one night he took a girl upstairs while her boyfriend's band were playing in the pub across the road. The guitarist had to stop the set and get off stage and back to the hotel room before Michael and his girlfriend. But there were no hard feelings — they became good friends after that, it was a male bonding sort of thing. When Michael turned on the charm he was impossible to resist. He'd tilt his head down and look up at you and totally focus his attention.'

Michael was far from traditional in his sexual appetites. A keen student of sexual literature — including the writings of the Marquis de Sade and contemporary British writer Angela Carter — he was fond of auto-eroticism, sado-masochism and multiple partners. On the X tour, at the same time as he was pushing his interest in drugs to its furthest limits, he was also experimenting wildly with sex. As one of the most desirable and available singers on the planet — and, for some, the most charismatic rock star of his generation — he was in a position to make love to virtually any woman he wanted, anywhere. For many periods of his life, he indulged this fantasy to the hilt. But in 1989, with the band in recess and with Michael working busily on *Max Q* and *Frankenstein Unbound*, his mind was turning towards a serious relationship once more. He had a very specific partner in mind.

Kylie Minogue was an intriguing choice for a girlfriend. At just 22, this petite Melbourne blonde had already captured the hearts of millions, firstly in the Australian soap opera *Neighbours* and then as a recording artist controlled by the hit-making UK creative team, Stock, Aitken and Waterman. Kylie commanded a massive and adoring audience throughout Australia, the UK and Europe; she was already worth millions of dollars and she was already in a stratosphere of fame and notoriety that Michael Hutchence could only dream of.

In the entertainment world, relationships between high-profile people are surprisingly common — with good reason.

Most 'normal' people with no experience of this world find a lifestyle of constant work, travel and partying exhausting and disorienting. If one partner in a relationship is famous and the other isn't, there's a tendency for all sorts of imbalances and resentments to come into play. But two famous people can exist on an altogether different plane. In theory, at least, neither partner feels threatened, and both understand the pressures and demands that are placed on the other.

Michael and Kylie first met in July 1987 when Michael almost literally bowled Kylie over at that year's Countdown Awards. Kylie had just picked up a slew of awards for her first album, and Michael was in an exuberant and somewhat mischievous mood. Legend has it that his first words to Minogue were 'I want to fuck you'. It's not a story that either Minogue or Hutchence ever confirmed, and others say that Hutchence was both drunk and attempting to make some public point about Minogue's lack of credibility.

Kylie and Michael met again in late 1988 when Kylie and then-boyfriend Jason Donovan went to an INXS show in Melbourne and later attended a post-show party. They talked, and Kylie later told friends that Michael had taken this opportunity to apologise for his public comments about her music. By 1989, Michael Hutchence was ready to take his casual acquaintance with Kylie Minogue a little further. When Kylie was due to play some shows in Hong Kong, he set about making contact.

Michael's Hong Kong life was always a well-guarded secret — not so much because the singer made any formal attempt to keep his affairs private, but more because of Hong Kong's distance from other western cities. Although there was a large expatriate community who may have been peripherally aware of the rock star in their midst, Hong Kong had its own hierachies of millionaires, socialites, models and high-flyers. It was a glamorous, sophisticated world in which Hutchence felt protected and comfortable — and between sojourns in the better known cities of the world, he loved his time in Hong Kong. The city afforded Michael privacy and anonymity, and, given its strict drug laws, it was as good a place as any for him to escape the temptations that were available elsewhere. True, he was known to indulge his passion for opium while based in Hong Kong, but this was not a daily phenomenon.

And there were other considerations that made Hong Kong an attractive base. Although Michael's professional relationship with his financial advisor Gordon Fisher had ended acrimoniously in 1988, he continued to employ highly secretive tax minimisation schemes in the years to follow. With the help of two former Fisher associates based in Hong Hong, Colin Diamond and Andrew Paul, Michael created a web of interlocking companies and trusts that would baffle even the most tenacious investigator. But in 1989 it was not money on Michael's mind, but love.

Michael Hutchence was a master of seduction, but he also knew how to play the role of gentleman suitor. He could be extraordinarily urbane, witty and charming when he wanted to be — and almost as soon as the Kylie Minogue tour party hit Hong Kong, Michael was very much in evidence as a host and guide to the city. He took Kylie and other members of her entourage water-skiing, shopping and sight-seeing. He also made a date with the singer, with the original plan being for Michael and Jon Farriss to accompany Kylie to dinner. In fact, if Farriss had had his way, things might have wound up differently.

'When I heard she was coming to Hong Kong I sort of said, "Hey, I'm going to take Kylie out, I hope you don't mind", explains Jon. 'And Michael sort of went, "Oh, now I'm taking Kylie out and I hope *you* don't mind". So we ended up organising a dinner together and it quickly turned into a kind of humorous thing. We were getting ready in opposite bathrooms and looking at each other going, "You're looking good, but I'm looking better".'

'We were just about to leave the house and we were both looking at each other with stupid smiles and Michael said, "Look Jon, I have to ask you a question, I hope you don't mind", and I said, "What?". And he said, "Do you mind if I go out alone tonight?" And I gave him this look, like, you've *got* to be kidding, and he said, "No, I'm sorry, I have to insist that I go out alone tonight. If you really want to come along that's fine but I think it would be better if it was just me". And I said, "OK, fair enough." And off he went.'

Kylie Minogue will probably never forget that night. At that time, she was very much the product of a highly protective, paternalistic organisation that not only determined what she would sing, what she should wear and what she should do with her career but also, to a large extent, how she should live her life. This organisation — which included her manager, Terry Blamey, as well as Stock, Aitken and Waterman, and her accountant father — was fiercely protective of Kylie. She was, after all, the goose that had laid the golden egg. The advent of Michael Hutchence was not in the five-year plan.

'It started badly,' she recalls. 'He was hours late. I was in my hotel room with my mother, my four dancers, my assistant and my manager, and they were getting more and more protective and annoyed. He finally arrived and he was confronted by all these angry faces. And then when we got to the restaurant, the food made me feel ill. But from that terrible start, we had a fantastic time. We talked and talked until we simply had to be separated.'

A week later, Michael followed Kylie to Japan. It was clear to all that the pair were besotted. Days later, Kylie had to dash off to London for some UK concert dates. As soon as they were over, she returned immediately to Hong Kong to spend a week with Michael before they both travelled to Sydney. She had work to do launching her new film, *The Delinquents*, while Michael was needed in Sydney for preproduction work on the new INXS album. The pair decided to rent an apartment in one of Sydney's most exclusive apartment buildings, The Connaught, overlooking Hyde Park. They set up camp for a Sydney summer of partying, love and work.

The affair proved to be a landmark moment in the careers of both Michael Hutchence and Kylie Minogue — and not just because of the intense level of media attention the lovers attracted. During their liaison, Minogue's public persona changed rapidly from being a frothy, one-dimensional teenager to something approaching a mature artist. And Hutchence, despite his fame with INXS, suddenly became tabloid fodder with many articles focusing on the apparent chasm between Kylie's clean-cut image and Michael's supposedly debauched lifestyle. He gained a place in the hearts of the British media from which he could never escape. 'It was shocking for everyone, including me,' says Kylie now. 'But he wasn't as bad as everyone thought, and I wasn't as good. We met somewhere in the middle.'

'We come from totally different situations,' Michael explained. 'Obviously all this affects me because I don't have that sort of image. People are saying, "What the hell are you two doing together?" I guess it shows how cruel I am, because I don't really care.

'Because she's copped so much criticism, she's a really strong person. She's formed her own philosophies because of that. It's made her a really good person because she can cut through people so fast it's not funny. It's scary how much she's toughening up. It just so happens that two people with a very high public profile got together. I think cynical people still think it's some sort of professional relationship, but it's definitely not. I'm not interested in publicising my personal life.'

Michael took perverse pleasure in all the attention — particularly in the widely held view that, as a lascivious rock star, he had taken an innocent young thing and corrupted her into becoming some kind of salivating sex vixen. But having comfortably avoided the tabloid media up until this point, he now found himself being stalked by paparazzi and, to his annoyance, he discovered that the British media were concocting stories out of thin air.

For weeks on end, Michael and Kylie appeared to be everywhere. While they might not have done more than any other young couple on holiday in Sydney, their every move was reported — from nightclubs to bookshops, from cafes and restaurants to rides around the city on Michael's Harley Davidson.

'There's a really evil, insidious part to being famous whereby the media can just make stuff up about you and there's absolutely nothing you can do to stop it,' Michael said at the time. 'They have this weird ability to mess with your life, all in the interests of selling a few newspapers.

'I pretend that this kind of thing doesn't affect me but . . . when I read things about my personal life that concern people who are close to me, it can really affect me quite badly . . . People do believe what they read. I mean, I do it

INXS in the early days.

1985: With *Listen Like Thieves* INXS had recorded the album that would make them international superstars.

INXS manager Chris Murphy in 1986.

L-R: Record producer Mark Opitz with Tim Farriss, unknown and Michael Hutchence.

INXS on Moon Plains (north of Coober Pedy, SA) making the video for 'Kiss the Dirt', from the *Listen Like Thieves* album.

Two of Michael's closest friends and confidants: Michelle Bennett and Richard Lowenstein, 1986.

Michael with his mother, Patricia Glassop, 1986.

Michael with Michelle Bennett: in the early eighties they were the hippest couple in Sydney.

Michael (Sam) with co-star Saskia Post (Anna) in a scene from *Dogs in Space*.

INXS celebrating the massive Australian success of *The Swing*, Sydney Harbour, 1984.

Paul Hogan (C), star of the hit movie *Crocodile Dundee*, with Andrew Farriss and Michael Hutchence on location in 1986. INXS were asked to contribute to the CD soundtrack — and wound up investing in the film.

Michael with LA model Jonnie at the MTV awards, 1988; the year INXS 'scooped the pool', winning five statuettes.

MIKE GUESTELLE/STAR FILE/APL

Rolling Stone Keith Richards backstage with Michael after a Madison Square Garden concert in 1988. INXS were always nervous playing New York or LA because the audience was always littered with celebrities.

J. B. DONNELLY/RETNA LTD/APL

1990: Michael with Kylie Minogue at his 30th birthday party. Kylie baked him a birthday cake.

Kirk Pengilly, Michael Hutchence and Tim Farriss on stage at Rock In Rio in 1991. With a crowd of 130,000 it was one of the biggest shows the band would ever play.

DAVE HOGAN/REX/AUSTRAL

Michael performs before 75,000 fans at Wembley Stadium, 1991.

ANDREW MURRAY/ALL ACTION/SYDNEY FREELANCE

1992's Concert for Life was to have been the most memorable outdoor show Sydney had ever seen. Instead, it turned into INXS's worst PR disaster.

Concert for Life: More than 60,000 fans swarmed to Centennial Park, Sydney, to witness sets from bands such as Diesel, Crowded House and INXS.

Michael with Helena Christensen, 1993. As one of the world's biggest rock stars and one of the world's top models, they made a beautiful couple.   ROSS BARNETT/APL

Michael with Paula Yates,
who once described him as 'old-
fashioned and very gentlemanly'.

Michael confronting paparazzi in
London: as his personal nightmare
worsened, the singer became
increasingly prone to violent
confrontations.

Sydney, 1996: Michael and Paula with Tiger Lily — just before opium was found in the couple's London home.

ROBERT ROSEN

Michael, shown here playing with Pixie, adapted surprisingly well to his new role as a family man.

BRENDAN BEIRNE/REX/AUSTRAL

In late 1996 Michael Hutchence rejoined INXS in Sydney to start rehearsals for the *Elegantly Wasted* promotional tour.

BRADLEY PATRICK/HEADPRESS

INXS at a press conference in Sydney late 1996. L-R: Kirk Pengilly, Andrew Farriss, Tim Farriss, Jon Farriss, Michael Hutchence and Garry Gary Beers.

BRADLEY PATRICK/HEADPRESS

Paula and Tiger Lily arriving at the funeral. The hours before and after Michael's funeral were fraught with intense family battles.

Michael's brother Rhett, wearing a striped suit that once belonged to the rock star, acts as pallbearer with members of INXS.

myself. And what can you do? Sue them? Get a skywriter to write "It's Not True" in the sky?'

With Kylie Minogue, Michael Hutchence discovered what it was like to be a media superstar. He was not simply of interest to rock journalists and screaming INXS fans, but to almost everybody. 'Up until Kylie, I'd never really been hassled in the streets or in clubs,' he observed a year later. 'I wouldn't act like a rock star, I wouldn't go out with body-guards or anything like that. But I had to change some of those attitudes because the way she works is the total anti-thesis of the way I work. If we went out for dinner anywhere in Europe, there'd be six cars full of photographers following us the whole time. We needed a racing-car driver to get us across Paris.

'We would never walk through the same doorway twice. It was always this rigmarole of going in the service entrance, hop into a car, change cars, go back there, enter through the basement — it was just ridiculous. But the thing is, the more you behave like a star, the more you get hassled. You create a sensation.

'It's funny to have some guy follow you around in a little Golf GTI all day and you don't even know it. You realise at the end of the day that's he's been taking photos of you holding hands and picking your nose. I just think it's boring. Who the fuck cares? Who gives a shit? We're just two people. I can think of much more important things. I don't like taking up space, you know? And they keep on writing bullshit about us.'

While Michael was enjoying the first flush of romance with Kylie — and reeling from the fact that photographers were being offered as much as A$50,000 for shots of him and Kylie kissing in the park — he had other, more pressing matters to contend with. Much as Kylie's transformation was fascinating the world, it was of only peripheral interest to Michael. By late November 1989, the six members of INXS had reconvened in Sydney at rehearsal rooms beneath Sydney's most memorable landmark, the Opera House, and things were not going at all well.

In the year since the band members had parted company, there had been plenty of changes on both a personal and professional level. Just as Michael had used his year off wisely, trying new working methods, expanding his experiences and finding a new love, the other members of INXS had been busy as well. While the band had been in hiatus, Chris Murphy (who had taken to calling himself C.M. Murphy to distinguish himself from a well-known Sydney lawyer of the same name) was building his business, consolidating both rooArt and MMA into major forces within the Australian industry. In 1989, *Australian Business* magazine named C.M. Murphy Entrepreneur of the Year.

Before the band reconvened, Michael had made grand pronouncements about the album, signalling (not too subtly) his intentions to take INXS into uncharted waters, to reflect some of the experimental edge he'd connected with in Max Q.

'This next album is going to be very important for us to do, and it's not as though we've sold 20 million albums,' he told a reporter. 'We've still got a lot to do. This is a symbolic time for us. The new decade is starting and we're older, we're not 22 any more. I think our energies, our attitudes have been directed in larger areas and I think the band is becoming more and more capable. There's a whole other side to INXS that hasn't been exposed, part of which has to do with the Melbourne connections to Max Q.

'I think above all, though, that there is an integrity to

INXS, in the music, that makes it worthwhile. God knows what the next album is going to be like but I know that I want it to be a more modern band.'

However, Michael Hutchence, in pushing his own musical agenda towards the left of centre, didn't necessarily have the band's support. Most of the band members had taken plenty of time out to relax, but their musical tastes had not progressed. If anything, some of them were becoming more conservative, looking into traditional musical forms for inspiration. Andrew Farriss, in particular, had rediscovered his love for country music, Bob Dylan and rhythm & blues — passions he'd been able to indulge in his work with Jenny Morris. When he and Michael first started tossing song ideas around for the new album, there was little common ground and plenty of conflict. As INXS struggled to make sense of Andrew Farriss's new songs, the mood at the Opera House was grim.

'It was kind of messy,' Michael Hutchence related. 'To be honest, it was pretty hard those first couple of weeks. I mean, INXS is not just sitting around holding hands, it's not like the fucking *Partridge Family*. At the same time we're very, very lucky that we've stuck together and gone as far as we have. We have a lot of respect for each other.'

'It was quite stressful and challenging when we regrouped to make *X*,' recalls Kirk Pengilly. 'The year off was really important to our development, because it was literally the first time we'd had the time and space to get our lives together. We hadn't previously had the opportunity to develop as individuals because we were always together and always working. It was like taking six lions who had been locked in a cage together for 12 years ... and just letting them go.

'There was a lot of tension when we first came back

together. We'd all gone off and done other things so there was a period when we had to re-establish where we all sat with one another. And I guess you have those nagging questions like, "Will it work? Will the magic still be there?" '

Some of the tension was professional: while Andrew and Michael struggled to make musical connections, several band members were making more noise than ever about the whole notion of a principal songwriting team within the band. The success of the *Kick* album had created a situation where Andrew and Michael were now far more wealthy than the other members of the band and, as they struggled to find a new identity, the entire band dynamic was shifting. Jon Farriss, in particular, had been writing with Michael in Hong Kong, and two songs from this collaboration were to make it onto the new album. For his own part, Andrew firmly believed that INXS songs could only ever be written by him and Michael, and if songs by other writers were allowed on an album, it was generally against his will.

But the differences weren't all about music. At a fundamental level, INXS were drifting apart. Egos were running rampant, as were some members' drug use. The six-way bond that had sustained them through more than a decade of hard work was bursting at the seams — and many members were seriously doubting their ability to carry on. Resentments over Michael's 'defection' to Max Q were openly aired. (If he had so many great ideas about songwriting, singing and production, why hadn't he used them for INXS?) In the first few weeks of rehearsals, Garry Gary Beers went so far as to resign from INXS. Even though he overturned his decision within days, it was a signal that the band's internal relations were strained to breaking point.

'The band wasn't getting on very well at all,' recalls David Nicholas. 'They'd been on the road for such a long time, and most of them hadn't really taken much of a break. Andrew and Michael, particularly, weren't getting on at all.'

The strain on the central creative relationship in INXS was only a sideshow compared with the deteriorating relationship between Andrew Farriss and producer Chris Thomas. The fraught hit-making partnership reached crisis point as the band moved from the Opera House to the newly installed Studio 1 at Rhinoceros. With a grand control room that resembled the bridge on Starship Enterprise, Rhinoceros was a testament to INXS's unbelievable success. But as the band started working on the X album with Chris Thomas, Rhinoceros was a great place to avoid.

Although Thomas was no stranger to excessive behaviour himself, he was also a consummate professional — and he was appalled by the band's disarray. Seeing the lack of focus and cohesion in the studio, Thomas attempted to take over the sessions in what quickly became a titanic struggle of anger, resentment, substance abuse and creative inertia.

'Chris can be very dictatorial in the studio, particularly if things are going badly,' says David Nicholas. 'He tends to just take control and start ordering people around. Andrew and Chris had always had a problem because they're both very similar, very strong willed. So, yeah, there were a great many heated moments. It was a very stressful time for the band, really hard.'

Late one night, the studio arguments became so intense that a very inebriated Chris Thomas announced that he was not only leaving the room — he was leaving the country for good. He stormed out of the studio and started charging up Oxford Street in the general direction of Sydney Airport.

David Nicholas had to run after him and physically drag him back to work.

'Chris was really pissed off with them because he took the view that they just got away with some things on *Kick*, but he felt that they couldn't afford to be that casual a second time,' says Clapton. 'The band had become flushed with the massive success of *Kick* and they were very self-confident. As far as Chris was concerned, they were overly confident — and as a result there was a kind of slack attitude in the studio. I remember Chris complaining to me that the band just didn't have the songs.'

The recording sessions for the album limped along, as much an exercise in compromise and getting the project finished as any kind of expression of creative enthusiasm. As with *Kick*, the band had insufficient material to create an entire album in one sitting, so Andrew and Michael were banished to New Zealand to write more material mid-way through the session. Upon their return, the album was completed at the rate of one song per week. While a number of tracks were very strong, including 'Bitter Tears', 'Disappear' and the first single, 'Suicide Blonde' (Michael's galloping personal tribute to Kylie Minogue), the album lacked either the rock attack of *Listen Like Thieves* or the irresistible pop hooks of *Kick*.

Nevertheless, X was still a strong album and it was certainly made more interesting by the involvement of outside players such as American bluesman Charlie Musselwhite. The album's attempts at musical sophistication were laudable and demonstrated a desire by the band for some ongoing musical progress, but X lacked the fire of its predecessors. Ultimately, X was saved by the band's instinctive musicianship and Chris Thomas's invaluable skills as a record producer.

The making of the X album marks a turning point, of sorts, in the career of INXS. For perhaps the first time in their adult lives, the band's six members were finding life in the band to be extremely tough. Much as their lives had always involved hard work and personal sacrifice, life in the band had always been intrinsically enjoyable. Now, it wasn't even that.

If it all seemed too hard — and during that unseasonably wet, humid Sydney summer, that's precisely how it felt — there was never any suggestion that the band had any alternative but to continue. One thing INXS still had going for them — perhaps their greatest asset — was their mutual commitment. They'd come a long way, but they hadn't reached the end of the journey.

'We haven't reached our goal yet,' Jon Farriss noted at the time. 'And this is a very idealistic, naïve goal which we sat around a table having a joint over about thirteen years ago, all being very young and cosmic and extremely excitable. The goal was essentially to go as far as we could go with our music and tap into as many people as we possibly could.'

Andrew Farriss's relationship with Chris Thomas was so bad that, for the first time ever, Andrew absented himself from the album's mixing sessions, leaving Michael and Chris to mix the album at London's Air Studios in June 1990. The short break that followed the album's completion gave Andrew the opportunity to tour briefly with Jenny Morris — including some European dates supporting Prince — while Tim Farriss continued his work with Crash Politics.

Although Kylie had remained a resident of Sydney throughout the early stages of the recording of X, she was eventually forced to return to her London base to resume her promotional duties for The Delinquents and to start recording a new album. Michael and Kylie remained in constant contact (after one brief period together, Kylie was busted going through Heathrow with a set of handcuffs) and after the mix of the album was completed in June, the couple took an extended European holiday which included two weeks in Italy and a trip to Provence. Michael had already fallen in love with southern France during a holiday there (with Australian friend Michael Hamlyn) in 1989 and, in an impulsive moment, he decided to buy a house there. Costing A$480,000, the couple's intended love-nest was a beautiful old white-washed cottage between the villages of Valbonne and Roque-fort Les Pins in the foothills of the Alpes Maritimes. The poetically named Ferme de Guerches was furnished with beau-tiful antiques from London dealer David Wainwright, and it was set in manicured gardens with swathes of lavender, olive groves, grape vines and a pool.

Michael and Kylie returned to London in fine style aboard the Venice–London Orient Express. Later that month, he pre-sented his lover with a diamond ring. For both of them, this was the stuff of whirlwind romance but, with INXS about to set off on another lengthy world tour, fate was not on their side. If Kylie hoped that the affair would develop into some-thing permanent, she was to wait in vain. Not only did the marriage proposal never eventuate, but the rumours of Michael's infidelities began surfacing virtually as soon as the tour kicked off.

As Minogue admits, her relationship with Hutchence brought an undeniable cachet of credibility to her highly manufactured pop career. In the months after she met Michael, she began taking control of her music in a way she had never done before. She started out on the long, slow path towards learning how to write songs and create music on her own — forging a personal style that owed nothing to the work of a controlling producer.

As the release of *X* rolled around, INXS started on their PR chores, enduring interminable interview junkets (in which media interviews were scheduled for up to ten hours a day) as they sold the album to fans all over the world. By this time, the other band members were becoming extremely wary of Michael; not only was he turning into a somewhat unpredictable force onstage and in the studio, but in interviews he was becoming something of a loose cannon. Interviews with Michael were largely about Kylie, sex, drugs, travel, the pressures of fame, world politics, matters pertaining to ecology and the Australian economy, and Max Q — but his comments were frequently flakey and rarely did they seem to be about INXS. As a result, a policy was instituted that other band members should be present at interviews to remind Michael of why he was there. It was to be a considerable time before Michael was allowed to be left off his leash alone.

chapter 7

X Marks the Spot

Although 'Suicide Blonde' was not a song in the same league as 'Need You Tonight', the pop radio stations of the world were ready for another single from INXS; the band's sound and their look were still synonymous with the high gloss of the late eighties and the new material was greeted with open arms. The single and the *X* album enjoyed massive success throughout all the markets INXS had broken with *Kick*, and quite a few that it hadn't. It was the album that turned the band into superstars in South America, the United Kingdom and Europe. Ultimately sales of *X* were less than half of *Kick*, but there are few bands anywhere who could be unhappy with sales in excess of four million units.

INXS had emerged from the *X* sessions feeling more confident about their future than they had at the outset. They felt good about the album, and they were excited at the prospect of playing some huge shows. They had finally achieved a level of success that made everything about their job much easier. And, on the basis of the offers that were coming through from promoters in every market, the *X* tour was clearly going to be a raging commercial success. INXS, who had always struggled to make a good living from touring because of their enormous overheads, finally looked set to make some serious money from their shows.

This time, the band decided, touring was going to be fun. They wanted to behave, and feel, less like a battalion of foot-soldiers or rats on a wheel and more like rock stars. If it were to be an exercise in luxury and indulgence, so be it. They were determined to avoid a repetition of the *Kick* tour, where the tedium of the road nearly brought the band asunder. Although there was an ample supply of French champagne, exotic beers and all manner of other temptations, the band were relishing the chance to have more healthy fun — taking up sports such as skiing and roller-blading as the tour progressed. For the first time in years, the band members started to look at the cities they were in, enjoying the experience of international travel in a way that only the truly rich can appreciate.

INXS could now afford to travel with the very best support staff that money could buy: not just top-notch sound and lighting guys but stylists, wardrobe staff, hair and make-up consultants and personal assistants. Such assistance was standard fare in the upper echelons of international rock 'n' roll, but it was relatively new to INXS. In adapting so many of the trappings of superstardom, there was also a feeling with the X tour that the band should put on the best shows of their career.

'When we all sat down to discuss the tour, we all agreed that we'd reached a level where we simply had to put on a great show,' Kirk Pengilly commented. 'We realised that we were literally competing with Prince and The Stones, and whoever else may be out there, for bums on seats.'

After a handful of warm-up dates in Australia, the band and their 62-person entourage headed straight to Europe, where they played 38 concerts and saw the X album top the British charts. For much of the European leg of the tour, the band acknowledged Tim Farriss's worsening fear of flying by travelling between a number of dates by train.

'It was kind of romantic, in a way,' Tim commented. 'Pulling up at a French provincial railway station in a fleet of limos was different and fun — and the best thing about trains is that the six of us can sit in a compartment and talk to each other. Having a six-way conversation in a plane is impossible.' Tim was one of several band members to take up semi-permanent residence in the northern hemisphere at this time. He and his family moved into a house overlooking the Thames at Chelsea Harbour, with Tim commuting from London to gigs in the UK and Europe.

Only a few shows into the tour, it was apparent that the band had reached new heights as a live act. This was due partly to production standards: INXS had invested well, and the band looked spectacular on the stage. But much of the success of the shows was attributable to the band's impressive musical prowess. Michael was evolving even further as front-man as he grew accustomed to the aesthetics of large-scale performing, and the band had developed an ensemble sound that was nothing less than formidable. The economy of the band's arrangements combined with the precise attack of the rhythm section to create a powerful and exciting concert sound.

'When we're onstage, I see the three of us in the rhythm section as being one half of the equation,' explained Jon Farriss. 'We're like a planet that Michael, Tim and Kirk can orbit around — and of course each needs the other to work.

We're the base, and we're not really in a position to go any-where either literally or metaphorically. We lay the basis for the other guys to decorate melodically.

'There's so much Garry Gary and I have developed over the years that's kind of extra-sensory, that's based on intui-tion. We can just look at each other onstage without even making an expression ... and the next minute we're both doing some amazing little thing. It's the sort of thing that's too subtle for 95 per cent of the audience to even notice, but it's something we just privately get off on. Right after that we'll get the giggles because we can't believe this shit's going on.'

INXS were setting high standards live — higher than they had ever set before — and demanding the most of themselves and their crew. The band had the capacity to rise above fatigue and exhaustion — and even boredom — to perform shows that were never less than awesome. After the gig, they were prone to intense post-mortems.

'We had a rule, which lasted about one night, that we wouldn't discuss the show straight afterwards,' says Garry Gary Beers. 'It's hard straight after a gig, because your ears are still ringing and you're pumped up with adrenaline. So we can find ourselves standing around shouting at each other.

'Sometimes we get very critical about things because we're so passionate about what we do. It's something we've been doing for half our lives, and although we're generally a pretty happy bunch, there are times when things get pretty heated. But on the whole, our discussions are very constructive. The idea is just to make the show as good as we possibly can.'

Typically, Michael had his own take on the experience. To him, performing was most fun when the entire night had a feeling of unreality. 'I enjoy it,' he said to one reporter. 'But it's a perverse situation that I don't think is really natural. Just being out there, watching all those people go crazy — it's kind of humorous really.

'I like trying to be really quiet before a gig. I like to feel the difference between being in a little room by myself and out in front of a huge crowd.'

The tour ran into foul weather in Britain — they were forced to cancel gigs in Glasgow after the semi-trailers carrying their stage and equipment were snowed in — and it was with some relief that INXS went into Christmas recess, with most members of the band returning to Sydney. In those few precious weeks before heading back out on the road, Garry Gary Beers took the opportunity to marry his girlfriend Jody.

By January, the band had kicked off the American leg of the X tour with shows in Mexico City. They were the first big-name Western rock band to play there in 20 years — since The Doors, legend had it — and the band had an absolute ball. In Buenos Aires, a girl brought a cake onstage for Michael's birthday. She was naked. At Rock in Rio, an enormous outdoor festival which featured some of the biggest names in the international music scene, the band played before 130,000 people while Prince watched from the wings. 'The night we headlined, we didn't come onstage until 2 am,' recalled Jon Farriss, 'so everyone in the audience was pretty drunk and exhausted. And let's face it, it wasn't easy for us to get to 2 am completely straight either.'

The band moved on to Los Angeles, where they appeared on the American Music Awards, appeared on the Arsenio Hall Show and posed for a Herb Ritts photo session. While in LA, they learnt that they had just won Britain's most prestigious music award, the British Photographic Institute (BPI) awards for Best International Rock Group and Most Popular Male

Singer. At the beginning of February, the band played a secret show at LA's famed Whisky Au Go Go.

'We'd said for ages that we wanted to slot a few more club gigs into the schedule because they're kind of different and fun,' said Michael. 'The Whisky show was weird. We all kept looking at each other and laughing because here we were a few days after playing to 130,000 at Rock in Rio . . . and we were all crammed onto this tiny stage playing to a small room full of music industry people.'

Trevor Smith is an Australian broadcaster who has interviewed INXS and travelled with them on several tours over the course of their career. Smith witnessed both the Whisky and Rio shows, and still remembers them vividly.

'At that point in their career, it wasn't hype,' recalls Smith. 'They weren't just the most successful band Australia had ever produced — they were one of the biggest bands in the world. Wherever you went, their songs were all over the radio. Wherever they played they were selling out. Men At Work, by contrast, had only ever been a media creation, but INXS were a global phenomenon. And their greatest strength was their stature as a live act; they'd worked all those years in the Australian pubs, playing to rooms full of angry drunks, and they could win over anybody.

'Standing there in this dodgy soccer stadium in Rio watching 130,000 people going absolutely nuts — dancing, singing along to all the songs — made you realise how incredibly big they'd become. As an Australian, I just felt incredibly proud.'

After playing Florida, INXS picked up a Gulfstream jet and flew to New York where they set up camp — for three solid weeks — at the luxurious Plaza Hotel. After years spent enduring the daily grind of life on the road — living in an overcrowded tour bus, alienated from their family and friends — the band were determined to reverse the equation. A tour regimen was implemented — one that was only possible for one of the ten biggest acts of the day — whereby the band were able to commute to gigs up and down the east coast of the United States.

Travelling by jet, they would leave for a gig in the late afternoon, arriving in time for a soundcheck and then a backstage dinner. After the show, the band would be transported to the nearest airport for the short hop back to New York. In the early hours of the new day, a fleet of limos would glide over the Hudson River and deposit their charges at the steps of the Plaza.

Mark Opitz had been invited to accompany INXS for a large section of the US tour as they wanted to record a number of shows for a live album. Opitz had been to dozens of INXS shows in his time, but he'd never witnessed international touring on this scale before. 'It was INXS in excess, it really was,' he laughs. 'The X tour was the tour where the band decided to really reward themselves for all the years of hard work. They went completely five star the whole way. I mean, they even had the name of the band painted on the side of the plane.

'When we did that stint at the Plaza, it was just amazing. We'd roll back into town at something like 4 am after playing a show in Philadelphia or somewhere like that and then we'd all head out to the O Bar until 7 o'clock in the morning. You'd sleep until early afternoon, and then at 4 pm, we'd pile back into the limos to make the trip back to Philly for the second show. It was a great lifestyle.'

INXS were on a triumphant roll, and show after show revealed them playing at the peak of their powers. But not all the gigs were perfect. One of the band's New York shows — headlining Madison Square Garden — has entered INXS legend as possibly their most embarrassing, Spinal Tap-like moment ever. As the Manhattan A-list watched attentively, the band's crew battled with a malfunctioning PA system (half of which had decided not to work at all), which, in turn, created a severe problem with the smoke machines. Despite the best efforts of the crew, who took to the equipment with a sledgehammer, the smoke kept billowing onto the stage, so that the band were unable to see each other and members of the audience could see even less. As could only happen at such a disastrous gig, Keith Richards was in the audience and came backstage after the show to compliment the band.

Despite the setbacks, INXS were enjoying themselves. 'With the *Kick* tour, I think we moved through life in a sort on blur,' Andrew commented. 'There was a lot of stuff happening to us but we couldn't take it in and it wasn't until the tour finished that we were able to sit back and look at what we'd achieved. But with the *X* shows we were somehow able to take things in as we went along. It actually made the touring far more enjoyable and far less stressful.'

In April 1991, the first leg of the world tour wound up with a triumphant Australian run — including six nights at the Sydney Entertainment Centre. In a sense, these gigs should have had the same feeling of triumph and pride that marked the final shows of the *Kick* tour, and in many respects they did. But the band was already becoming wary of the tendency for the Australian media to lead a backlash (there had been some very negative reviews of *X*), and were beginning to feel resentful at their perceived need to re-prove themselves on home turf.

'In many ways, Australia is where we're at our most

nervous,' says Kirk Pengilly. 'I think it may be because Australia is where most of our friends are, and we all get a little self-conscious about that. You're up in front of people who've watched you grow up.' Unfortunately, the touring — and the associated partying — had taken its toll on Michael. By the time he reached Australia his voice was in tatters and he was barely able to speak.

'I really shouldn't have done the Australian tour at all,' Michael said in 1992. 'My voice was in such bad shape that they had to give me cortisone just to allow me to sing. But that's pretty scary because it suppresses your immune system, so you never really know how much damage you're doing to your voice. Looking back on it, I think that I did do quite a bit of damage on that tour, and a year later it's only just recovering.'

INXS could never be accused of mistiming their breaks: in May, while the band rested for six weeks, Andrew Farriss's wife Shelley gave birth to their second child. Michael, mean-while, had publicly split with Kylie after rumours began cir-culating of his liaisons with other women around the world (the names bandied about included actors Patsy Kensit, Claudia Carvan and Kristen Zang as well as supermodels Elle MacPherson and Helena Christensen).

Michael's lifestyle was now radically different from any other member of INXS. While most of the band were still confirmed party animals, and enjoyed their share of whatever was going around, they never became overtly fond of life in the spotlight or the club scene. After shows, most band members were just as happy to go back to their hotels and spend time in the bar or their rooms — alone, together, with other friends or whatever — as party till dawn in a large noisy club.

Michael was made of different stock. 'I'll very happily admit that I really enjoy going to clubs. I do it most nights I'm on tour, so I guess I have a lot of stamina, although I find that if I overdo it, it's to the detriment of my health. But I don't go out as a rock star, with an entourage of photographers and bodyguards and hangers-on. I go as myself, like I'm any other person going out, and I usually find that people respect that. I never do that thing Prince and Madonna do where they clear a private area of the club and have these huge guys standing guard. I just blend into the crowd.

'To me, clubbing is a way of staying in touch with what's really happening. I know it isn't the most professional thing for me to do after a gig, but I personally can't bear the thought of being a professional. The thought that I'm doing this as a career really revolts me. I know that sounds perverse, but I'm a perverse person.'

Michael was living large as a post-modern hipster playboy, enjoying his life to the maximum. While it would be simplistic to characterise the other members of the band as conservative family men with no vices, the fact remains that the five other guys *were* more settled. Now in their early thirties with children and other interests (three members of INXS would ultimately own and manage large country properties), they were less inclined to act like a group of teenagers. They worried about their lead singer and wondered where all his strangeness would lead.

'I don't see my behaviour as being all that abnormal by the standards of most of the people I know,' Michael countered. 'By the standards of most normal people — or even the rest of the band — sure, I'm a bit different. I haven't found my one true love and settled down. I think it's wonderful that they have, of course, but it's not the way my life is.'

After the break, INXS returned to Europe for a leisurely three-week summer run of giant festival shows and headline concerts. 'We loved that leg of the tour so much,' Tim Farriss commented later. 'Partly I think because it was so short. Three weeks is about the shortest international tour we've done in something like six years. The result was that everyone stopped worrying about the grind of being on the road and just had some fun.'

In Nuremberg, Germany, the band were joined by Dave Stewart for a rousing rendition of 'Suicide Blonde' — but nothing could compare with the thrill of headlining Wembley Stadium before a crowd of almost 75,000 people in July 1991. INXS used the gig to its fullest: they allowed UK radio to broadcast the gig live, and recorded it for a live album, while 15 cameras shot the show for a live video.

'Wembley was a very significant show for us,' said Garry Gary Beers the following year, 'because we'd had to fight really hard to be accepted in England. We'd had to tour there year after year, slowly building up a live following, and the chart success was always a bit elusive. So to finally reach a point where we could sell out Wembley was just fantastic.'

INXS were on a roll and, even though the tour was coming to an end, they were in no mood to stop creating music. Andrew and Tim, particularly, felt that it would be in the band's best interests to keep the ball rolling — and to prevent Michael and other members from getting sidetracked by other projects. 'We faced a lot of challenges with *X*,' Kirk observed. 'It was a very stressful time, but we emerged from the making of the record and from the tour that followed feeling stronger and more unified than we'd ever been.'

The day after the Wembley show, INXS went into London's Metropolis Studios and recorded a new song called

'Shining Star'. Most of the band members had been up all night partying, but Andrew was there to prove a point about what kind of band he wanted INXS to be. Somehow, despite their ragged and chemically assisted state, they recorded the track. INXS completed the last dates of the tour and returned to Australia, where they immediately set to work at Rhinoceros selecting tracks and mixing a live album — to be titled *Live Baby Live*.

By the time they emerged from the X tour, the band were able to look at their bank accounts and realise that they were very wealthy. Prior to *Kick*, only Michael and Andrew earned significant income from INXS. But as the touring started to become seriously profitable, and as *Kick* and X started to sell by the million, they all became multi-millionaires.

'As far as the money goes, what can I say?' said Kirk when asked about his fortunes. 'Who wouldn't want to win Lotto? In some ways I still feel guilty about the money, especially when all these articles start coming out saying, "INXS — Multi-millionaires", and then it's weird going and seeing your old friends, it's like, "Ah, hi guys, it's old Kirk here".

'In some ways there's probably a few friends that I lost out of that situation and to me that hurts more than the desire to have money. I couldn't say I could retire now and not work again, there's no way any of us could do that.'

With some 15 years of live performances under their belts, it felt as if the time was right for INXS to document their performing prowess with a live album and video. The aptly titled *Live Baby Live* captured the band at the peak of their stadium-headlining powers: they were dynamic, powerful and completely captivating. The band had already had a large number of tracks selected by the time of their May break.

After finishing their final commitments in Europe, Mark Opitz and several band members — most notably Andrew — holed up at Rhinoceros to make a final track selection and commence the mixing. By August 16, 1991, the album was complete and by November, *Live Baby Live* was released. (The video of the same name, released at the same time, had a different track-listing and was, in fact, the edited highlights of the Wembley concert.)

The decision by Chris Murphy and INXS to release a live album and video was a controversial one. For most of the band's labels around the world, *X* had been a difficult album. None of the singles had been massive hits, and if it hadn't been for the wildly successful concert tour, the album might have been a far more spectacular stiff. Instinctively, the executives at Phonogram in Europe, Atlantic in the USA and WEA in Australia knew that *Live Baby Live* was a poorly-timed vanity exercise. But where once they felt like participants in the decision-making process, they were now feeling distinctly on the outer, and felt that they had fewer and fewer opportunities to interact with the band or make a creative contribution to the game plan.

But the decision to bring out a live album was motivated by more than pride: the band were also working to a secret agenda. Privately, the members of INXS had reached a decision to halt all touring operations for the foreseeable future. The decision was far from unanimous: Kirk and Garry Gary had always been quite fond of the road, and believed it to be a central plank of the band's success. However, their arguments were outweighed.

'I don't seem to get as exhausted by touring as some of the guys — so I don't have a problem with it,' observed Kirk at the time. 'It can be a bit of a drag to do meet-and-greet sessions with record retailers and radio people before every gig ... but they serve a very important purpose. I think if people leave these things feeling good about the band because you've bothered to talk to them, then they're going to sell your records with a lot more enthusiasm. It's just good business practice, really.'

Jon Farriss was also inclined to see the benefits of touring — even though he was all too aware of the pitfalls. 'The thing about touring is that you're only onstage for two hours out of every 24. So you spend the rest of time getting there, preparing and waiting. But somehow I find that those two hours onstage make up for the other 22 hours of weirdness and boredom.'

Michael indicated that he had no problem with touring if there was a definite demand. 'My problem with the touring is not the actual touring itself, but the fact that you can't do anything else. Eighteen months is a huge chunk out of your life, really, and you can get to the end of it and wonder what you've accomplished. But generally my attitude to touring is that I don't mind doing it if there's a genuine demand for us to play.

'When I had all the problems with my throat on the Australian tour, I went to see a Sydney throat specialist who is one of the very best in the world. He looked at my throat, and then he asked to see how much work I'd done over the past five years. So we pulled out a few bits of paper and showed him our touring itinerary since the mid-eighties. He took one look at this and said I was incredibly lucky to have any voice left at all. He said what we'd done was ridiculous, and I think I agree with him.'

Of all the members of the band, it was Andrew who was adamant. Some of his reasons were professional: as the band's main songwriter and undisputed leader in the studio, he found the endless months of touring to be an unproductive grind. (He later decided to lug a small portable studio with him so he could at least write songs in his hotel room.) Some of his reasons were personal: Andrew was the one member of the band who never had time for drugs, drinking or partying. An intense, dogmatic man with a powerful imagination and a will of steel, Andrew Farriss was always bound to be the band's Brian Wilson. And right now, Mr Wilson wanted to remain in Malibu.

'I suppose people imagine that INXS only ever travel around in limos staying in the best hotels and playing the biggest arenas,' he told a stunned reporter in 1991. 'It makes me really angry when I hear that because even now, when I look back on all the years of touring, the vast majority of those years weren't spent that way at all. They were in fact conducted in very threatening, confronting, depressing and emotionally draining situations where we were literally playing seven nights a week.

'We used to spend most of our early years in Australia driving from town to town, and the early days in America were just as bad, getting around in a clapped-out and over-crowded coach.

'Look, in many ways we have a fortunate life. We travel to lots of incredible places, we stay — these days at least — in luxurious hotels, we play before all these adoring fans and we take home a bit of money. I'm sure a lot of people must wonder what the problem is. All I can really offer by way of explanation is that in order to have all those things we sacrifice a lot. Not just our personal privacy, but our entire private lives. For many people, their families and friends and homes are what their lives are all about. For us, touring all the time, our work becomes our life and that's obviously a huge compromise. We've been successful, but at a price. We've given a large part of ourselves away.'

Having completed their touring duties for the X project and made the decision not to tour, INXS felt as if a huge weight had been lifted from their shoulders. Europe and the UK were under their spell, and North America, South America and Japan were in their thrall. From where they stood, a limitless future as one of the biggest bands in the world awaited them. All they had to do was make more great music.

Unfortunately for INXS, their luck was about to change. They were not to know — but they were about to find out — that the path down the mountain would be faster and more frightening than anything they had encountered on the way up.

'After X, the members of the band really became individuals,' Trevor Smith observed years later. 'I mean, they probably always were, but up until then they had subjugated their personal ambitions — and to a great extent their personal feelings and personal lives — on the road up that incredibly steep mountain. But once any band reaches the top of that mountain, there's an inevitable process of fragmentation, because you're free to go off and do whatever you want. Success can numb you, it can take away your creativity. Your choices become greater, and that really diminishes your focus.'

chapter 8

Wherever You Are

D espite the increasing difficulties the band were experiencing in dealing with each other, INXS didn't emerge from the X tour feeling as bad as they had after *Kick*. Partly because the album/ tour cycle had been preceded by a lengthy break, and partly because the tour had been shorter and less arduous than previous runs, the band felt neither exhausted nor angry with each other. Although the X project had started on a very bad note, the cycle ended on a positive one: INXS were excited about the music they could make together, buoyed by the success of the large European shows and keen to remain on a creative roll.

As soon as X was complete, they had decided that it would be the last INXS album to feature Chris Thomas as producer. Without this source of conflict and tension, they were convinced that they could make some excellent records under their own direction. Much as Thomas had delivered the band three hugely successful albums — effectively presiding over the international breakthrough of the band — they were now confident enough of their own abilities to work without him.

To some, it may have appeared that INXS were arrogant to think that they *could* do it all themselves — knowing how much Thomas had contributed to the sessions.

Despite cautionary words from many associates, the band's resolve to break the touring cycle was now strengthening. They hatched a plan to record two studio albums in relatively quick succession without taking any time out to tour. For a while, they even toyed with the idea of a double-album — an artistic move the record industry usually views as a form of commercial suicide. The idea was to give INXS an opportunity to develop creatively without the intense pressures of the road bearing down upon them. At this stage in their trajectory, there were few people who would dare tell INXS they were wrong. They had earned the right to do whatever they wanted to do.

Increasingly, and perhaps inevitably, the band were growing apart. While Tim and Kirk remained good friends, and while Jon and Michael still nominally shared an address in Hong Kong, the members of the band were seeing less and less of each other — to the point where the six members of INXS were only ever together to record or play. The demands of family life are naturally insulating and as each member grew older, and as they put more geographical distance between each other, they found that their interests were less and less alike. 'I don't think people realise that we're very, very different people,' Michael pointed out. 'And that's *why* we're still together, I suppose. Otherwise we'd bore each other stupid.'

The bond between Andrew and Michael was now fragile, at best. While the pair still had a flair for writing songs together, they had virtually nothing in common. 'When I see Michael these days, it's generally because we're working together,' Andrew commented at the time. 'For some reason, people expect us to be like the Seven Dwarfs. Hi-ho, hi-ho.'

Because he was barely present in Australia, Michael's involvement with the band was far less than the other members' involvement. Tim Farriss once observed that Michael never helped load their equipment after a show because he was too busy chatting to fans. Years later, that same attitude was manifesting itself. While Michael was undeniably the focal point of INXS, as the singer, the star of the videos and the only person the media really wanted to talk to, the rest of the band attended to the time-consuming business of running their affairs.

'We're the ones that have to do the machinations: writing the music, recording, getting the equipment together, that sort of stuff,' Garry Gary Beers noted dryly. 'And Michael does his lyrics and turns up.'

As the members of INXS settled back into what passed for real life at a rarefied altitude, personal changes seemed to be coming thick and fast. After an intense four-year relationship with an American girlfriend, Lisa, Jon Farriss was now madly in love once more — with LA based actor Leslie Bega. He had also splashed out A\$2.4 million for a historic mansion in the upmarket Sydney suburb of Woollahra. Kirk Pengilly had undergone a painful split from his longtime partner Karen, had moved into a house in the heart of Sydney's bohemian Kings Cross and had started seeing Australian singer Deni Hines. And somewhat embarrassingly, Andrew Farriss and Michael Hutchence were named on Australian *Business Review Weekly*'s Rich List, a register of the country's biggest earners.

To the surprise of many, Michael was entering a new phase of stability. After breaking up with Kylie he'd gone through a period in which he was seen dating different girls, and showing up in altered states at different nightclubs, on an almost nightly basis. His fondness for the British and European dance clubs — and his ability to withstand days of back-to-back partying — was legendary. But luckily for the band's sanity (and Michael's health), he had become involved with a gorgeous 19-year-old model (half-Danish, half-Peruvian) by the name of Helena Christensen.

Helena was everything that Michael's club pals weren't: she was intelligent (with a love of poetry and the ability to speak six languages), she was sophisticated and she was naturally reserved, possibly even conservative. 'It's so embarrassing for both of us to explain,' Hutchence was to say of the relationship, 'because we both hate that whole thing about rock stars and models. It's such a cliché.'

Hutchence knew little of Helena's career, and she knew little of his. But on almost every level, they were well-matched. Hutchence recalled that he first saw the model in a picture taken by celebrity photographer Herb Ritts. 'She was sitting on this beautiful white horse, bare-legged, like an Amazon. And I remember thinking, "My God, I'll never have those legs wrapped around me". But funnily enough . . .' he trailed off, laughing.

'We actually met on the telephone, and talked for two hours without taking it any further. It was a very strange relationship, you know, because we didn't really know what we both looked like. We weren't actually going to meet. We were having such a great time just talking to each other on the phone, communicating with our minds instead of our bodies. We were going to keep it like . . . I don't know, pen pals, but I capitulated. We couldn't help ourselves. I'm a physical guy and . . . well, she's a pretty physical guy too.'

After spending two months in France with Helena, Michael

travelled alone to Australia to join up with the band. In October 1991, after recording a video for 'Shining Star' at Sydney's Phoenician Club (the single was being released as a bonus studio track for the *Live Baby Live* album), Michael and Andrew sat down at Andrew's enormous home in the Sydney suburb of Belrose (not coincidentally within kilometres of where he had grown up and gone to school) for their first proper attempt at songwriting for some time.

Andrew had become philosophical about his partnership with Michael: he knew that the pair had reaped some terrific results, but he was also tired of being let down by Michael's erratic behaviour, his unpredictable mood swings and his careless disregard for his own creativity. Andrew had come to take the view that the pair would write songs when they could; it was not an issue he was prepared to force.

'Let's face it, Michael is not the most reliable person in the world,' he said at the time. 'I've had to learn to be a little philosophical about the whole songwriting thing these days — and I certainly refuse to chase Michael around to write songs. If he calls me up, fine. If I call him up and he doesn't return my call, that's fine too. All I know is that it only works if we both want to do it — and if not, I can always write a song by myself.

'Michael and I never took our songwriting relationship that seriously. It was just something that happened and we took it in our stride. But very recently we've learnt to value it a bit more because we've seen some fantastic results from it over the years. I hope it's something we can hang onto.'

A surprise visitor at these songwriting sessions was Australian actor Kym Wilson. One of several pretty young women who had a habit of periodically appearing in Michael's life as geography and timing allowed — for weeks, days, or perhaps only hours — Wilson was to achieve a certain fame and fortune when she became one of the last people to see Michael Hutchence alive. Back in 1991, she was seen by Andrew as an obstacle between the two writers, and yet another distraction in what had become an extremely difficult writing partnership.

So who *was* in charge of INXS at this point? In some respects, the band had been steered by Chris Thomas and Chris Murphy for the past few years. But Thomas was now out of the picture, and Murphy — who was now commuting between his Sydney business hub and the home base he had established in London with his young family — held less and less sway over his wealthy charges. In the early days, Kirk and Tim — by virtue of being older — appeared to control the band's destiny. But as INXS entered the nineties, it often appeared that the decision-making process had fallen into disarray. Little could be done without Michael's approval, and Michael veered between listening to Andrew (who had penned so many hits for the band, after all) and Jon (who he probably regarded as a closer friend and a more hip, worldly collaborator).

Other members of INXS felt a certain frustration that the band wasn't being run along more democratic lines, but they were wise enough to acknowledge that it could be no other way. Creative differences in any band are inevitable, but in a band as large as INXS, they often became unbearable — and Andrew's dogmatic approach to his work sometimes made any discussion impossible. But behind the united front they presented to the world, INXS was always a hotbed of shifting alliances and temporary loyalties.

As they prepared to record once more, there were more subtle shifts of loyalty and allegiance as the notes began to fall. 'INXS keeps evolving and changing,' Kirk Pengilly explained. 'Individual roles in the band shift around, members' input into different areas is always increasing or decreasing. It's very fluid, but it's also very volatile because we're six very creative people.'

In the studio, with INXS nominally sharing production duties with Mark Opitz, the band were said to be relishing their new creative freedom as they worked on *Welcome to Wherever You Are*. For three albums, virtually everything they had done had been at the direction of Chris Thomas and the producer had kept a firm lid on many of the band's more radical suggestions and ideas. Without this overbearing discipline, the band informed the media, the six members of INXS would be giving full reign to every idea and impulse they'd been harbouring.

'I think it's immediately obvious with this album that we've reached a whole new level,' Kirk observed at the time. 'We're feeling really positive — and also very confident in our own abilities. This album hasn't been difficult at all — in fact we've had so many ideas it's just ridiculous. The motto for this album was, "We'll try any idea", and believe me, we have. I think this album is going to shock a lot of people.

'These days we seem to progress even more from one album to the next. We realise that we're now in a position to try just about anything, to experiment with all sorts of things. We're not like a heavy metal band that can only do a small range of things — we feel as if we're working in a wide open space.'

In truth, *Welcome to Wherever You Are* was another troubled album. The sessions were frequently indulgent, as individual members sought to place their stamp on the band's new sound, but the experimentation ultimately gave way to a frustrating dissipation of creative focus as one member after another became distracted by external events.

'For a start, Tim was really incapacitated with Reiter's syndrome, so he barely played a note,' reports one of the studio personnel. 'I mean, honestly, most of the guitar on the album was played by Andrew. Kirk was in the middle of a very messy and upsetting divorce, so his head was somewhere else. Jon was preparing to get married to Leslie, so you had him running off to make all these arrangements . . . with the result that most of the album was put down using drum machines and then overdubbed later.

'And in the midst of all that, Garry Gary and Jodie were expecting a baby, so he's running around going to classes and all sorts of stuff. Michael was only around some of the time because he had to stay out of the country, and when he did show up he was really out of it, and we'd have to just shove a mike in front of him and get him to improvise until something sensible emerged. In all honesty, the album was made by Andrew Farriss, Mark Opitz and [engineer] Niven Garland.'

For all his success, Michael remained a bundle of insecurity. He had started his career a curious contradiction of shyness and captivating poise, and this internal dynamic only intensified with time and the immense pressures of fame. 'He really hated being alone,' said one friend, 'so he'd sit around the studio getting completely wasted, just hanging out with whoever was there after the rest of the band had gone home. The thing was, he wasn't confident in his own talent. He still wasn't sure that he had what it takes.'

By March 1992, *Welcome to Wherever You Are* was complete. Andrew Farriss was understandably delighted with the album, feeling that it was a personal vindication after the pitched battles with Chris Thomas. The album had given him his first serious chance to explore his musical imagination since *The Swing* — and he seized the opportunity with both hands. From the mysterious opening strains of 'Questions' through rockers 'All Around' and 'Only Time', it's an album of appealing texture. Some songs, the epic 'Men and Women' and 'Baby Don't Cry', even featured a 60-piece concert orchestra — a penchant that Andrew had wanted to indulge for many years.

'*Welcome to Wherever You Are* is actually an amazing album,' Andrew Farriss said at the time. 'It's full of musical experimentation, which is always dangerous for a successful band. It's not a predictable rock record, by any means; we managed to capture a lot of diversity.'

Andrew delighted in telling people about working with the orchestra. 'It was actually my idea,' he laughed. 'I claim responsibility for good and bad! I'm a big fan of that era of sixties pop music that had lots of brassy, almost jazzy things woven in there. I like that. And in some ways, I thought that approach might suit the band because we don't really have any great attachment to one specific era of music. We don't say things like, "We're really into this", and end up only doing that. We'll try anything. I mean, that's the beauty of the band.'

Garry Gary Beers summed up the band's mood perfectly when he made this observation mid-way through the album sessions: 'We're really excited with the music that's coming out. We're all producing it, which is something we'd never allowed ourselves to do together. I guess we never had faith in ourselves. I think we're beginning a whole new chapter of INXS.

'We want to really immortalise ourselves over the next few years. I think we've reached the heights as a touring band, and we're proud of those achievements. But right at the moment, we're not entirely convinced that we've made the best record we're capable of. We want to be remembered for our music, not our lifestyles. We want to make some albums in the nineties that'll blow the tits off everyone.'

But behind the doors of his enormous, beautifully appointed Sydney offices in Crown Street, Darlinghurst, Chris Murphy was deeply concerned with the direction the band was taking. Not only had the X album sold less than half what *Kick* had (it was the first time in INXS's career that they hadn't increased their record sales), but the *Live Baby Live* album and video had been met largely with indifference. The music world was waking up to a whole new era in which bands like Nirvana and Pearl Jam were emerging from Seattle, in the north-west of the United States with a no-frills punk-pop sound. Everywhere, the successful bands were dressing down — forgoing the aid of a stylist, design company or hair consultant — and playing down their celebrity. The economy was in recession and the era of grunge had begun.

For bands who had become successful in the big-spending eighties, the trend presented an enormous challenge. Just as the advent of punk rock in the late seventies had made all the long-haired art-rock of the mid seventies look indulgent and irrelevant, so now a new generation of punks was sneering at the arena rockers. Almost overnight, acts like Guns 'N' Roses went from being multi-platinum heroes to the object of snide jokes. U2 were one act that cleverly rode the new mood by making monumental adjustments to their whole artistic rationale: where once they had strutted proudly with their anthemic rock songs and heroic posturing, they now adopted an ironic distance. We love our success, they were saying, but we don't take ourselves seriously.

INXS were also keen to strip back — demonstrated by much of the music on *Welcome to Wherever You Are*, and the album's title and cover concept. The fact that the cover didn't feature the band's image — the first album not to do so since *Underneath the Colours* — was a significant gesture.

'The thing is, we burst our own bubble,' Michael Hutchence observed some years later. 'The eighties were a golden era for many people, but they were also a period of excess that couldn't last. I'm not sure that we ever really enjoyed it, or felt totally comfortable with it, but we went along with it. We wanted a change.'

Unfortunately for INXS, fate was conspiring to rob them of their moment of new-found glory. U2's ground-breaking album *Achtung Baby* had come out while INXS were in the early stages of recording sessions for *Welcome to Wherever You Are*. Even if — as they subsequently claimed — INXS did not listen to U2's album while recording their own, U2's release certainly stole INXS's thunder. Much as *Welcome* stands up well today as one of the band's strongest albums, it was no match for the postmodern apocalypse of noise that was *Achtung Baby*. U2's album had single-handedly redefined the role of the superstar act in the new pop era; by contrast, INXS' album was somehow less than its parts.

'When we were making *Welcome*, we really thought that it would be a head-turner,' says Mark Opitz. 'But, largely because of *Achtung Baby*, it sort of wasn't. They were doing something that was radically different, but still using a lot of guitar, and *Welcome* just didn't slam people the way it was supposed to. We all felt a bit ripped off, really.'

Welcome to Wherever You Are was scheduled for April release and as the months ticked by, Chris Murphy knew that INXS needed to address the issue of their declining sales. Mutterings from within the international labels (particularly Atlantic in the US) suggested that the band was in decline. Murphy suspected, perhaps rightly, that the band's Australian audience had missed the full extent of their European and American success. The members of INXS who still resided in Australia were acutely aware of the way the local media represented the band; they were concerned that coverage tended to focus on the band's wealth and inaccessibility rather than their hard work and proud achievements. What they craved more than anything else was recognition.

After lengthy meetings, and even a confidential crisis report from a well-known industry figure, INXS felt that their needs would perhaps be best served by mounting a major outdoor concert: something that would serve as a visible emblem of all that they had accomplished over the past 15 years and something that would set up *Welcome to Wherever You Are* to be the enormous success it deserved to be. It was essential that the album open with strong sales in Australia so that Murphy would have the ammunition to convince the European and American record labels that INXS were still commercially viable. So, even though the band were not intending to tour to support the album, they recognised the need for some kind of spectacular live event.

While INXS put the finishing touches on the new album, the opportunity presented itself to stage such a show. Two Sydney-based executives — Tim Koster, an investment banker, and Warwick Hastie, an events organiser — had approached Chris Murphy with the idea of getting INXS to play a one-off charity show to benefit the widely respected Cardiac Unit at Sydney's St Vincent's Hospital. After the unit's leading surgeon, Victor Chang, was shot dead (in a bizarre bungled extortion attempt) in 1991, the unit, subsequently named after Chang, became an immensely popular cause. Koster and Hastie had already raised money for the unit by staging a charity Rugby League match.

When the pair — who had established a company called Meridien Marketing — approached Murphy to investigate the chances of INXS appearing, they were pleasantly surprised to receive a positive response. Unlike Midnight Oil, INXS had never shown much interest in charity shows, but this time they had their own reasons for giving their time freely. The parties agreed that a new venture should be established, so a company was formed with two MMA executives, Gary Grant and Matthew Alderton, joining Koster and Hastie as directors. At the band's insistence, it was decided that the concert proceeds should also be allocated to the St Vincent's AIDS Patient Services and Research Unit.

A number of major sponsors were approached, with TV stations pledging free airtime and the advertising agency George Patterson Bates pledging free consultation on the creation of a media campaign. The team had decided to called the show the Concert for Life and their plan was to stage the concert in Sydney's enormous green space, Centennial Park. Like New York's Central Park or London's Hyde Park, Centennial Park is handy to a number of the city's richest residents but, unlike those other well-known spaces, Centennial Park had rarely been a site for public entertainment and a rock concert had never been staged there. Nevertheless, coopting the support of a number of the city's most influential lobbyists (including arts baron Leo Schofield and former NSW premier Neville Wran), permission for the concert was negotiated with Sydney City Council.

'I can't tell you how much shit we went through to put that concert on,' recalls Gary Grant. 'A lot of it had to do with the venue and the difficulties we experienced with the council, and of course a lot of it had to do with all the things that can go wrong with an enormous outdoor concert. It was easily the most stressful thing that I've ever been through.'

By late February 1992, the organisers were ready to officially announce the Concert for Life. The bill was to include Crowded House, Diesel, Yothu Yindi, Ratcat, Def FX, Deborah Conway, Kate Ceberano and Troy Newman. It was announced that the concert would attract between 70,000 and 120,000 people and earn between $500,000 and $1,500,000 for the St Vincent's units. Tickets were to be sold at $21.

In the lead-up to the show, it appeared the Concert for Life would give INXS a much needed boost of public support; for the first time in a while, they could be the good guys. After rehearsing for several days at the ABC's Gore Hill TV studios, the band undertook two semi-secret pub gigs (at Avalon RSL and Paddington RSL) billed as The Farriss Brothers. Proceeds from these shows went to the Wayside Chapel, another popular Sydney charity, which has cared for the homeless and desperate of Kings Cross for many years.

But even before INXS took to the stage there were dark rumblings in the media. Whether this was petty sniping or legitimate reporting is a matter of opinion, but the press was ready to pounce. The Australian music industry and media had been quietly miffed that INXS had not bothered to show up en masse to accept awards at the two major awards shows screened in Australia in 1991, the ARIAs and the AMAs. Under Murphy's guidance, the band had become increasingly unavailable — and while this may have been perfectly understandable in view of their intense workload through much of the preceding year, it was interpreted as arrogance.

At a special press conference several days before the event, the then deputy prime minister, Brian Howe, and senior St Vincent's staff were insulted when Michael Hutchence failed to appear (although three other band members did) and it was reported by the media as an outright snub. Disclaimers that the singer was 'rehearsing' were clearly false, and many were beginning to seriously reconsider the band's commitment to the cause.

Although the weather on the day of the concert — Saturday, March 28 — was less than perfect by Sydney's impossibly high standards and arguably may have prevented the audience from swelling to anticipated levels, the rain that threatened never eventuated, and the show went off without a hitch. Behind the scenes, however, it was a different story. The very first equipment truck to enter the park succeeded in knocking the top off a century-old sandstone pillar and from that point on there ensued a pitched battle between park administrators and concert organisers.

Despite a crowd officially estimated at 70,000, police reported that there were virtually no instances of injury or crime. And despite loudly voiced concerns by local residents that the audience would trash the park, damage was kept to an absolute minimum. Senior Sergeant Geoff Woodgate of Waverley police was quoted as describing the concert as 'one of the smoothest operations that most of the police have been involved in'.

After memorable sets from Diesel and Crowded House (possibly the first act all day to really reach out and grab the boisterous crowd), INXS hit the stage at 5.00 pm and played through until 6.30 pm. As the afternoon sunlight softened, production elements such as lights and smoke, and a 36-piece orchestra, were wheeled out to enhance the magic of the main attraction.

Backstage, the mood was far from charitable. Members of several other bands were furious that INXS had inexplicably received larger billing on all concert advertising (despite assurances from MMA that all bands would receive equal billing). On the day, musicians from other acts arrived to discover that INXS were to be housed in their own, highly exclusive, enclosure. Rumours began to circulate that other bands had been heavied by INXS security and told to stand aside when the headliners passed to walk onstage. Given that most of the bands on the bill had known INXS for many years, this behaviour scandalised those in the backstage area. Worst of all, INXS were being afforded production values, lights and extra sound, that had not been made available to other acts — values that instantly improved the quality of their show.

INXS had broken a number of unspoken rules, concerning etiquette, that govern musicians, and the music industry, all over the world. As the other bands stood backstage listening to the sounds of an orchestra that had been hired at considerable expense to enhance just two songs — one of which was being filmed, so it was said, for a future promotional video — the thought occurred to one and all that they were the victims of a very clever scam. It would take some days before these rumblings were audible in the wider community.

Initially, at least, the media was supportive of INXS. The *Sun-Herald* ran a positive piece the morning after the concert bannered 'Sydney Celebrates' and reported that 90,000 people had attended. The paper reported that the show had been hot and indeed it was hot near the front where the crowd had compressed into a tightly packed sea of bodies and sweat. Two hundred and fifty people had collapsed and a hundred 44-gallon drums of water had been sprayed on the front rows. But the paper also noted that only seven people were taken to hospital — most of them with minor injuries caused by falling out of trees. Rival paper the *Sunday Telegraph* ran with the headline 'The Day Rock Lost Its Bad Name'.

Praise was duly given in several newspapers for the exemplary way in which the concert stage was rapidly dismounted and the concert area cleaned. That section of the park was back to normal and ready for Sunday's picnickers by the time the park opened at 6 am the following day.

By Monday, however, the tide was beginning to turn. The *Sydney Morning Herald* ran a joke that was doing the rounds of the Australian music business (*Q*: What's the name of the new INXS album? *A*: Life) and questioned the motivations behind such an event, pointing out that artists derive tremendous promotional value from big charity concerts. The paper noted that many of the acts performing at the Concert for Life had new albums in the works, and that they mentioned them more readily than heart and AIDS research when doing their promotional interviews for the show. Other commentators noted sourly that there appeared to be a disproportionate number of MMA acts on the bill.

Deborah Conway was one artist who wasn't afraid to speak the truth: 'I don't think we should fool ourselves that this event is purely cause-driven, but I also don't think we should be so pompous as to suggest that it should be,' she said, noting that the fans had simply come to see their favourite bands. 'But a big part of the money they have paid is going to help research into AIDS and the work of a fantastic heart transplant team — and that has to be a good thing.'

By mid-May, the *Sydney Morning Herald* had managed to

get its hands on a financial statement for the concert, which revealed a number of serious concerns. The biggest concern was the relatively paltry sum the show had raised. Not counting $255,000 in donations (from the Department of Health and Community Services and others) and revenue from catering and merchandising concessions, the money left from ticket sales after costs were deducted was said to be a staggeringly low $153,000. While part of the reason for this was that attendances and revenue were lower than anticipated (only 62,000 punters actually passed through the gates, generating revenue of $1.36 million), the real reason was with the costs incurred in staging the show.

Promotions and publicity, which included the price of the public radio station 2JJJ recording and broadcasting the show, were said to have cost $215,634. Artist accommodation, catering and rehearsals came in at a staggering $85,235. The orchestra cost $16,576 and the lights — only used in INXS's set, when it was still daylight — cost a further $34,000. Industry pundits also questioned the logic of flying in well-known UK stage manager Lee Charteris (at a cost of at least $40,000) when equally qualified people were available here. And, of course, the overriding question was why the organisers had insisted on mounting the show at Centennial Park when far cheaper venues (such as Sydney's Domain, the Showground or the Opera House steps) were readily available.

When it emerged that INXS had a crew shooting parts of the concert to make a video for their new single 'Baby Don't Cry' (one of the two songs that featured the orchestra), the tide of media support turned against INXS.

With some of the industry's most senior figures offering themselves to the media to voice their feelings about the Concert for Life (legendary promoter Michael Chugg, for example, called it a 'disgrace'), the Concert for Life became one of the biggest scandals Australian music has ever seen. INXS members and the concert organisers might have argued — as they did privately — that the aforementioned costs were wildly inaccurate and misleading. They might also have argued that many of the concert costs were ultimately designed to simply make a better show — and none of the expense would have mattered if they'd pulled an additional 10,000 or 15,000 people (thus generating a further $200,000–$300,000 in gate takings). But, outraged by the media and industry backlash, Chris Murphy denied any media requests to talk to the band — no-one from INXS publicly commented on the allegations or uttered a single word in their own defence.

'We were all totally devastated,' says Gary Grant. 'I mean, I personally put months of work into the event and wound up giving myself an ulcer. Sure, some of the costs were high — but we really just wanted to put on an amazing show. It was what people expected of INXS at that time, after all. We did nothing wrong, but it all turned into this massive disaster. It turned into an opportunity to fire off a few bullets at Chris, but the problem was that the bullet hit me and then ricocheted into the band. I was so disgusted that I resigned from MMA and hopped on the first plane I could out of Australia.'

Although the St Vincent's hospital administrators were actually delighted with the event — a high-profile PR exercise that had netted the hospital some valuable funds — they were also shocked when INXS refused to defend themselves against an increasingly hostile press.

Richard Wilkins was the onstage MC for the Concert for Life, and witnessed the entire day's events from the privileged surrounds of the backstage enclave. 'I can almost see both sides of the story,' he admits. 'I mean, on the one hand, I can see it from the band's perspective: they put on a great show for free at a time when they could make a fortune from everything they did. They raised awareness for a good cause. Their hearts were in the right place.

'But, for the other bands, it must have seemed like they'd been duped a little bit, sure. They thought they were there to do this charity show, but when they turned up it was all a bit like a giant INXS showcase. I mean, it was clearly the band's baby. Chris Murphy and Gary Grant had organised it. And yes, they had that aloofness and arrogance that comes from being international superstars. Murphy kind of encouraged that — and no, it didn't go down too well with some of the other bands.'

For their own part, the members of INXS were appalled. It has often been observed that wealth and fame have a negative impact on anyone's ability to grasp reality — and INXS were showing signs that their own grip was slipping fast. The band were convinced that the Concert for Life had been motivated by the purest of reasons (they could have simply staged a concert in the park and charged people money — and no-one would have minded) and they were dumb-struck by the negative publicity, seeing it as a personal attack rather than a valid criticism. To make matters worse, the adverse publicity had completely killed sales of *Welcome to Wherever You Are*.

'They were totally distraught about it,' says a close friend. 'They couldn't understand how something with such good intentions was just being ripped down around their ears. Everything they'd built up in this country was just draining out the door, and they were beside themselves. Many people who were close to the band had to point out to them that this wasn't about INXS, it was about Chris Murphy.

'Chris had worked as this maverick outside the accepted rock 'n' roll mafia that runs the industry in this country. He'd always played by his own rules and avoided working with those guys. In a sense, he established an alternative to their system, and for them it must have been incredibly annoying to see him have so much success, so quickly. With Concert for Life, all those people finally got their chance to put the boot in — and that's exactly what they did.

'The really strange thing is the band didn't know how to manage the disaster. They really had never had to ride out any major PR disasters before, and when it finally hit them, they were hopeless.'

When the band finally emerged later in the year to comment, it was clear that their pride was still extremely fragile. 'It was supposed to be a great show — something on a grandiose level, of the quality that we are known for around the world,' said Kirk of the initial idea. 'It's often said that our bands make it big overseas and then forget about Australia, so we wanted to put on something on the level of our Madison Square Garden shows or our Wembley Stadium concert in London, where we played to nearly 80,000. It was always going to be expensive to put it on.

'Perhaps it was a mistake that we didn't talk to the press when the thing exploded because, to be honest, there was nothing to hide,' continued Kirk. 'We all took it hard because it was our home ... I'm a strong believer in karma and I know we did nothing wrong. We tried to do a good, charitable thing and we got crucified for it. It was a great concert which raised $600,000 for a hospital which was absolutely ecstatic. It seemed quite obvious to us that a small number of losers within the music industry were motivated by jealousy against us or our manager. It's a fickle, childish attitude, trying to tear down a band such as ours, and if Australian music keeps doing it, it'll end up disappearing up its own arse.'

'We were jumped on,' said Michael in the same interview, 'but we have no bitch with Australia — we love the place. I guess we're still disappointed that we could put together the biggest rock show in Australian history, take no profit and create an amazing amount of awareness, and then have to put up with all that stuff. You know, maybe there were some mistakes but I really can't find them. Maybe it was because we'd tried our best not to just make it a money-making venture for those concerned but to make it a big, wild, exciting day.

'It would have been easy, after the whole Concert for Life thing, for us to say, "Right, we'll never do anything for anybody for nothing again", or even, "We'll never come back here again", but I don't think our real fans took all that much notice of what other people said. Australians will always look into it for themselves.'

The band's decision to not speak to the media in the aftermath to the Concert for Life may well be remembered as the worst decision of their career. In refusing to comment, they only exacerbated the problem. In a rare interview in 1994, Chris Murphy gave his reasons for the media blackout and hinted at the paranoia creeping into the band's ranks.

'I could see what was closing in on us because I'd seen it in various forms ever since our Australian Made tour in 1986,' explained Murphy, 'so I took a very firm policy on our response. The guys were all hurt and confused and Andrew Farriss was really freaking out about it but I said, "I'm not going to let myself or you guys be dragged down to this level.

We've done nothing wrong, in fact we've delayed our next album to put this show together. So let's maintain our dignity about it". I was expecting intelligent people in the business to understand our silence and back us but I'm afraid we were too naïve. The bandwagon jumping just flabbergasted me.'

Ironically, *Welcome to Wherever You Are*, released worldwide in April 1992, was one of the band's best albums. While it lacked the commercial polish that Chris Thomas had given to the previous three albums, it was an album of spirit and diversity, and clearly the band's toughest sounding album since *Listen Like Thieves*. Without openly acknowledging it, INXS were taking on some of the rawness of grunge — and perhaps just a little of the glam/camp posturing of U2's *Achtung Baby* — to reinvent themselves for the new decade. Whatever else it was, *Welcome to Wherever You Are* was far from being the creative output of an increasingly irrelevant band: if anything, it showed just how much promise INXS still had.

'*Welcome* had the best critical reaction of anything we've ever done,' Michael Hutchence observed in 1993. 'That was the kiss of death for the sales. But to me that means a real lot ... except that I always feel that I deserve more than I get. It's the ugly truth behind this baby-kissing rock star facade that I have.'

Although the album debuted on the UK charts at Number One and made a strong showing in a number of world charts, its presence was staggeringly brief and its impact minimal. Without the band's touring activities to keep their name in front of their American and European audiences — and without the opportunity to showcase the new material in a live show — the band's audiences looked elsewhere. In the USA, where INXS had once been able to sell several million albums, sales peaked at just 700,000.

'We knew we were taking a lot of time out from flogging ourselves around America, where you pretty much have to be in people's faces with music all the time,' Hutchence noted dryly. 'With due respect to them, we love playing there but Americans are kind of fickle. Talk to anyone who's done the American thing on a big scale and they'll say the same thing: they love you, but you're only a part of them for as long as they feel like it. That's OK, we sort of expected that and it is inevitable to lose a bit after six years of being there constantly, but it does concern me a little when I think of how much we put into it in the first place.'

Interestingly, record company politics may have also played a part in the rapid sales decline of INXS. In the first decade of the band's life Chris Murphy had nurtured cordial, collaborative relationships with all the band's labels: people like Atlantic's Doug Morris or Phonogram Europe's Alain Levy were made to feel that they had played a critical role in the band's success. But in the later, heady days of *Kick* and *X*, some senior executives at the various labels began to feel excluded from decision making in regard to the band's plans and future. As INXS sales slipped no doubt new acts took pride of place on the 'priority lists' that determine the level of a record company's commitment to its acts.

'This business is all about relationships,' says one manager. 'If you're good to people on your way up, they'll be kind to you if you deliver an album that isn't so good. That blow is kind of cushioned, because everyone likes you — and that goes for the media, radio, everybody. If you've spent your career fucking people, you fall hard. Everyone is just waiting for the moment when you have an album with no hit singles and then, bang, they *screw* you.'

Welcome to Wherever You Are sold just two million units —

enough to earn the band a lot more money and a highly respectable figure by the standards of most performers, but not enough to hide the fact that INXS's record sales were halving with every release. This was nothing less than a free-fall, and it created panic in the band's ranks. For some band members, the solution lay in a return to the sound of their most successful albums. Others believed they needed to become a tougher, more extreme rock band. Others felt the answer lay in dance music.

Michael Hutchence captured INXS's mood when he observed: 'We have three options: one, we can become a pale imitation of ourselves and keep churning out the same old stuff; two, we bland out, take the middle road and make nice inoffensive records that make lots of money; or three, we attempt to reinvent ourselves completely.'

chapter 9 | # Life in Exile

After performing a round of international promotional chores for *Welcome to Wherever You Are*, including intensive media interviews in Europe and the USA, the members of INXS scattered with the loose intention of reconvening later in the year to record again. If the band had initially been enthused with the idea of recording two albums back to back, the debacle of the Concert for Life and the extremely disappointing sales of *Welcome To Wherever You Are* had left them deflated and nervous.

Not only were INXS going backwards quickly in markets that they had worked tirelessly to conquer, but their reputation was severely tarnished in Australia. For a band that had been perceived as heroes just two short years ago, this was difficult to deal with. So desperate was Andrew Farriss that he announced he was leaving Australia for good, and promptly decamped for London with his wife and children. Andrew wasn't the only member of the band who was putting distance between himself and his homeland. Jon Farriss and his wife Leslie were now living principally in Los Angeles, while

Michael was living in France with Helena Christensen. Manager Chris Murphy had relocated with his family to London prior to the release of *X*, and had maintained his base there ever since. Despite the magnitude of his Australian business operations, he was just as disinclined as some of the band members to return home.

The culture of blame was becoming endemic in the INXS camp. Many artists experience sales slumps, it should be noted. Many highly respected acts have experienced massive career troughs, but most artists maintain their dignity through an implicit belief in their own creativity. Rarely have they been so naïve as to blame external forces, such as the media, for their fallow periods. But fatally, INXS were convinced that they had behaved impeccably and delivered fine albums; it never occurred to them that the root of the problem might be found within themselves.

For many band members, it was now getting just a little too hard. After the monumental stiff that was *Welcome to Wherever You Are*, the band retreated into their personal lives — hoping against hope that when they looked up again, their problems might have disappeared.

Michael and Helena were deeply in love. Dividing their time between Helena's Paris apartment (a necessity given her regular modelling assignments in the city) and the house in Provence, the pair settled easily into a blissful existence. Michael was again pulling back from his self-destructive tendencies and was, for once, feeding the intellectual side of his nature. With Helena as a willing partner, the pair spent their spare moments walking, reading and talking. They began hosting dinner parties in Paris — with Michael often doing the cooking — and frequently entertained house-guests in Valbonne. It might not have been a normal suburban existence, but it was a long way from the marathon sessions of sex and drugs that had consumed at least part of the previous decade. It was a sophisticated and pleasant way of life — but it was rudely interrupted in September 1992.

In an altercation with a cab driver in Paris that month, Michael was seriously assaulted, sustaining a heavy blow to his head when he fell to the pavement. Although Michael had been bashed several times over the years, this was a lot more serious. His injuries were so bad that he suffered severe headaches, slurred speech and, perhaps worst of all, the complete loss of his senses of smell and taste. He began falling into black depressions that would last for days. Michael and Helena were concerned that the singer had sustained some form of mild brain damage, and consulted a number of doctors and neurosurgeons. The tests proved inconclusive, but Michael was prescribed anti-depressants.

'That definitely changed him,' Richard Lowenstein later observed. 'He loved good food and wine and beautiful women, and suddenly he lost some of his senses. I can remember having him in my arms crying, saying, "I can't smell or taste my girlfriend".'

Helena nursed Michael back to health in Valbonne. His physical recovery was quite quick, but the mental scars remained. Yet, for all that, Michael was determined not to further delay the recording of the new INXS album. Confused as he was with the band's lack of success, he was also convinced that they could move in exciting new directions. If previously Michael had allowed other band members to determine the musical direction of INXS, he was convinced that things would be different this time: he was going to take control.

It was time to make some tough decisions. INXS were now at the end of their recording contracts with WEA in Australia,

Phonogram in Europe and Atlantic in the US. Relations with Atlantic had deteriorated to such an extent that the band knew they would receive little or no support from the label upon the new album's release. They knew they could depend on Phonogram to wave the flag — particularly as Chris Murphy was privately indicating to the label that they were in the running to pick up the band's new contract worldwide. The relationship between MMA and Phillip Mortlock and his staff at WEA Australia, which had once been particularly tight and creative, had reached a stalemate and there were many disputes

On the one hand, the band felt the way many bands do at the end of a contract: they simply wanted to be free to make new arrangements. But, on the other hand, they were acutely aware that INXS could not afford another dud album.

One thing they were completely unanimous on was that the new album should not be recorded in Australia. Not only had Rhinoceros Studios been closed down but Andrew and Michael had no interest in returning to the country at all. It was also agreed that the band needed to work somewhere remote where individual members could not be distracted by personal issues. Michael suggested that the band travel to Valbonne for writing and demo sessions, and to spend some time discussing and mapping out their future direction. So, in October 1992, the members of INXS found themselves travelling through rural France in search of their increasingly enigmatic lead singer.

It was decided that the room in the house with the best acoustics was the dining room — so all the furniture was removed and the band set up to play in this tiny stone room. The two-week writing session started badly. Michael was in an argumentative mood — no doubt exacerbated by both alcohol and anti-depressants — and felt it was his mission to shake the band out of their perceived complacency. 'I was going through a really bad personal time,' he admitted later. 'I hated myself for all kinds of reasons, mostly because I'd lost sight of who I was. I was an unhappy boy.'

Part of the problem lay in the fact that Michael had a sound in his head that he thought would bring INXS out of their late-eighties bubble and thrust them into the musical maelstrom of the nineties. Before the rest of the band arrived, he spent several days with Jon working on a track that captured the music in his head — music that was intense, aggressive and threatening. Between them, the pair concocted the primal, in-your-face explosion that became 'The Gift'. Much as this sat at odds with Andrew's fervent belief that the band simply needed to return to the commercial rock and funk of *Kick* and *X*, Michael was determined to have his way.

A month later, after performing some European promotional chores, INXS reconvened to record their new album, again with producer Mark Opitz, at an obscure residential studio complex on the Italian island of Capri. It might have sounded glamorous (the studio came with its own villas and its own private restaurant) but the reality was a little different. The food was excellent and the views sublime, but recording was tough from the outset, with a multitude of equipment-related problems piling on top of the band's tense internal dynamic.

For many observers, the questions were simple: in the age of grunge and exciting new alternative music coming from people's garages and bedrooms, what kind of band flies to a hideously expensive Italian coastal resort to record an album? What kind of band releases a commercial flop — and then follows it up with another album recorded by the same producer? The answer, clearly enough, was that it was the behaviour of a band that had lost its way.

INXS recorded in Capri for two months, and then called a halt to the sessions so that everyone could return to their families for Christmas. After the break, Andrew and Michael returned to the studio a week before the rest of the band with producer Mark Opitz and engineer Niven Garland. The pair wrote and substantially recorded a further six tracks before the rest of the band members arrived.

'It was a kind of messy session,' admits Mark Opitz. 'I have to be diplomatic here ... but let's say that, early on, there were people getting involved in the sessions who maybe shouldn't have, and it was all turning out pretty badly. When we returned after Christmas with Andrew and Michael, it was very much a question of Andrew reclaiming control. The thing you always have to remember in this band is that the dynamics are quite complex. It's not one guy's band.'

Garry Gary Beers believes the time on Capri was one of the worst in the band's history. 'Michael was being an absolute fuckwit,' he was to recall in Q magazine. 'No-one could reason with him about anything. He pulled a knife on me one night while we were recording — and I'll tell you, he was lucky I didn't disembowel him. Michael was a serious cunt on that album, and he'd never been that much of a cunt before. It made us angry at the time, but now we know he was reaching out to us as friends.'

INXS were attempting to reinvent their sound. They realised the era of the stadium rock show — at least as it was known in the eighties — was well and truly over. The airwaves were ruled by the music of club culture and a new generation of nihilist rock acts. Anthemic stadium songs like 'Never Tear Us Apart' (or even sleek funk numbers like 'Need You Tonight') suddenly sounded dated and somewhat vacuous. Music had entered an era that was dominated by bands that stared at their feet behind a wall of hair for an entire show. A band like INXS — with their prancing, high-kicking stage movements and their singer's extravagant, hair-flicking physicality — suddenly appeared to look like something from the cabaret circuit. The fundamentals of entertainment that they had picked up over 15 years on stage — qualities that had helped them achieve world fame — now appeared camp, almost kitsch.

INXS were being sucked into the vortex of irrelevant disposability that had consumed British bands such as the Simple Minds and Duran Duran — and they knew it. The music on *Full Moon Dirty Hearts* revealed the extent to which they were determined to fight the backslide with songs that were tough, earthy and without artifice.

Although the finished album had some strong commercial elements (including duets with both Chrissie Hynde and Ray Charles), there was no denying that this album was a statement. In keeping with the spirit of the age, it even contained a track mixed by Brian Eno.

'We're stepping back from the funk,' Michael observed. 'There's still a groove there but it's more of a groove that sits on itself. We've re-established our sound. It still sounds like us but it also sounds fresh. It's the INXS that I personally like the most. It's not kind to listeners, it's nothing like "Baby Don't Cry".'

By February 1993, *Full Moon Dirty Hearts* was effectively complete — although the duet with Ray Charles was not recorded until September in Los Angeles, just a few weeks before the album's November release. But because only 12 months had elapsed since the underwhelming release *of Welcome to Wherever You Are*, it was decided that a tour would be a good strategy to place the band back in the public eye and set up the release of the new album.

This idea presented some problems: given the downturn in the economy, and the lacklustre performance of the last album, it seemed likely that INXS would face the prospect of playing to much smaller crowds than they had played to on the X tour. Even though this was a dilemma facing many major rock acts in the early nineties, it was not one that INXS were ready to come to terms with. Up until this point, each INXS tour had been bigger and more spectacular than the last, and moving back down the food-chain — at the same time as U2 were radically changing the playing field with their extraordinary *Zoo TV* multimedia spectacular — was difficult to stomach. In addition, INXS had publicly pledged to give themselves a break from major-scale touring less than two years earlier, and they were not interested in going back out on the stadium trail.

Instead, INXS hit upon a radical idea. Rather than play smaller or fewer arenas, and attract comment about their shrinking audience, they would play *much* smaller venues. In brief, they would play the sort of large clubs and small theatres they used to play in the early eighties. It was a deliberate attempt on the band's part to reconnect with their roots, to find a bond with their audience that had been broken by years of large shows, and a way of deconstructing their image as rich rock stars removed from the reality of everyday life. INXS felt that too much emphasis had been placed on the grunge phenomenon. In their own minds, their early days in the Australian pubs were far more elemental than anything that was happening in the bars of Seattle. Perhaps naïvely, they felt that they could recreate those days again for the benefit of themselves and their audience.

Almost as soon as it had been announced, the Get Out of the House tour looked like a bad idea. Much as the history of rock 'n' roll is littered with examples of massive bands surprising their fans by playing secret shows in small clubs (The Rolling Stones make a habit of it), this may have been the first time it was attempted on a world scale.

The tour was dogged by the perception — particularly in the US — that INXS were only playing small venues because they couldn't fill larger rooms. The entire world tour lasted three months, with just 11 dates allocated to the US, including the 4,000 seat Barker Hangar in Santa Monica (which sold out in three minutes) and the 5,000 seat Academy Theatre in New York. In all, just 16,000 US fans saw the band play — fewer than they were accustomed to playing to in a single night. The band that had once played arena shows in the US for months on end suddenly seemed to be yesterday's heroes and, much as most of the shows were sold-out riots of energy and sweat, the perception proved more powerful than the reality.

'It's all business in America,' Andrew despaired at the time. 'They can't work out why, if you're a big band, you're not playing big venues and making a lot of money.'

Despite the advice of many in the INXS management camp, the band were convinced they were right and they were determined to carry through their plan. After their three-month run between April and June, they undertook more sporadic touring and promotional work between November 1993 and March 1994. While Chris Murphy relaxed the rules sufficiently to sneak in a number of larger shows during the second run (including some festival bills in Europe), he could do little to alter the inevitable backward slide.

The band even took a new crack at the South East Asian market with a string of shows. Although they put a lot of work into Asia and Japan during the early stages of their career, these territories had been largely ignored during the meteoric years of their success in the US and Europe. Now, when INXS would have benefited from a loyal Asian fan-base, they found that they had left their run too late. Much as the band could attract paying customers, they had failed to truly conquer the region. Yet, throughout the process, they proved that their PR skills were well and truly intact. In one inter- view after another, they defended their approach.

'This is a sort of rebirth for us,' Michael Hutchence told *Rolling Stone*. 'We've done just about everything except play five nights at Shea Stadium and maybe that'll come later. But I think if I did another nine-month run around arenas I might go insane. We're looking forward to seeing what a band on our level can do with an idea like this. Big bands will tell you they're jaded and they're sick of stadiums, but they'll never do anything about it because the dollars are waved in front of them.

'But we're different because we're a live band, that's who we are, where we came from. Before anyone knew who the hell we were, we were doing that, and I guess in a way that's our connection to each other. Live rock 'n' roll is really only freely enjoyable and exciting when you can make mistakes; when you don't have the guy from *New Musical Express* stand- ing there and you know you can try something and get away with it, even if it doesn't work. That's very important and it's the sort of atmosphere we need to recreate. It's a buzz and we love doing it.'

With a scaled-down crew of just 12 people, the INXS club shows of 1993 were well remembered by the fans who managed to secure a ticket. In the intimate surrounds of a rock club, the band's formidable unity and precision were combined with a ragged energy. While the stages invariably looked too small and while the rooms they played could barely contain their awesome sound (let alone the audience), the shows were visceral experiences that proved the band's extraordinary ability.

'There's not a lot of hangers-on with this tour,' Michael was to observe mid-way through the run, 'probably because there's no food and drinks backstage! We've even gone back to changing our clothes in toilets. Getting in and out is a bit hard but, so far, it's all worked. We're reclaiming some of the old excitement, proving to ourselves that we're not old and cynical yet.'

Although America's *Performance* magazine dubbed it Club Tour of the Year, the pub and club dates of mid-1993 (and a number of larger shows in parts of Australia, Asia and South America in early 1994) failed in their task of igniting new interest in and excitement about INXS. The shows were well received, and there were many positive reviews, but they did little more than keep the faith with the band's most devoted fans. As the moments ticked by towards the new album's November release, even Chris Murphy started doing interviews to talk up the album.

'One of the things that audiences are going to discover is that Michael Hutchence is a new man,' he noted. 'He's hit a point in his life where he has a strong sense of who he is and what he is capable of. On Capri I saw and heard his best writing, his best singing and his best energy. Whatever hesitation there might have been with the

Welcome album, I don't think will exist when the new one goes out.'

The album was met with generally positive reviews — although few were overwhelming. American *Rolling Stone* gave the album three stars, pausing to comment that its predecessor had been 'woefully underrated'.

A rave notice in *Stereo Review* said: 'Combining the fire-power of The Stones at their most taut and brutal with the edgy, dark-side polemics of The Doors, and setting this boldly outlined alchemy to an elemental dance-club beat, INXS makes music that mirrors the mood of the age — agile, troubled, determined, angry, uncertain of a final destination but speeding there on a steady course just the same.'

Many of the reviews were not so wildly enthusiastic, but they were largely kind, and deservedly so, for *Full Moon Dirty Hearts* was by no means a bad album. The fact remained, however, that INXS were sliding inexorably into a black hole. If they were at the cutting edge of pop music in the late eighties, they certainly no longer inhabited that ground now. And they had not achieved international fame for long enough to be respected as elder statesmen. If they had ever been perceived in that light in Australia, this image had been largely dashed by the Concert for Life.

It's worth noting that a great many acts have ridden out sales slumps — and retained credibility and respect. David Bowie spent 20 years building one of the most spectacular careers in pop music, only to forsake pop stardom for challenging, experimental music that was guaranteed to alienate the bulk of his fans. Even though he now sells a fraction of his former album sales, he is regarded with reverence simply because he has stuck to his guns. The same can be said of Lou

Reed, Paul Weller, The Artist Formerly Known As Prince, Sting and George Michael.

Pearl Jam were one of the biggest bands in the world in the early nineties, but because of their perverse creative decisions, sporadic touring schedule and virtually non-existent PR skills, each album they've released has been half as successful as the last. Yet they are still regarded as one of the most important rock bands of the nineties. INXS's compatriots Midnight Oil have also been in an extended sales decline since 1991, but no-one has ever questioned the validity of the band's music or their motivations for remaining together.

For INXS, the respect seemed hard to come by. There were bands like Pearl Jam who were rocking harder. There were bands like The Red Hot Chilli Peppers who were blending rock and funk more convincingly. There were bands like U2 who were redefining pop music in a far more sophisticated, intelligent way. But the band that was once renowned for its irresistible, hedonistic pop/rock was now notable for releasing half-baked singles of dubious commercial appeal. The photo of INXS on the front cover of *Full Moon Dirty Hearts* shows six men rapidly approaching middle age, looking — well — dazed and confused.

'There's no magic formula for success in this business,' notes their friend Richard Wilkins. 'A band can happen because of a particular group of people and the music they make together — and then a few years later that exact same combination can have no success at all. People change, the music business changes, music evolves. If it was easy, everyone would do it.'

Realising that he needed to do something to focus media

attention on the new album, Chris Murphy concocted a brilliant scheme. Drafting their old friend Richard Lowenstein, Murphy announced to the band's record labels that they would be undertaking a special project: they would be making videos for every one of the album's 12 tracks, to be screened on TV prior to the album's release.

It was a novel idea for its time, albeit an expensive one. Lowenstein set to work securing the services of a number of promising young Australian film-makers (as well as crews and technicians) who had emerged from either Swinburne Institute of Technology in Melbourne or the Australian Film and Television School in Sydney. The plan was to make two or three big-budget videos (for potential singles such as 'The Gift') and a series of low-budget videos for the remainder of the tracks. It was further determined that INXS would only make themselves available for ten days of shooting, so not all the clips would feature the band.

'Very few bands have attempted to make a video for every song on an album,' Michael Hutchence proudly announced as the plans fell into place. 'We wanted interesting ideas from film-makers who weren't corrupted by management or record company expectations.'

'We wanted to make anti-videos, in a way,' Lowenstein told *Billboard*. 'We wanted to avoid the clichés and accepted forms of the music video, and tried to steer away from any directors who'd made videos before. It would be pretty hard (for a young director) to make a low-budget film with six millionaires standing around, but there was more a feeling of exuberance among the film-makers because they felt they were making short cinema pieces rather than video clips.

'Frankly, I think the music video boom is over. There is very little that sticks in your mind these days as ideas have become increasingly bland. We have attempted to make something that is an alternative to what you would normally see. It is also giving young film-makers a chance to be seen. For them, it's an opportunity to make a short film without going through the bureaucratic morass of government funding bodies.'

There was little doubt that INXS were ahead of their time. In years to come, with the advent of media such as the Internet and Digital Video Disc (DVD) emphasis on the visual side of music will increase and the demand for conceptual audio-visual works will grow. In 1993, the idea was limited in its usefulness. Nevertheless, Kirk Pengilly enthused, 'It's a real turnaround for us. Nearly every video we've done has been performance based. I think it's the way of the future. In five years it may be expected that the whole album be a visual piece, as something you play on your computer or interact with on some level.'

The project was certainly interesting. Aboriginal director Tracey Moffatt (who had directed the feature film *Bedevil*), created a blaxploitation send-up on 'The Messenger', while Stavros Efthymiou turned the title track into a complex concept piece featuring actors Ben Mendelsson and Alice Garner. Emma-Kate Croghan (who went on to direct the cult hit *Love and Other Catastrophes*) directed the video for 'I'm Only Looking', while a long-time Richard Lowenstein associate, Lyn-Maree Milburn, shot three others.

Richard Lowenstein, unfortunately, was right. By 1994, the excitement had largely drained from the music video revolution. While MTV and its imitators were still extremely popular worldwide, creating impressive profits for its parent company Viacom, the feeling in the music industry was that video had become little more than a very expensive way to promote music.

In Australia, INXS were still a big enough name for the band's record label to convince the country's biggest TV network, Nine Network Australia, to screen the *Full Moon Dirty Hearts* video collection — in its entirety — on late-night television during the week prior to the album's release. In the US, a limited number of Leow's cinemas ran the videos for a short period. It was a measure of how low the band's fortunes had sunk that the collection was never released on video.

Atlantic did nothing to promote *Full Moon Dirty Hearts* in the US and, despite the possibilities of the band's duet with Ray Charles (the venerable rhythm & blues pioneer even appeared with INXS on David Letterman's *Late Show*), the album barely registered on the *Billboard* charts. It went on to sell a woeful 150,000 units in the US. Matters were only slightly better in Europe, where INXS had taken the wise step of appearing on a number of festival bills earlier in the year — but there was no changing the fact that the album was another monumental stiff.

The band dutifully worked their way through their promotional chores — and two months of shows — with wounded pride in check. When asked about the band's future, Michael Hutchence responded with typical defiance. 'The only thing that matters is INXS. After all we've done together we owe each other that. Everything else doesn't matter except the people who have been into it. We'll keep doing it unless we start getting stoned with rocks when we step outside our front doors. If a band breaks up just because the last record happened to sell three million copies less than the previous one, then they weren't worth it in the first place.'

But, beyond the rhetoric, the band were devastated. Everything they had built up over the years of work was falling around their ears. There was a growing distance between the band's members brought about partly by where they chose to live, partly because they were no longer spending their lives on tour together and partly because they were growing apart as people.

A band of three or four members have fewer directions to splinter. For the six members of INXS, the act of holding the engine together, maintaining the fundamental bond that had already carried them through so much, seemed like too much effort. When INXS parted company in early 1994 after a final run of shows in Asia, there was no date mentioned for new recording or new tours. Much as the band's members were reluctant to face it, the prospect of an uncertain future loomed large. In honest moments, many members acknowledged that INXS were effectively defunct.

chapter 10 | # The Nightmare Begins

By early 1994, Michael Hutchence's philandering days appeared to be largely over. Although there was still the occasional fling (such as the incident in January, when, while on tour, Michael allegedly received a visit from old flame Kylie Minogue and disappeared into a backstage toilet cubicle for well over an hour), he seemed deeply committed to his relationship with Helena Christensen.

The couple became a fixture of the social set of Paris and southern France, appearing regularly at film festivals, fashion parades and exclusive parties. The Valbonne house became a favourite haunt not only for Michael's and Helena's families, who frequently visited, but for a constant procession of the world's rich and famous. During the summer of 1994, visitors to Valbonne included Evan Dando, Adam Clayton, Bono, Lenny Kravitz and Prince Albert of Monaco. Australian rock star Jimmy Barnes — living his own life of self-imposed exile in nearby Aix-En-Provence with his wife Jane and their three children — was also a regular visitor.

For this brief period, Michael Hutchence lived the comfortable life that the world expects of its millionaire rock stars. Michael and Helena ate well, entertained lavishly and drank beautiful French wines. Michael developed a penchant for Havana cigars. Living up to the image of the rock star as much as he could, he ensured that the garage housed an Aston Martin car and a Ducati motorcycle as well as a slightly more practical Jeep. On warm days, Michael and Helena would occasionally drive down the hill to visit idyllic beach resorts such as Saint-Tropez.

Although INXS were in a period of extended hiatus, the wheels of industry were still turning. While the band members had gone their separate ways, Chris Murphy had been quietly negotiating a new worldwide record deal that would see Polygram Records pay A$40 million for rights to the band's entire back-catalogue as well as five future releases. Murphy was keen to preserve the value of the band's recordings and see that their financial future was secure. In view of the distance INXS had fallen, it was an impressive deal.

There was, however, a catch: like all record deals, the $40 million was not being paid up-front in a lump sum. The payment was entirely contingent on the band delivering a series of albums over the coming decade. The company made no secret of its concerns about the band's long-term viability (and even their existence as a unit). Still, INXS were undeniably pleased to receive an up-front cash payment of almost A$15 million. Even if they never recorded a note, they had come out ahead.

As the new deal was being finalised, the band's original labels — including Warners in Australia and Atlantic in the

USA — played out the final stages of their contract with INXS by releasing a Greatest Hits album. The disc traced the band's 17-year history and included two new tracks, which were, in fact, salvaged from a secret, aborted session with Chris Thomas. The timing of the album was appalling; nobody was remotely interested in a history of the band's music. INXS did little to promote the album. It fared badly in the charts and did nothing to revive the band's flagging fortunes.

In June 1994, Michael revealed how far he had travelled from the heights of rock credibility — and how much he had accepted his girlfriend's world — when he and Helena appeared in a lavish fashion spread shot by Peter Lindbergh for *Harper's Bazaar*. Titled 'Time Out: Helena Christensen and INXS Singer Michael Hutchence at Play on the Beach', the spread featured shots of the lovers modelling clothes on a deserted beach. At the same time, Helena's international profile received a further boost when she appeared in Robert Altman's movie about the French fashion industry, *Prêt à Porter*.

Michael was in danger of becoming a supermodel's boyfriend and an ex-rock star, and the relationship was showing signs of stress. If life with a beautiful model in the south of France would be heaven for many men, Michael was already finding his life a little *too* comfortable. His wanderlust was beginning to get the better of him, and he was yearning to spend time with new people in different places. Perhaps most importantly of all, Michael was itching to work.

Helena, for her part, was becoming frustrated by Michael's inability to commit to a long-term relationship. The couple had discussed marriage, and plans were underway for a wedding in Copenhagen later in the year. Helena had bought a A$3,000 wedding dress and was keen to issue invitations but, in October, Michael told her that he was not yet ready to marry. Over the next three months the relationship cooled rapidly and the couple spent long periods apart. Coincidentally, Kirk Pengilly's 17-month marriage to Deni Hines was collapsing in a spectacular blaze of publicity on the other side of the world.

By February 1995, Michael was spending more and more time in London, largely because he wanted to start work on a long-promised solo album, and because he wanted to be closer to the music capitals of the world.

He purchased a three-storey mews building in Smith Terrace, Chelsea, just a stone's throw from Sloane Square, and commissioned Paris-based Australian architect Robert Grace (a former protégé of Renzo Piano and a design partner of celebrated Australian Marc Newson) to handle the renovation. An old joinery workshop, the building had a blunt industrial flavour that Grace planned to accentuate — creating a strikingly modern home with radically sloping walls and a gently sloping floor. It was clearly intended for only one or two people, and had a bathroom with no door.

London was a particularly bad place for Michael to settle. While the American rock industry was rapidly emerging from its 30-year obsession with chronic drug use, and many of the most notorious drug-users were now proclaiming their newly clean status, London was still a hot-bed of dangerous drugs and risky behaviour. Drugs were in plentiful supply — and so were British pop and rock stars who were more than happy to party with Michael at any one of the city's hundreds of clubs. It was a recipe for disaster but, for the moment, Michael had other problems.

Almost as soon as he'd arrived in London, rumours began to circulate that he was having an affair with Bob Geldof's wife, Paula Yates. (The pair had known each other casually for many years, and are believed to have instigated a sexual relationship as early as 1989.) Just as the new rumours began to surface, Yates and Geldof publicly announced a six-month trial separation — an action which tended to indicate that their marriage was in less than perfect health. But Michael and Helena had not announced a split — and as the rumours began to gather momentum, both Bob Geldof and Helena Christensen were beginning to feel somewhat ridiculous. 'I've been made to look like a fool, like the biggest shit in the world,' Geldof spat at a reporter as the story began to unfold. Although the Hutchence–Yates liaison was still unconfirmed, and while both parties steadfastly denied the gossip, Christensen was determined that she should emerge from the wreckage with some semblance of dignity.

'Michael and I haven't been getting on for quite a while,' she told reporters defiantly, noting that she was now seeing actor Stephen Dorff. 'We most definitely aren't seeing each other at the moment. I haven't talked to him. I've heard from mutual friends that he is seeing Paula Yates. All I know is that we are no longer together and I'm not bothered by that.'

It's unlikely that Michael Hutchence had really considered the consequences of a relationship with Paula Yates; it's unlikely that Michael had spent much time considering the consequences of anything he did, come to think of it.

If he'd thought about it, he might have realised that, as the wife of Sir Bob Geldof and the mother of three children, Yates was a very poor choice of lover. While she had always been viewed as a somewhat shallow, publicity-seeking figure (she had variously hosted TV shows, written books and filed a weekly newspaper column) there was a great deal of public affection for this scruffy, bohemian family and their eccentrically named offspring. Since Live Aid — the singer's ambitious and undoubtedly heroic attempt to feed the world's starving millions through a series of massive concerts — Geldof had been viewed as a kind of living saint. And while his musical career had foundered in the years following Live Aid, he had turned his hand to television production with great success — the production company he co-owned, Planet 24, had become one of the most successful in the UK.

Privately, friends of the couple freely admitted that Geldof was a dominating, overbearing husband with an inclination to have his own way. In 'stealing' Geldof's wife and children, Michael Hutchence — certainly no saint himself — was condemning himself to a hell he had never dreamt of. It was a move that guaranteed Yates and Hutchence constant media attention of an order they had never experienced before — and, worse, it placed them in a position where they were ruthlessly criticised and vilified.

In early March, Hutchence and Yates were spotted by a reporter leaving the singer's exclusive London hotel, The Halcyon. It was clearly only a matter of time before the pair would be snared by the paparazzi. In the meantime, efforts were being made to rebuild the two longer term relationships that were about to be destroyed by the affair. U2's Bono — whose relationship with his wife Ali is said to be among the most secure in the music world — was trying to play cupid to the warring couples. At his insistence, Bob and Paula made the trip to his A$3 million castle in Killiney, near Dublin (known to Bono's friends as The Love Hut) for a weekend of reconciliation. The following weekend, Michael and Helena were dispatched to the same location.

As it happened, it was all for nought. On March 20, Michael and Paula disappeared for a springtime frolic in the home counties. The pair checked into a beautiful country guest house, the Chilston Park Hotel in Kent. Unbeknown to them, however, most of the other rooms were occupied by reporters and photographers who had been tipped off about the booking. When the couple emerged the next morning, the media were ready to snap them. Michael's attempts to halt the inevitable consequences — by hitting one of the photographers — only resulted in an assault charge.

Months later, Paula Yates's former publicist alleged that Yates herself had tipped off the media about Chilston Park, apparently in an effort to force Michael to publicly split with Helena. If this was the case, the plan worked beautifully. Within hours of the media ambush, Paula told Sir Bob she was leaving him forever. After a tearful meeting at their Chelsea home, Yates collected a few of her children's most treasured possessions and packed the kids into a taxi for the short ride to rented accommodation in Mount Row, Mayfair.

Within two days, Michael was dining with Helena at London's Ivy restaurant, not in an attempt at reconciliation, but to draft a joint announcement. By March 24, a touchingly gentle statement was released by INXS publicists Poole Edwards stating that the couple would be 'spending time apart' although they were 'sad and still loving each other'. In contrast to Helena's bitter comments to the media, the joint statement revealed no rancour: 'Despite the current media furore, the parting is perfectly amiable and they still love and are in contact with each other. Both parties expressed sadness at the decision'.

Displaying a certain ability to play the media game even at the nadir of their relationship, Yates and Geldof also managed to release a statement on March 24 announcing their permanent separation. Geldof was said to be completely devastated. Although he and Paula had maintained a reasonably open marriage, he never believed for a moment that it would come to a crashing halt. He quickly adopted Michael Hutchence as his lifetime *bête noire*, and in one celebrated aside to a journalist, he was heard to refer to Michael as a 'neo-junkie philanderer'.

As this story was unfolding, Michael's manager and bandmates stood back and watched with horror. Not only was the band's singer showing no interest in making new music with INXS — he was turning into the object of the tabloid media's daily attention. For the band, it all seemed too bizarre for words. For Chris Murphy, it was the last straw.

In June 1995, after a week of tense phone conversations between Michael (who was in New York recording the first songs of what would eventually become a solo album) and Andrew (who was still resident in London), Chris Murphy announced that he was stepping down as manager of INXS. After some 18 years working the band from pub-rock obscurity to the heights of Madison Square Garden and Wembley Stadium, and after four years in Britain, he'd had enough. He had also just turned 40, and he desperately needed to pay some attention to his other business interests. In addition, he had split from his second wife and had assumed the role of principal parent for his children Stevey and Jeri. He was yearning to take his kids home for a simpler life.

Murphy's final days as manager of the band were fraught, with some band members learning of Murphy's decision before he had an opportunity to tell them himself. The band had had their fair share of disputes with their manager over the years but they were now in deep shock.

'I didn't want to create any fanfare or do any damage to INXS,' Murphy told journalist Stuart Coupe with more than his customary optimism in the week the story broke. 'I didn't even want it public — I just wanted to let them get everything together first. It was all very emotional; there were a lot of tears for a couple of us.

'I still love them, and after 15 years I think the last thing INXS really need, to be honest, with all the Michael and Kirk press now, is people seeing this guy who's been with them so long departing. I was going to try and do it quietly and just make sure that I could help them through all the business they've got to do now and help them put it all together.'

Tim Farriss and Kirk Pengilly were the first band members to go to press with comments. 'After 15 years, it's almost like going through a divorce,' said Tim. 'In some ways that's frightening, but we also see it as being the beginning of a new era for INXS.' Pengilly added, 'No matter what people might say, Murphy tries to do the best thing, especially by us.'

Executives at Polygram Records were furious with Chris Murphy. For one, they felt they'd been misled: they had offered INXS a new record deal at least partly because they felt that Murphy was the kind of visionary manager who would ensure that the band would have some long-term longevity and ongoing relevance. They were also privately appalled that a manager could tie up a massive international recording deal, take his hefty commission from the advance, and then simply walk away.

Of all the members of INXS, Andrew Farriss has the capacity for being the most blunt. Although he is inclined to indulge in a form of blinkered self-justification, he can also be quite acute in his observations. A year after Murphy's departure, in a *Billboard* interview, Farriss put the band's feelings into perspective: 'We'd worked together for 16 years. You can't say that meant nothing. We had great moments and bad moments. That's all there is to it, really, and it's finished.'

INXS announced that they would henceforth be managed by Paul Craig (an Englishman who had worked for Murphy out of MMA's London office), with their American affairs still being attended to by the New York-based husband-and-wife team: attorney Bill Liebowitz and the band's longstanding New York representative, Martha Troup. In reality, these three individuals had relatively little to concern themselves with, other than Michael's sporadic recording activities for his solo album.

At the same time as the INXS announcement, Murphy announced that he had re-structured the three-year licensing deal between rooArt (along with sub-labels Ra and Le Digue) and Warner Music Australia, changing the arrangement to a straight pressing and distribution deal. This meant that rooArt was now a stand-alone independent, with none of the financial backing of a major label (Warners had sunk a reputed A$15 million into rooArt and had received little in return). Nevertheless, Murphy pressed forward with an ambitious release schedule, financing big-budget albums from the likes of Jenny Morris, the Screaming Jets and Wendy Matthews out of his own pocket. A little over a year later, Murphy wound down MMA's management division and sold off both rooArt and MMA Music, divesting himself of all music business interests.

Over the next two years, Murphy remained in the limelight with a number of business ventures, including his purchase of Sydney radio station 2SM (which he relaunched, unsuccessfully, with a country music format) and his backing of the magazine *Australian Style*. With his decision to pursue relatively low-profile investments, and his choice to forgo rock 'n' roll for life on a polo pony stud in Wagga, NSW, it became apparent that Chris Murphy had made a decision to remove himself from the music industry. After all that he'd achieved and experienced and the vast wealth he'd accumulated during his years with INXS, it was hard to blame him.

Life was not improving for Paula Yates. While Michael and Paula were blissfully happy together, and while Michael was adapting surprisingly well to his new role as a surrogate father to Fifi Trixibelle (aged 12), Peaches (aged 6), and Pixie (aged 3), the attention of the London press was wearing the couple down. Much of the coverage was nasty, for example an edition of UK *GQ* magazine that featured a shot of Helena Christensen on its cover with the headline 'WOULD *YOU* TRADE HER IN FOR PAULA YATES?'. Michael was so incensed by the headline that he rang the editor and abused him.

According to their friends, press reports like this were incredibly upsetting to both Michael and Paula. The pair were madly, irrevocably in love — and it was a source of constant distress to them to discover that the world at large couldn't understand their feelings. 'The thing that nobody seemed to understand then, or now, is that Paula is an absolutely amazing woman,' said one friend. 'She's really bright, she's very funny and she has all these amazing stories. She's an incredible person, really — like a cartoon. And of course, like Michael, she had this incredible libido. She was the kind of person where if you ever met her, say at a dinner party or something, you'd always feel glad that you'd had the opportunity.'

Domestically — and financially — Paula and Michael's lives seemed to be in a state of perpetual turmoil. As soon as she'd split from Geldof, Yates was unceremoniously dumped from her on-camera role for TV show *The Big Breakfast* (produced by Geldof's Planet 24). With her principal source of income removed (she was receiving only minimal maintenance from Geldof, and was a long way from receiving her share of their joint property assets), Paula was racking up debts and she quickly fell behind on the rent payments for the Mayfair townhouse.

Realising that eviction was a distinct possibility and recognising that she didn't have the necessary funds for a Mayfair address, she sought out a suitable house to buy. A house was located in the somewhat less desirable south London suburb of Clapham. Paula promptly arranged a hefty mortgage and moved her children in. Michael had not yet committed to full-scale co-habitation, and the couple remained financially independent of each other. Michael's assets were thought to run to tens of millions of dollars (some posthumous estimates placed the figure as high as A$40 million) but the vast majority of the money was invested in complex trust arrangements and was by no means readily accessible. Generous as he may have been at certain times, Michael had become extremely cautious with his money. He was not about to give the financially troubled Yates easy access to his fortune.

However, between trips to Valbonne and occasional jaunts to New York and Los Angeles to record tracks for the solo project, Michael had effectively moved into Yates's decidedly suburban house in Clapham. By the middle of the year, family life was settled enough for Michael's father, Kell, and his stepmother to visit him in Clapham.

Paula Yates had lived most her adult life in the glare of

intense media attention and the current crisis was not about to stop her continuing this noble tradition. If many people might have run for cover at such a difficult time, Paula had other agendas. Just when she least needed publicity — but was desperate for hard currency — she decided to write her autobiography. Published in record time, it hit the bookstores in September 1995, with time to spare for the Christmas rush.

While the *News of the World* published a report from an old flatmate who claimed Yates was a heroin user (*and* bisexual!) and while her mother declared the contents of the book to be fiction, Yates stoically did the media rounds, discussing such important issues as her father's addiction to lithium and his passion for playing a Wurlitzer organ late at night while Paula sat in an orange box with a balaclava on her head. True or not, the book made a damn good read.

Writing about her marriage to Geldof, she says: 'I did everything and became everything I thought he would like. Then suddenly I was 35 years old and I was no longer willing to be told when I could chat on the phone or redecorate the bedroom. Bob is the most controlling person in the world. But, God, we lasted 18 years and we did so much; it has been incredibly difficult.'

By late 1995, the media frenzy in the UK was reaching fever pitch. 'It's a national obsession,' Paula told a reporter. 'It has reached the point of Princess Di and I doing alternate weeks. It's like being in the middle of some hideous nightmare.

'They have chased the kids and shoved them around. They have slept outside our bedroom in sleeping bags. You feel contaminated, poisoned. When I left Bob, they followed me for four months, non-stop. The night they broke the story of Michael and I in a country hotel, they apparently had all their equipment in the fire extinguisher at the hotel. We had no idea.'

In all the madness, there remained an incredibly strong attraction between Michael and Paula. Michael's closest friends might have doubted his ability to commit to a long-term relationship, especially one with such an enormous amount of very heavy baggage, but the couple rode the storm with admirable poise. 'He's like Cary Grant — old-fashioned, very gentlemanly and very dry,' Yates claimed. 'When I was with Bob I was so frenzied, trying to make everything perfect. Michael is a different kind of person. Now that I'm with him I don't feel the same need to flirt and I don't feel the same need to work. He has made me very laid-back. It has taken that whole drive out of me. It has been an incredible feat of will on his part to see it all through. I have been very distressed and he has been incredibly strong.'

In October 1995, Paula discovered that she was pregnant. Michael was over the moon with the news he was to be a father and celebrated by presenting Paula with a A$25,000 Van Cleef & Arpels diamond ring.

That Christmas, the happy couple left the children in Sir Bob's care and departed for a summer holiday in Australia. They relaxed for a few days on a Queensland island before travelling to the Gold Coast to meet Michael's mother, Patricia, and attend to some business. After that it was down the coast to Byron Bay for the christening of Michael's nephew Zoe Angel, the child of his brother Rhett and his partner Mandy. By New Year's Eve, Michael and Paula were in Sydney enjoying the party season. Most members of the band were glad to see Michael back in town, and Kirk (living in rented digs at the upmarket suburb of Palm Beach) threw a party for them during their brief stay. For just a few short days, it felt as if their London nightmare was a million miles away.

Upon returning to London, Michael threw himself back into the solo album — an incredibly expensive recording project that he was funding from his own pocket. Dictated as much by his creative whims and busy social life as the availability of collaborative partners, the solo album was always going to be a loosely structured affair with a diverse list of credits. Over the three-year period that the album was in progress — from the beginning of 1995 to the end of 1997 — Michael worked with a veritable Who's Who of contemporary music. In a sense, much of the recording fulfilled the function of therapy for the angst in his personal life. Studio bookings were certainly welcome relief from the madness of the custody battle. Some sessions were known to go on for two or three days.

In the process, Michael created several tracks with the husband-and-wife Talking Heads rhythm section, Tina Weymouth and Chris Frantz. He had worked with Danny Saber, celebrated producer of Black Grape and The Rolling Stones; Andy Gill, a former member of the Gang of Four and now an emerging producer in his own right; Tim Simenon, formerly the brains behind UK chart-toppers Bomb the Bass; and Nellee Hooper the terminally hip producer of Bjork, Soul II Soul and U2. Working sporadically, and with no apparent game-plan, Michael also booked studios for lengthy celebrity jams with the likes of Dave Stewart, former Clash frontman Joe Strummer and Black Grape's notorious leader Shaun Ryder.

Many of the sessions resulted in dead ends but, in three cases, tracks were deemed good enough to sell as one-off songs for inclusion on soundtracks and project albums. 'The King

Is Gone', a song Hutchence worked up with the Talking Heads crew, saw the light of day on the MCA album *No Talking Just Head*. (It featured contributions from other vocalists.) A Tim Simenon-produced cover of the Iggy Pop song 'The Passenger' was released on the *Batman Forever* soundtrack, while another cover — of the Eric Burdon classic 'Spill the Wine' — made it onto the forgettable soundtrack for the equally forgettable Pamela Anderson vehicle *Barb Wire*. Wallowing in a certain lack of artistic direction, Michael even fitted in a contribution to an album titled *The Symphonic Music of the Rolling Stones*, which featured the London Symphony Orchestra working their way through the Jagger/Richards catalogue. Hutchence chose 'Under My Thumb'.

By late 1995, the solo album had a working title — *GBH* — title which reflected both the criminal act of assault (grievous bodily harm) and the chemical anagram for a dangerous new designer drug that was popular in the London clubs at the time. Of all the tracks recorded, the final sessions — completed largely in France with Andy Gill — produced material that was the closest to finished work.

When asked to describe the music, Gill commented, 'There's a deeper, richer kind of feel. A kind of cinematic ... wide quality to it. It isn't kind of very up pop songs — it's more mid-tempo and there's a sort of darker feel to it. Lyrically it's fairly autobiographical. It's kind of a mature record.'

One track in particular, 'Put the Pieces Back Together', was a vitriolic work that chronicled Michael's relationship with Bob Geldof (each verse ends with the line 'sue me, sue me, sue me') over distorted industrial loops. On another song, 'Don't Save Me from Myself', Michael sings of his depression arising from his personal problems. 'She Flirts for England' was recorded as a tribute to Paula. Michael insisted that a bed should be placed in the studio so that his partner could lie on it while he sang his vocal.

'These songs were from Michael's heart and explain just how he was feeling, especially towards Geldof,' says Gill. 'Michael was a very happy man by nature but the situation with Bob, Paula and the children would always send him into a very black mood.'

Co-collaborator Danny Saber was impressed by Hutchence's work in the studio. 'His voice was so vibed,' remembers the producer. 'This was a liberation for him. He was a gentleman and a dude, like Shaun Ryder, a real "of the moment" kind of guy.'

Lengthy feature stories on the new album began to appear in some of Britain's most respected music magazines. The protracted recording process was clearly nearing completion, and Michael was already talking up the release. But suddenly, and inexplicably, he had a change of heart. Instead of wrapping up some final loose ends and releasing the long-awaited album, he shelved the process — at least temporarily — and rang Andrew Farriss with the suggestion that the pair commence writing songs for a new INXS album.

The timing was bizarre. Not only was the band still reeling from the poor sales of *Full Moon Dirty Hearts* (even their Greatest Hits album had failed to spark any interest), but Michael was soon to become a father. It would have been far easier to put the finishing touches to the solo album and launch the release with a few well-chosen TV appearances than it would be to commence the difficult, possibly overwhelming task of bringing INXS back from the brink of extinction. But Michael was not convinced that *GBH* was ready for release. As a career move, the album needed to be staggeringly brilliant — and Michael wasn't at all sure that it was.

And there was more: Michael felt under siege during the media battle between Bob and Paula. He had never experienced anything this horrific in his entire life. He was also badly stung by the baiting he'd been receiving at the hands of Oasis. In December, at the MTV Europe Awards, Oasis frontman Liam Gallagher referred to Paula Yates as 'sad' and he and Hutchence wound up having a drunken fist-fight later that evening. Two months later, at the Brit Awards, Gallagher publicly challenged Hutchence to another fight. Michael was generous enough to still agree to present the band with an award for Best Video. For his efforts, Noel Gallagher called Michael a 'fucking has-been'. As Oasis ruled the charts with a succession of monstrously successful hit singles, it was difficult for Michael to ignore just how much had changed in a very short time.

For better or worse, Michael began to crave the security and comfort of the five musicians he had spent his life with and, ironically, the personal turmoil had stirred him to write a brace of new songs of which he was immensely proud. With the birth of Michael's first child imminent and with Andrew Farriss's wife Shelley pregnant with their third child, it was decided that Michael and Andrew should clear their schedule and start working on new music immediately. By February 1996, the pair were ensconced in a hotel in Dublin working on new songs together. 'I was warmed up by the work on the solo album,' Michael declared, 'so for the INXS album I wrote a song a day for two weeks.'

By March, the band had convened in London for two weeks of rehearsals before travelling to Canada — to the Vancouver studio of producer Bruce Fairbairn — to commence work on their tenth studio album. Fairbairn was a strangely conservative choice of producer — he was best-known for the polished rock sound he had given multi-platinum acts such as The Cranberries and Bon Jovi. Just when INXS needed a challenging, cutting-edge young producer with the capacity to really push the band creatively, they chose a producer who was better known for radio-friendly sounds and efficient recording methods. In just three weeks — their fastest recording session since their earliest days — the new album was complete.

More quickly than anyone might have predicted, INXS were a reality once more.

chapter 11

New Life

In the countdown to the birth of their child, Michael and Paula's lives were not becoming stable. Paula's financial affairs were going from bad to worse, with London newspapers widely reporting her mounting debts to include A$46,000 in credit card bills, a claim from her Mayfair landlords for A$90,000 in damages and unpaid rent, and unpaid commissions due to the agents who sold her the Clapham house. She was also said to be behind in her mortgage and, by June, it appeared likely that the bank would soon seize the property.

Michael appeared either unwilling or unable to help. Although he had millions of dollars tied up in international real estate and numerous band investments (including an extensive Australian property portfolio), he was exhausting his cash reserves at an alarming speed. Not coincidentally, he listed the first house he ever owned — the terrace in Paddington, Sydney — for immediate sale. The house netted him a tidy A$285,000 (not bad for an investment of just over $100,000 in 1984) but it's unlikely the money lasted long.

In Michael's mind, it was Bob Geldof who should have

been shouldering the burden of keeping Paula and her children in comfortable circumstances. They were Geldof's family, reasoned Hutchence, not his and he was concerned that an offer of financial assistance might lead to an avalanche of claims. If two decades in the limelight had taught Michael anything, it was to be extremely careful with his money. He realised, however, that his failure to place Paula and her family in large and comfortable lodgings reflected poorly on his financial worth — and his capacity to accept his new responsibilities.

'If Paula and the kids are likely to lose their home then I'll stop that happening,' he offered gallantly. 'I have enough to help, and that's what I'll do.'

Behind the scenes, Michael had behaved far more gallantly than anyone realised. Although he stopped short of offering Paula a massive cash bailout, he did something just as useful: he gave a personal guarantee for the full extent of Paula's extensive (and escalating) legal bills pertaining to her divorce and custody battles. Months after his death it was still not clear what the full cost of these bills would be, but it was certainly feasible that the final bill would run to well over A$1 million.

For Paula, however, the immediate solution lay in pleading with Bob Geldof to allow her and the children back into the couple's family home in Chelsea. Geldof had not been using the house much — he was living in his mansion in Haversham, Kent, with his new girlfriend Jeanne Marine — and only used the Chelsea house as a city address. But, so far, he had resisted Paula's requests to have use of their former home.

Paula took her fight to the High Court but, after several days of legal wrangling, Geldof and Yates reached an out-of-court settlement. Without recognising Yates's right of legal ownership, he agreed to give her the use of the Chelsea terrace. In return, he and Marine would have the use of Hutchence's expensively renovated Smith Terrace *pied-à-terre* (again, Hutchence remained the owner of the property). It was a deal done out of expedience, but it was one that suited the needs of all parties. Ironically, Michael had never had the chance to sleep even a single night in the Smith Terrace house.

In a joint press release, Yates and Geldof announced in a handwritten note: 'After three days of complete bloody night-mare in the High Court of Justice, Bob and Paula have with collective sighs of relief arrived amicably at a half-decent solu-tion to their housing arrangements. Paula and the kids will move into the house in Chelsea. Bob will move into Michael's house down the road. Thanks very much.' The note was signed by both parties.

On July 22, 1996, at home, Paula Yates gave birth to a 3.1 kilogram (6-pound 14-ounce) baby girl, Heavenly Hiraani Tiger Lily. Even by the high standards set by Yates and Geldof, it was a bizarre name. (Heavenly is from the Tennessee Williams play *Sweet Bird of Youth*. Hiraani was an old friend of Michael's and supposedly means 'beautiful sky' in a Poly-nesian language. Tiger Lily was also chosen by Michael, appar-ently in tribute to Hong Kong.) This was one of the greatest moments in Michael's life. The couple named singer Nick Cave — also a resident of London and a close friend of Michael's — as the baby's godfather. Cave and Michael had in fact been business partners for some time; the unlikely pair had held shares in the Portobello Café in Portobello Road, London. Now, Michael was strengthening their bond with a request to help care for his only child.

For Michael, the arrival of Tiger was the completion of a cycle that had begun with the disintegration of his own family

20 years earlier. Ever since his early teens, Michael's family life had been difficult to the point of being dysfunctional. While his mother remained unpredictable and often smothered him with attention when he least expected it, relations with his step-sister Tina and brother Rhett were frequently strained. Rhett was the member of Michael's family who had been adversely affected by his brother's fame and fortune. Not only had Rhett failed to resolve his jealousy and sense of inbuilt failure, he actually acted out his frustration. When there was a mess — and there was frequently a mess — it was usually Michael who provided the necessary funds to pay for the clean-up. Michael's relationship with his father continued to be strong. Indeed, Kell Hutchence had often been enlisted as a silent partner in a number of Michael's complex investment and tax minimisation schemes. Kell was, demonstrably, the only member of his family Michael truly trusted.

With Paula and her three daughters — and Tiger as well — Michael had a family of his own. After a full life, he felt ready for the commitment and self-denial that is implicit in parenthood. If his life would now include making kids' breakfasts, doing the family driving or reading books at bedtime, so be it. This would be a crazy, yet happy, family of Easters and birthdays and Christmases.

For a few days, at least, that dream remained intact. Michael was deliriously happy, and the couple even received Bob Geldof as a visitor in the nursery. Exercising his rights of ownership before the attending paparazzi, Geldof casually let himself in the front door with his own key, and remained in the house for some time.

On August 12, the proud parents posed with the baby for the benefit of photographers. 'Watching Michael with our daughter is just fantastic,' Paula told the press. 'He's a natural father, as I knew he would be. Tiger Lily is a very lucky girl.'

Michael responded, 'Every time I look at her I start beaming. She is beautiful. I still can't believe that I'm a Dad.'

But on top of his professional insecurities and the ongoing battle with Bob Geldof, parenthood placed an enormous pressure on Michael — and his temper frequently cracked over the coming weeks as he sought to protect his new family from the intrusions of the media. While he had never been a violent person, the years since his head injury in 1992 had seen him increasingly inclined to swing fists with little provocation.

The violence had started at the same time as Michael's affair with Paula was gathering steam; subjected to pressure that he'd never previously experienced, he lashed out with alarming frequency. The incident with the photographer at Chilston Park resulted in an assault charge, and in September 1996 he was convicted and ordered to pay A$200 compensation for personal injury, A$800 for assault and A$3,000 for damage to the victim's camera. Between the Gallagher brothers and the paparazzi who threatened to ruin his private life, Michael was swinging his fists with alarming regularity.

During his first public outing with Paula and the new baby, Hutchence became so agitated by the press photographers who were stalking the couple that he leaped out of his cab to push one of them away. A few days later, while Paula was visiting her solicitor, Michael again jumped from a parked car to threaten another photographer. Understandable as his actions might have been, they were neither rational nor productive; it was clear that he was not coping.

Michael needed to escape, and a welcome excuse came in the form of Australia's ARIA Awards — the equivalent of America's Grammys or the Brit Awards. The producers of the show were keen to have INXS perform on the program, and even though release plans for the new album were still up in the air (Phonogram had toyed with the idea of releasing it in August 1996 before shelving the project until March 1997), the band were excited at the prospect of playing new material to a large Australian TV audience. It would be a way of telegraphing the fact that the band were still together and making new music. The trip would be a good opportunity to escape the oppressive attention of the British media, and Michael and Paula would also have the chance to introduce Tiger Lily to her Australian grandparents.

So, in September 1996, after a brief holiday in France, Michael, Paula and Tiger — followed by a sizeable pack of British paparazzi — arrived in Sydney for the ARIAs.

In an expansive mood, Yates entertained reporters at the couple's Sydney hotel — the Ritz Carlton in Double Bay — and waxed lyrical about her plans for the future. 'I really love Australia,' Yates told the *Sydney Morning Herald*. 'There is no comparison with Britain. Australia is special to me. My new daughter is Australian. When my children are older I think we will definitely move here, although we would have to arrange it with Bob so he could see them as much as possible.'

'In London they [the paparazzi] chase my children down the street until they fall over. Then they take pictures of them crying and run them with a headline saying "Paula's children cry over her divorce". I'm happy to say the Australian media have been really nice. I'm going to have as many [children] as I possibly can. Michael is fine about it. He loves fatherhood. But he's still a wild man, of course.'

Scoffing at persistent rumours that the couple were to marry during their lightning Australian visit, she said, 'As if anyone with three other children would ever get married without them! I would never get married without my girls.

They are going to be bridesmaids. Outfits have been planned, sketches have been drawn, begging letters have been written . . .'

The producers of the ARIAS and the representatives of the major record labels who plan the show were always lukewarm at the idea of an INXS performance on the show. Although Polygram bravely presented the band's appearance as an exciting exclusive preview, there were many doubters — and on the night, INXS changed few minds with their performance. The band chose one of the slower songs from the new album, a brooding, almost hymn-like piece called 'Searching'. Many felt that the song was an all too visible metaphor for the band's distressing lack of direction but for many INXS fans, it was great to see the band on a stage at all. As it happened, other events transpired that quickly made the appearance fade into irrelevance and brought Michael and Paula's happy Australian honeymoon to a crashing halt.

On September 29, London police raided the couple's Chelsea home and found 'substances' that were later identified as opium and pipes, as well as pornographic photos and fetishistic sex equipment. The police had been tipped off by Paula's nanny of 12 years, Anita Debney, who claimed she was looking for instructions for the car alarm. She was looking for them in a Smarties box hidden within a shoebox under the couple's bed, as you do.

Michael's friends certainly weren't surprised. In the past two years in London, he'd been known to snort coke, smoke heroin and take virtually every designer drug known to humanity. As one close friend put it, 'The only surprise to anyone who knew Michael was the idea that he'd leave a stash of drugs at the house in the first place. When you were with Michael, you tended to stay until *everything* was gone.'

The media went into a frenzy, hunting Hutchence and Yates down in the midst of their Sydney holiday. In London, Geldof seized his opportunity, and within days he had brought an action in the British High Court applying for custody of his three daughters. (Paula raced home immediately to fight the action, but failed.) Geldof's application was successful, at least temporarily, and Fifi Trixibelle, Peaches and Pixie returned to their father.

Michael and Paula were distraught. If there was a time in Michael's life when a drug bust of this nature might have been little more than an amusing incident to laugh about after the lawyers had done their work, that time had passed. Not only had the bust ruined their Australian sojourn — throwing a negative pall over the couple just as Michael was showing off his child to his Australian friends and family — but it also had all kinds of implications for Paula's custody of her three daughters and the legal battles over custody and property settlement she would eventually have to face with Bob Geldof. The media even suggested that Michael and Paula's custody of their own daughter might be at risk if the charge were proven.

'I was incredibly worried about him because I'd never seen him so beside himself,' Michael's friend Greg Perano related after his death. 'He was absolutely stressed about a horrible situation and there was nothing he could do about it. It was a great moment in his life. He was a father and he was out here showing off his child and he thought it was one of the greatest things that had ever happened to him. And once again he was being put in a situation where his security was being threatened.'

Geldof, clearly using the media for all it was worth, stated that he was 'concerned' about Paula's plans to move the family to Australia and told the *Sunday Express*: 'Believe me, I love my three children more than anything in the world. I would do anything to protect them from harm. Without them, I am nothing.'

Not surprisingly, nanny Anita Debney resigned days later. Then Paula's PR consultant, the widely respected Gerry Agar, resigned. The *Sun* suspended Paula's newspaper column — her last source of income since *The Big Breakfast* dropped her in February — and a new hate campaign commenced against Michael and Paula in the British tabloids. A drugs scandal, on top of all that had preceded it, sent the hounds into a frenzy. This time, they were baying for blood.

Upon his return to London in mid-October, Michael voluntarily appeared at Chelsea police station where he answered questions but was not charged. (Paula had appeared at the same station two days earlier.) Michael and Paula later claimed the drugs had been planted in their home, and it was ultimately impossible for police to gather sufficient evidence to charge either of them. The charges were eventually dropped.

Although he had escaped the ugliness of a criminal trial, Michael and Paula's lives were becoming a travesty of family life because of media intrusion and their worsening paranoia. Both believed that their house and phone were bugged — and they were convinced that many current or former associates were spying on them. Michael's drug use was escalating under the pressure.

'Along with Anita, I was blamed for planting the drugs,' Gerry Agar related later with astonishment. 'That was ridiculous, it shocked and surprised me. I felt Michael and Paula were in a mutual fantasy.'

chapter 12

The Last Time

To create songs for the tenth INXS studio album, Andrew and Michael had deliberately isolated themselves in Dublin. Taking the creative process one step further, they had started to demo tracks before bringing the rest of the band into the picture. In a clear attempt to avoid the friction and emotional turmoil of a six-way argument, the band's two key men were attempting to settle the creative questions in advance. This was not going to be another painful album to make. Indeed so successful were they in controlling the creative process that this was to be the very first INXS album — and ultimately the last — to feature a collection of songs written exclusively by Andrew Farriss and Michael Hutchence.

Once again, they were also determined to avoid the distractions of recording in Sydney (or London, for that matter), which is why Vancouver seemed to be an ideal location. Not only was Bruce Fairbairn's Armoury Studio located there, but it was exactly the kind of modern, yet anonymous, city the band needed to work in. No supermodels, no distractions. The tracks for the album were largely recorded in just eight days using state-of-the-art equipment set up in the band's rehearsal room.

As Andrew explained, 'We made sure that whatever came out of our mouths or our guitars was something that could be kept. We didn't want to end up in that situation where we go, "Oh shit, how do we make that happen again?"'

The band were relieved to be working together again and felt upbeat about the sessions. Optimistic as this might have seemed, they had their fingers crossed that this would be their opportunity to overcome the disasters of the past few years and rise above the debris. 'This is our attempt to reclaim some of the territory I think we helped pioneer,' Andrew announced. 'The album combines elements of dance music and rock, and that's been an INXS tradition since the beginning — we were experimenting with remixes back in the early eighties. Of course, when you write and record, you never know if what you're doing is valid at all. It's only looking back that you can see what connected. But with us, even though we've incorporated a lot of different kinds of music, we always sound like us.

'Michael and I have known each other since high school and been through some incredible ups and downs personally and professionally since then. So in writing the new songs, our attitude was, "What have we got to lose?". The thing we stressed was spontaneity. We've spent a lot of time in the past labouring over songs that probably didn't benefit from it. I think the more off the cuff Michael and I are, the better the music comes off. I mean, I wrote "Need You Tonight" while I was waiting for a cab.'

In his interviews to promote the album, Hutchence sounded positive but, reading between the lines, it's clear that he was uncertain about the album and the rationale behind the band's existence. 'I don't know where we'll fit in now,' he pondered during one interview. 'I've always had a horror of that. Ever since the success of *Kick*, I've had a terror of being lumped in with bands that were popular then, but are now extinct. We come from a generation of which there aren't too many survivors left. A generation wedged somewhere between punk and disco. There's U2, the Cure, REM, Depeche Mode, maybe. It's a strange place to be.

'Come to think of it, I don't think we've ever fitted. Maybe it's a generational thing, or maybe it's because there's always been six of us pulling in six different directions.'

Because of the arrival of Michael's and Andrew's babies — and the possibility that the album would become lost in the major releases that swamped the market in Christmas 1996 — it was decided to hold the release of INXS's new album until March. This was a blow to some members of the band; they had never had to endure a delayed release before, although many bands have found themselves in this situation. Waiting almost a year to drop an album was unheard of for INXS but, because they were in the hands of a new record company, they chose not to put up too much resistance to the plan. Looking at the upside, it was decided that the long lead-up would be used to extensively pre-promote the album, to warm the international media to the idea that INXS were back again.

In early December 1996, the band travelled to LA to shoot the video for the album's first single with celebrated director Walter Stern and to pose for the surreal desert shots that would ultimately grace the cover of the new album. Immediately afterwards, Michael and Paula — with Peaches, Fifi, Pixie and Tiger, and an entourage of support staff in tow — travelled to Australia for a brief holiday prior to the start of Michael's promotional commitments for the album. While

Fifi attended a horse-riding camp, the rest of the party travelled to Magnetic Island on the Great Barrier Reef. There they witnessed the modest New Year's Eve fireworks at Picnic Bay.

The band reconvened in January for rehearsals at the ABC studios in Gore Hill. They even invited a handful of Australian media and record company personnel to attend a show in one of the studios. INXS played well, and were clearly chuffed that some of the most powerful players in the Australian industry seemed prepared to accept them back with open arms.

Although INXS had acquired a reputation in their home country as aloof rock stars, the band remained, as they had always been, perfectly charming and affable people — as pleasant a bunch of guys to hang out with as any in the international music business.

But Murphy's independent way of working, and the band's unwillingness over many years to make themselves available for endless Australian media requests, had resulted in the burning of a lot of bridges between INXS and the Australian music media and industry. The debacle of the Concert for Life had worsened the situation. Now, the band was determined to rebuild those bridges and, over the summer, band members took the unusual step of inviting selected media representatives to a series of post-rehearsal dinners. Confused as they might have been by the decline in their fortunes, they had certainly never reached a point where they had lost confidence in their music or lost the will to continue. They still loved being together, loved playing together and, most importantly, they weren't too proud to go out and share the feeling.

Straight after playing the show at the ABC studios, INXS flew to the US to appear on a VH1 (a US cable channel) special being shot in Aspen, Colorado. Thus three solid months of interviews and TV appearances designed to build their public profile and prepare the world for the release of the new album commenced.

It was decided that the album — which was, realistically, the release that would ultimately determine the band's future — should be titled *Elegantly Wasted*. Named after a track on the album, it was a term that had been originally applied to members of The Rolling Stones (particularly Keith Richards) at the height of their dalliance with hard drugs in the 1970s. To most observers, it seemed a particularly inappropriate title, but it had come from a highly credible source (U2's Bono had suggested it to Michael during a drinking session in Dublin) and the band were not changing their minds.

Three years may not be a terribly long time for most people, but it's a very long time in pop music. After some time away from the limelight, INXS found themselves inhabiting a different world. They noted, with some relief, that the media were still interested in them and showed them considerable respect. The band had also become adept at maintaining contact with their international fans via the Internet. But they also came to understand that the ground rules had changed. If they wanted to be noticed, they would need to reconsider their attitude to certain forms of promotion.

Specifically, they had to be prepared to do what so many young bands were doing: they had to be prepared to sing for their supper at in-store appearances, media interviews and even record company functions. For a band who had only ever presented themselves in full six-man flying formation — with all the bells and whistles — this was a tough transformation. Despite their 20 years in the business, the members of INXS took to the promotional challenge with gusto, crisscrossing

Europe, South America, the United States and Canada with a seemingly endless stream of showcase performances, radio interviews, TV appearances and photo opportunities. While they were re-exposing the world to the band and its music, INXS left virtually no stone unturned.

'We did a hell of a lot of impromptu acoustic performances,' says Garry Gary Beers, 'where we'd just hop up and play a few songs in whatever configuration was available. It might be Michael and me and Andrew, it might be Michael and Tim. It really forced us to think again, as musicians.'

Tim Farriss recalls one hilarious afternoon in Barcelona when he and Michael were invited along to a large record store for an 'in-store appearance'. In-stores are one of those ugly realities of the modern music business: fans and potential record buyers are encouraged to crowd into a store for a glimpse of one or two captive stars. At a good in-store, artists perform acoustically for the privileged few; at bad in-stores, bands sit behind a table and autograph a handful of CD slicks (covers). In Barcelona, Tim and Michael found themselves somewhere in between.

'This guy introduced us and then someone thrust microphones into our hands and we were kind of pushed out on stage,' recalls the guitarist. 'So we're standing there in front of about 2,000 people with absolutely *no idea* what to do. The next minute the PA started pumping out "Need You Tonight" so we just stood there dancing and singing along looking like complete turkeys. Michael really got into it and the crowd went nuts, of course. It was totally bizarre.'

When the band started planning their live set for the concert tour, this experience proved to be a valuable one. 'I think on this tour we really de-structured our set a lot,' said Michael. 'We'd done a lot of acoustic things, like with two or three of us playing at a radio station or whatever, and that really helped to break things down. We also started to leave room in the set for jamming, for inspired things to happen.'

'We've been doing all sorts of different things with the songs,' agreed Andrew Farriss. 'Instead of just doing a faithful version of the album track, we've been injecting some energy and fun into the proceedings, putting a bit of flexibility into it. Some of the older songs have really benefited from that kind of treatment; they're still recognisable for the audience, but we get something from it as well. In some cases, we've actually improved on the original.'

But before they could hit the road once more — something the band was genuinely looking forward to — there was a mountain of interviews to climb. For many of these appointments, Michael carried his customary packet of Marlboro Lights and a Zippo lighter, which he delighted in showing to every journalist he met. A present from Paula, it was engraved with the words: 'You're gorgeous. Please fuck me.'

During one revealing interview, Hutchence was asked whether the pressure of the past two years could have serious implications for his emotional wellbeing. 'Yes, it certainly could,' replied Hutchence. 'But, you know, I guess I'm stronger than I realised. I've got important people to take care of here. People and children. I've got to make sure everyone's OK.

'When you're very young, in your teens and 20s, you're basically useless to society. It's just, "Heads down, let's go!". But eventually you start to raise your head above the horizon a bit and other things start to come into view and you realise that there are other things in life apart from yourself.'

Elegantly Wasted was released in June 1997, and immediately garnered a positive response from radio programmers and music media all over the world. At first, American radio responded particularly well, with the band picking up more playlist additions than any other act in the album's first week of release but, sadly, the initial enthusiasm quickly gave way to inertia. Despite all the efforts of INXS and Polygram, the sales picture was only marginally better than *Full Moon Dirty Hearts* and the single never really gained the necessary momentum to become a hit. The album debuted in the Top 20 in most of the band's core markets but it slipped quickly thereafter.

Much as the band's many fans had genuinely wanted to like the album, the fact remained that INXS had not progressed. They had not even remained on the tougher, more contemporary course they'd set themselves with *Welcome to Wherever You Are* and *Full Moon Dirty Hearts*. Instead, they appeared to have reverted to a limp, unconvincing pastiche of their late-eighties sound that was often alarmingly uninspired — and few were prepared to let them get away with it. In a searing review in American *Rolling Stone* by Elysa Gardner, the gloves were well and truly off.

'The latest offering from those ageing Aussie pinup boys in INXS, seems like an exercise in nostalgia. INXS haven't lost their flair for making sexy, streamlined funk-rock confections, but ten years after "Need You Tonight" hit the top of the charts, the sinuous dance grooves and crackling bursts of guitar in new songs like "Elegantly Wasted" and "Don't Lose Your Head" don't seem very fresh. At least Men at Work knew when to call it quits.'

Trevor Smith says it pithily: 'Privately, I know Chris Murphy's view was that the band should have left it longer.

I mean, if you're going to go away, then go away for a few years and then come back when there's a real demand. Instead, they came back with a pretty ordinary album, and that was a kiss of death. I don't know one person who thought that "Elegantly Wasted" was a good song title, or a good song. I mean, I'm sorry, but this is the late nineties, and there's no such thing as elegantly wasted.'

The band launched into a concert tour — their first proper world jaunt since the conclusion of the X tour in 1991, albeit at a far more modest level — with a series of South African shows in June. At a concert at the Mohegan Sun Casino in Cape Town (not the kind of venue the band had played for many years, it should be noted) Michael was in fine form. From the stage, he ordered six martinis for the band — and invited the waitress onstage to deliver them. He then gave one to Andrew and made him drink it. Jumping from the stage, he hopped onto the table of a honeymoon couple, drinking their drinks and chatting to them. 'By the end of the night,' he told them, 'I expect you to be doing it on the table.'

A 25-year-old local model by the name of Carolina Rorich claimed to have spent that night with Michael at Cape Town's Peninsula Hotel. Faithfully recounting the details for London's *Sunday Mirror*, she described an evening of champagne, cocaine and wild sex, and even confirmed the dimensions of Michael's penis for the newspaper's readers. It was the kind of night that Michael might have had a thousand times before, but this time it was bad timing.

Few people had cared what Michael got up to in his leisure up until a few years before. Now the whole world wanted every gory detail. But if the British public were scandalised — and, let's face it, they invariably were — Paula appeared happy to forgive him. Later in the tour, she appeared onstage at New York's Beacon Theatre with Tiger Lily in her arms, so that Michael could show off his family to the audience.

The band proceeded through Europe, the UK, Canada and the USA — playing theatres and large clubs to full houses and receiving excellent reviews. Much as nobody could deny the extent to which INXS had slipped in the popularity stakes, there was a sense that, for the first time in years, they were clawing back some ground. In London, for example, the band headlined the 10,000 seat Wembley Arena rather than the enormous Wembley Stadium they had headlined six years earlier — but the reviews were still ecstatic. With the support of a new record company that was keen to prove its enthusiasm, the band worked their way through the United States with a new-found sense of purpose.

On the road, INXS were having fun again. Several members of the band had turned their back on music during the layoff (Jon Farriss, in particular, had not picked up a pair of drumsticks for more than two years), but now they were back in the swing and relishing the joy of being onstage together once more. Now, as ever, the band used their keen sense of humour to carry them through the tedium and inevitable disappointments of life on the road. All six members of the band had become somewhat obsessed with the cult comedy film *Austin Powers: International Man of Mystery*, and long hours on the tour bus were spent mimicking key scenes from the movie.

'I reckon we're playing better now than we ever have before,' Kirk Pengilly enthused mid-way through the tour. 'We've had great ticket sales, great reviews and fantastic audience response. We've been through a lot of adversity these past few years, but it has actually worked at bringing the band closer together. We're playing really well, and Michael is more confident onstage than I've ever seen him. It's still the same six of us, six against the world.'

Michael was similarly energised by the shows. 'This tour has been one of the best ever, for me. I think after this many years it's clear that we're not in it for the money, or the novelty value of stepping out in front of an audience or seeing all the pretty girls in the front row. We got over all that years ago, and now we're mainly interested in doing this as well as we can, developing what we do. We're doing it for ourselves, I guess.

'One of the things that interests me at this point is that you do develop as an artist over a period of time,' he continued. 'The experiences in your life, all the things you know and understand, bring something new to your songs — even the old ones that you probably thought you got right years ago. I just can't wait to get to Australia and play as well as we've been playing lately, because for us it's a really neat completion of the circle.'

The entire band were revitalised. Playing in front of concert audiences for the first time in years, even when many of those concerts were far from sold out, they realised that for all the negativity in the media and the problems they had experienced with record companies, management and their internal dynamics, there was still a strong and loyal INXS audience that was interested in the band and, excitingly, loved their most recent work. In focusing on the failure of their recent albums to reach the heights of *Kick* and *X*, they had lost sight of the bleeding obvious: a million people is *still* a million people.

While there were several disappointing nights that saw them playing to half-empty halls, there were also nights on which the band felt as if they were recapturing their former glory. Headlining festival bills in Europe, INXS were playing to crowds of up to 40,000 people. One night in Chicago, they pulled 17,000. This was not the stuff of abject failure.

'I honestly think that this tour is the best we've ever played,' says Jon Farriss. 'We've been playing a lot of new material, because we're basically representing three whole albums that were never promoted live in a concert setting, plus the greatest hits album. With this tour we've made very sure that the songs from albums like *Full Moon* and *Welcome* are given the same weight and attention as the other songs because we're very proud of them. A lot of our fans are very familiar with the older songs, but they don't realise how well they know the more recent material until they hear us live.'

'It dawned on us recently just how many people have gotten into INXS since the *Kick* era, like the last three albums,' said Tim Farriss. 'If you look on the Internet there are so many people talking about those albums — and because we haven't toured much since the early nineties, we haven't really come into contact with them and they haven't been exposed to us as a live act.'

Undoubtedly, INXS were attempting to convince themselves, and Michael, that the band had a future. Australian journalist Susan Chenery travelled with them through several US dates and found them upbeat and optimistic, despite the visible signs of their declining audience. 'The band were lovely,' she recalls, 'and always very uplifting to be around. There were lots of jokes, lots of laughter. But I also sensed that Michael was really weighed down because of what was happening with Paula and Bob. The thing you have to understand is that Michael was really very soft and gentle — and Bob can be a real bully. He was frightened of Geldof. He hated him, actually, although he was very careful not to say as much because the court proceedings made it all very sensitive. But it was really obviously on his mind a lot.'

In New York, Michael submitted himself to a revealing interview with journalist Sharon Krum in which he discussed fame, the British media and the recent deaths of Princess Diana and Dodi Al Fayed. His words in this interview graphically illustrated his state of mind — a swirling mixture of fear, anger, frustration and rampant paranoia.

'I think the equation is very simple and sad,' he said of the role of the British and European paparazzi. 'The press, especially in England, makes a construct of a human, and then they either do two things with that person. They make them beyond human, or they dehumanise them. Bob Geldof was taken beyond human to sainthood — so if you left him, that leaves one choice. You are bad, you are wrong. It's as simple as that.

'The situation is quite the opposite, if only you knew. It's all lies. People don't know the truth, and I can't talk about it now.

'You see the destruction of the person you love in front of your eyes, the attempted destruction, and to fight it is to be violated all over again. The question I have is, where are the human beings in all this? The stuff that has happened to us, it could make you lose your faith in human nature.

'It's against the law to destroy blacks, Jews, people for religious causes. That law and parliament have stopped discrimination like that. All we have left is celebrity, and every society has to kick a dog, it's a fact. Someone to raise and someone to burn. It's human nature. Celebrities are the last bastion, and it's not against the law.

'They say you asked for it. That's bullshit. I am not a cynical manipulator of the media, I never have been. I think

230 Burn

there should be limits. The average Joe Blow is living vicariously through MTV and Planet Hollywoods and what does it say about us? People have forgotten that celebrities are human beings.'

Hutchence told Krum that he had known Princess Di and her lover — and that their deaths 'knocked us for six. This has to be a wakeup call for people. Your appetite for celebrity has led to this. Your vicarious pleasure for 25p has cost the life of magic.

'I would hate for people to say, "Oh, stop whingeing". I'm not whingeing, but I consider myself to a point a creative artist, and people like us aren't built for this stuff. Madonna is built for it, even though she has gone through hell. Overall she has been the winner because her art is media, and power to her. But overall, we don't have such thick skins, and the irony is you are trying to write your song or make your film and your life is vulgarised and bastardised.'

Asked how he keeps sane, he answered, 'I'm barely doing it.'

In September, INXS parted company with their manager of two years, Paul Craig. The move was bloodless, and had less to do with the disastrous reaction to the album than it did with the power that their US representative, Martha Troup, held over the band. In conjunction with husband Liebowitz, Troup had always been one of their most trusted advisors — and had been handling their North American management for some time. Now Troup would manage INXS on a worldwide basis.

'A lot of people thought that the band should have hired a more heavyweight manager after Chris Murphy,' says one Australian artist manager. 'Whatever else Chris was, he had this incredible vision and drive — and at that stage of their career, the band really needed someone who could re-focus the band and give them some real direction. They needed someone who could help them choose songs and put some sort of plan together. Paul and Martha are both very nice people, but they're not heavy hitters.'

After the US tour the band went their separate ways with the aim of reconvening in November for a short string of Australian shows. The band had mixed feelings about returning to their birthplace after what they felt were too many nasty reviews of *Elegantly Wasted* and they were particularly stung by the way Australia's ultra-hip JJJ network had responded to the album (not only had station programmers rejected all tracks, but announcers had publicly mauled the band for releasing such an ordinary album). For all that, they also sensed that there would be a certain resonance in a homecoming tour that would coincide with their twentieth anniversary. (The anniversary proper occurred while they were on a brief tour break. Most members of INXS celebrated the occasion in Sydney with a party that also marked Tim Farriss's fortieth birthday.)

It was sad and terribly poignant that — at the point in their career when they should have been celebrating their achievements and relishing the distance they had travelled — INXS were considering the possibility of not even playing Australia. As the dates approached, they were acutely conscious of the tour's implications.

'We were going to just not come to Australia on this tour,' Tim Farriss warned. 'But we figured the whole reason we wanted to play was that we're playing such great live shows at the moment, and if the band comes into the country, picks a bunch of great shows to do and people are blown away, then that says more than any printed word. That's our best retaliation, to come in and play great shows, not to run away. We're a lot more resilient than that.'

'This tour is a celebration for us,' added Jon Farriss in an upbeat moment just weeks before the tour. 'It's a home-coming, a resolution, the completion of a two-decade cycle that's seen us travel into pretty much every little corner of the world. So now we're back where we started, carrying all the weight of our experiences. It means so much to be able to share this.'

chapter 13

The Journey Home

A fter the last shows in the United States in late September, Michael flew home to Paula and the kids in London, and the remainder of the band returned to Australia. The plan was to rest up for two months, and then launch into the final leg of the tour with a run of concert dates around Australia. After the qualified success of the international shows and promotional work (qualified because they had failed to sell the album to any degree) the mood among the band members was cautiously optimistic.

The first single from *Elegantly Wasted* — the album's title track — wasn't a hit, but INXS's morale received a welcome boost with the news that another song, 'Don't Lose Your Head', was to be used on the soundtrack for the Nicholas Cage/John Travolta movie *Face/Off*. In Australia, 'Don't Lose Your Head' was promptly released as a single, and with some help from the publicity surrounding the film, it appeared that INXS were on their way to their first hit single in years.

Plans were progressing for the Australian tour. Because the band no longer had an Australian-based management company, it was decided that their old colleague Gary Grant (who now managed a number of local artists, including Wendy Matthews) should be given the role of agent. Grant quickly became the band's unofficial Australian manager, a role he had accepted during his many years with INXS. Grant sold the tour to Frontier Touring, one of Australia's largest concert promoters, and set about organising the logistics of the 15 dates.

From the outset, the Australian-resident members of INXS were highly active in organising the tour. Once they might have left others to do this work, but suddenly they were placing a lot of importance on the details. While Jon Farriss was conscripted to deal with the art direction of posters and tour programs, and everyone did their share of interviews and meetings, Tim, Kirk and Garry looked closely at venues.

'We've put a lot of thought and discussion into this Australian tour,' Tim Farriss explained as the days counted down to the first show. 'I've given more thought to these dates than any tour we've done — certainly any tour we've done since I used to manage the band. We went through all the venues for this tour in a lot of detail. We've played most of them at some point, so it's all full of memories for us. These are the venues we wanted to play.'

Although they were proud that the tour was marking their twentieth anniversary as a live act, INXS didn't want to make too much of a fuss about it — just in case anyone did their sums and realised how old they were. So the tour was dubbed Lose Your Head in an effort to maximise interest in the single. A decision was made to put a simple XX on the back page of the tour program as a subtle acknowledgment of its historical importance, and the band went to work devising a setlist that was packed with songs from their two decade history, including many songs they hadn't played live in years.

INXS were already aware that *Elegantly Wasted* had been a mistake. While they believed in the music — and, in fact, believed the album to be among the best of their career — they acknowledged that the name of the album was wrong. There was a degree of recognition within the band that the album's imaging and artwork were less than ideal. But true to form, they felt that the album's poor showing (worldwide sales amounted to just 650,000) was due largely to media persecution; they were convinced they were still the subject of a media vendetta, and were extremely sensitive to criticism. More than anything else, they were worried about the way the Australian shows would be received. It was a strange mixture of feelings: great pride on the one hand and a sense of persecution on the other. It all added up to a certain defiance that was at odds with the band's standing in the industry. The shows were selling well, and INXS had every reason to think they'd go well but they couldn't overcome the feeling that they all had something to prove.

'We've all had to deal with the negative publicity and criticism in our different ways,' said Kirk Pengilly. 'Obviously you deal with the fact that not every album you release is going to be super-successful, but some of the nasty stuff that gets written is hard to bear. Andrew, particularly, is really hurt by it and takes it very much to heart.

'We are still really proud of the music we make, regardless of whether it's a hit or not. We're not discouraged by some of the bad things that have happened because, at the end of the day, we think that the last album, the last few for that matter, are pretty damn good. That means we'll do whatever we have to do to get our message across.'

'I'm incredibly passionate about INXS,' Andrew Farriss

emphasised in the days leading up to the tour. 'I don't care how many records we sell, or what other people think of us — we just believe in what we do. Our live performances are incredibly important to us and I think with these shows you'll really see what we're about. We've been very fortunate as a band — and for a very long time — and that's worth cele-brating. We've put a lot of work in, for a lot of years, and we're proud of what we've done.'

For Kirk Pengilly, Garry Gary Beers and Andrew, Jon and Tim Farriss, such sentiments of solidarity and defiance were more than just the words of a band trying to talk up ticket sales (most shows were close to being sold out). They had a strong vested interest in keeping their band alive — even if the project appeared to be on its last legs.

INXS were failing to address some of their most funda-mental problems: the declining quality of their music, their alarming lack of musical direction and their increasing irrel-evance. In a sense, they were back where they started in the late seventies — a great live band who were yet to make a great album. And because their shows were the one place the band still really clicked, they were understandably keen to present the Lose Your Head tour as a turning point in their fortunes. It was an opportunity to celebrate two decades of achievement with their Australian fans, to reclaim some of the ground they had lost in the nineties, and re-motivate their audience — and perhaps themselves — for the future.

But the one person they *really* needed to re-motivate was thousands of kilometres away, in a terrace house in Chelsea, with a lot of other things on his mind. Hutchence had also enjoyed the American shows, and he was looking forward to playing Australia — but he was also aware that the album had not clicked commercially. Thinking selfishly, he knew that it was time to take some decisive steps towards building a new future. At the age of 37, he clearly had plenty of potential left in him and his only challenge was to find a suitable vehicle for his talents.

Decisiveness was not something that came easily to Michael — and now, weighed down by serious depression and a load of prescription anti-depressants, including Prozac, he was having trouble getting through most days. What could he do? Although his property assets were substantial, he had not earned any real income from INXS for some years — other than his share of the Polygram advance, and that was effectively only a loan against future earnings. Unless he started to sell off those assets, or strip back his lavish lifestyle, he needed to find some ways to earn more money. Radical action was required.

Michael knew that he had the solo album — and that once he returned from the Australian dates he needed to polish up the best tracks, perhaps record several more, and then release the album. In the meantime, his thoughts were turning once again to a film career.

Since making *Frankenstein Unbound*, he'd flirted with the idea of appearing in another feature but between all the recording and touring, and his busy social whirl, he'd never found the time. In 1990, American director Oliver Stone had called Hutchence to see if he'd be interested in starring in his biopic on Jim Morrison, *The Doors*. Apparently Billy Idol had been cast, but had been injured in a motorbike accident. Hutchence declined — partly because he was about to mount the X tour, partly because he had always feared comparisons to Jim Morrison and partly because he doubted his abilities to star in a major Hollywood feature.

'I told him I thought Billy would be a better person to do

it and I thought he should wait until Billy was well again,' Michael told a reporter. 'I love movies and I love acting, but I don't know how good I am at this stage.'

In 1994, a more tempting offer was made by Michael Hamlyn. The Australian-born film producer was one of Hutchence's closest London friends, and Hamlyn had recently teamed up with an Australian director, Stephan Elliott, to make an outrageous road film about the adventures of a group of drag queens who travel through the Australian desert. Michael was interested enough to hold a number of meetings about the movie, and met with Elliott to discuss his character. However, after months of negotiations, and after discussions with Chris Murphy, Hutchence decided not to do the film. When Elliott was unable to secure Michael's commitment, he cast Australian actor Guy Pearce in the role. *Priscilla, Queen of the Desert* went on to become an international cult hit — and Michael was privately furious that he'd been talked into missing what might well have been a turning point in his career.

During the band's visit to Vancouver to record *Elegantly Wasted*, Michael found time to shoot a cameo role (as a record company A&R man) in a independent film titled *Limp*. In the months leading up to the Australian tour, Michael had been keenly investigating his film prospects once again. On November 6, he travelled to New York to have lunch with Michael Douglas; the pair first met when Douglas approached Michael to allow him to use 'Don't Lose Your Head' in *Face/Off*. Now Douglas was returning the favour by advising Michael on possible strategies for a full-tilt launch into Hollywood. After the New York meeting, with Paula and Tiger in tow, he travelled to Los Angeles where (between impromptu appearances at the Viper Room and one last session for the solo album with Danny Saber) he met with a number of directors and even submitted himself to a screen test for a new Quentin Tarantino project. Like dozens of rock stars before him, Michael was giving Hollywood his very best shot.

Michael and Paula were also looking at other career parachutes. It was clear that Paula would never be given fair treatment in London, and the couple began thinking about starting a new life — and possibly even a new career path — in Australia. Paula instigated a conversation with Australian TV production company Artist Services, with a view to producing a show for the Australian market. She had performed guest hosting duties for another Artist Services program, *Tonight Live* (a Letterman-style tonight show hosted by Steve Vizard), in the early nineties, and discussions now centred on the idea of Paula hosting a Ruby Wax-style chat show. Paula told Artist Services that Michael would be involved in the show as a creative consultant. Further meetings with Artist Services were scheduled to take place in December.

The plans were starting to fall into place. Michael and Paula would travel to Australia with the children for the INXS Australian tour. They could have their meetings with Artist Services, enjoy some holiday time with friends and family, and look more closely at the practicalities of relocating their lives to Australia. Michael asked friends to look out for suitable houses to rent for the Sydney summer, and he had already confirmed to his father Kell that he, Paula and Tiger would be spending Christmas Day at Kell's Sydney apartment.

According to Paula, the couple secretly planned to marry on the Tahitian island of Bora Bora in January 1998. Clearly, this would only be possible if Paula's three daughters were able to attend the ceremony. (In the aftermath of Michael's death, members of the singer's family were at pains to deny that this was ever the case.)

The one obstacle preventing their plans from coming to fruition was Bob Geldof; since the custody hearing in 1996, the couple's three daughters had been living mostly with their father. Bob was not keen to allow Paula to take the children to Australia for Christmas, partly because he feared that they might not return. So while Michael flew to Australia to commence tour rehearsals, Paula remained in London to fight her former husband in court. It was another tense and uncomfortable time in the Hutchence/Yates household.

Michael arrived in Sydney on the evening of Tuesday, November 18 and went straight to the Ritz Carlton, checking in as Murray River. He stayed up late, making phone calls to the UK to check on the progress of Paula's legal proceedings, and then slept until lunchtime. Later on Wednesday, he met with Gary Grant and tour manager John Martin before he filled a prescription for anti-depressants and returned to his room to rest. On Thursday, Michael drove himself to band rehearsals in a rented car, returning to the Ritz Carlton at 5 pm. Fatigued by jet-lag and numbed by the cocktail of anti-depressants in his system, he lay down on his bed to take a short nap before attending a fundraising party for his friend Kym Wilson's production company, Pork Chop Productions, but he slept through the alarm and remained in bed until Friday morning.

On Friday, Michael again drove himself across the Sydney Harbour Bridge in the warm spring sunshine to join INXS for rehearsals at the ABC. He spent the day with the band — and a number of journalists who were invited to attend the sessions — before returning to the hotel at 6.00 pm. For the band and media alike, there was a shared understanding that INXS were preparing not just for their first Australian tour in four years, but also for their twentieth anniversary. In an unspoken way, it was acknowledged that INXS had something to celebrate: they had survived.

TV reporter Richard Wilkins was originally scheduled to interview Michael at rehearsals on the Friday but, at the last minute, their meeting was rescheduled for the following Monday. Because Wilkins wanted the interview — for *The Today Show* — to feature footage of the band's rehearsals, he sent a camera crew to the ABC studios to capture INXS at work.

'I've looked back at that tape quite a few times,' Wilkins confesses, 'but honestly, there's nothing there that would suggest that he was unhappy or depressed or anything. Looking back at it, he's winking, flirting with the camera — and just very confident and self-assured. He looked happy with what he was doing and, you know, really charged-up about the tour.'

Wilkins emphatically denies that the tape — the last footage ever shot of the star — showed Michael to be badly affected by alcohol or drugs. 'He was drinking, but he definitely wasn't wasted. Michael could be pretty excessive, but there's a difference between slightly tipsy and smashed — and he definitely wasn't smashed. If anything, looking back, he seemed so happy that it made me wonder whether he had already made his decision.'

At 7.30 pm, Michael was picked up by his father Kell and his step-mother Susan and taken to dinner at an eastern suburbs restaurant, the Flavour of India.

Michael had been drinking wine throughout the day's rehearsals, and he continued drinking quite heavily through dinner — showing only passing interest in the food his father had ordered. According to interviews with Kell Hutchence, Michael was in a good mood, and dismissed his father's concerns about the pressures of life in the British media spotlight. He also told his father that he'd received strong feedback from Hollywood on his screen test, and there was a suggestion that he should travel to Los Angeles for further meetings. According to his father, Michael scoffed at the idea of leaving Australia before the tour, and indicated that he would pursue the offer after the tour was over.

In what has become a frequently recounted exchange, Kell Hutchence leaned forward and asked his son whether he was all right. Hutchence sr was understandably worried that the pressures of the legal battles with Sir Bob Geldof were taking their toll on a person he knew to be more fragile and sensitive than he ever admitted. But Michael was adamant he was fine, and dismissed his father's concerns with a wave of his hand.

By 10.30 pm, Michael was back at the hotel. He returned to his room — where he apparently met briefly with an unidentified woman in what many now believe to have been a pre-arranged cocaine purchase — before coming downstairs to the hotel bar at approximately 11.00 pm. Michael sat and listened to the female singer who was entertaining the hotel guests, and clapped approvingly at the end of the song. He started up a conversation with two girls at the bar, but was soon joined by Kym Wilson and her barrister boyfriend, Andrew Rayment, whom Hutchence had not previously met. After a round of drinks at the bar, Michael repaired to his room with Wilson and Rayment.

According to Wilson's account of the evening, the trio spent the next four and a half hours talking and drinking.

(They ordered strawberry daiquiris and a bottle of French champagne and also drank from Michael's mini-bar.) Wilson explained that Michael was awaiting a phone call that would tell him whether Paula would have the court's permission to bring her children to Australia. But when the phone did ring, it was to inform Hutchence that the court hearing had been delayed because a judge had not been allocated. Michael took another call from LA concerning his forthcoming Tarantino role. Sensing that he would be battling his demons for many hours to come, Wilson and Rayment eventually left the room before 5.00 am.

No-one knows precisely what Michael Hutchence did for the next five hours — but one thing he didn't do was fall asleep. We know that shortly before 5.30 am he spoke to Paula, who informed him that the court had delayed the hearing until December 18. For a person who had always felt a chronic fear of being left alone — and spent most of his adult life successfully avoiding it — this was terrible news. Not only would he not have Paula and Tiger at his side for the Australian tour dates, but now there was the prospect that they would probably not even make it to Sydney for Christmas — thus throwing all their family plans into confusion. Furious, Hutchence then rang Sir Bob Geldof and pleaded with him to allow the children to come to Australia. Geldof has since said that Hutchence was drunk to the point of being virtually unintelligible, characterising the singer's tone as 'hectoring, abusive and threatening', and he eventually hung up on him.

After dawn broke over Sydney and the first soft light turned into blazing sunshine, Michael made more calls — firstly to Martha Troup in New York and then to his old girlfriend Michelle Bennett. The message he left on Troup's answering machine at 9.38 am Sydney time, was slurred: 'Martha, I fucking had enough.' When she rang him back minutes later, the phone rang out. Michael tried to call her again, and again found the answering machine switched on. On this last message, according to NSW State Coroner Derrick Hand, Michael sounded 'as if he was affected by something and was slow and deep'.

Michelle Bennett received two calls from Michael. The first was intercepted by her answering machine shortly after 9.00 am, and police officers would later describe his tone of voice as 'wasted', but the second call, at 9.54, she took in person. Michael was crying and sounded so upset that she immediately left her Bellevue Hill apartment — a mere five minutes from the hotel — to visit him. But after arriving at the Ritz Carlton and going to his room, she could not raise him. She returned to reception and tried calling him, but again received no reply. Vexed, she left a note for Michael at reception and left the hotel.

The band knew that their singer wasn't going to make it to rehearsals. In the hour before his death, Hutchence left a note for tour manager John Martin at the Ritz Carlton's reception desk, to inform him that he would not be making it to the studio. The band members may have wondered at the reasons for the note but, at this stage of their career together, it's unlikely they gave it a second thought. Annoying as it was that Michael was missing a vitally important appointment, the fact remained that the singer had behaved erratically many times before. He had, in truth, let the band down too many times to mention. Although INXS were due to start the tour with a warm-up date the following night, and they'd barely had two days' rehearsal, this was really nothing unusual.

When the band found out that Michael was dead, the impact was devastating.

Almost as soon as Michael's body was discovered, a Ritz Carlton staffer bounded onto the footpath outside the hotel and blurted the news to a handful of reporters and photographers. Before a single member of the INXS entourage knew anything of the singer's death, the news — initially reported as a rumour — was spreading like wildfire through the electronic media.

John Martin was the first INXS staffer to be officially informed of the death. Martin called Gary Grant, who in turn agreed to drive to the ABC studios — a mere ten minutes away from his home — to intercept the band. En route, Grant placed a call to Michael's mother; she had already heard the news on the radio. It would later transpire that Kell Hutchence also discovered his son's death via a phone call from a reporter seeking comment.

As Grant pulled into the studio carpark, he encountered Kirk and Tim bounding out of their cars. The pair had pulled up at exactly the same time, and now the two old friends were exchanging jokes as they stood waiting for Grant to park his car. Farriss and Pengilly started firing one-liners at Grant, who was by now struggling to speak. 'Guys, guys, I have some terrible news,' he blurted.

Upstairs, Grant, Farriss and Pengilly encountered the other three members of the band. Fearful that they would hear it on the radio first, John Martin had called the band and told them the news. The five band members and the handful of friends and staffers in the rehearsal room were shocked into disbelieving silence. Some time later, as they stood embracing each other and crying, Gary Grant pulled out his mobile phone and called Chris Murphy on the home number of his rural property in Wagga, NSW. As soon as Murphy picked up, both men began sobbing uncontrollably. For all the battles and animosity, the INXS family were united once more in this moment of grief.

While it would take the band some time to fully come to terms with what had happened, the implications of the news were plain enough: Michael was gone for good, and INXS as we knew them were no more.

In the only interview any member of INXS has given since that fateful day in November 1997, Andrew Farriss recalled how he'd felt when he heard that his friend of more than 25 years had just killed himself.

'We were at the rehearsal studios and we were told that Michael was dead. I remember my first reaction was just tremendous loss. I still feel that and I will always feel that. I think the why isn't tremendously important, it's the loss of the person that's important.'

By 6.00 o'clock that night, as the evening news bulletins reached those who hadn't already heard the radio reports or the rumours that were circulating in the city, households all over the country went into shock. Australia had lost one of its most famous sons — a pop culture icon who had grown from a gangly suburban youth into an international superstar. A performer who had stood in the glare of a thousand spotlights and held us fascinated in his gaze. At 37, Michael Hutchence might not have been young — but he was too young to die. Like Princess Diana, he had been transformed by the media into a player in our daily lives. On that warm Saturday in November, something died in us all.

Tributes for the singer began pouring in from all over the world. Approached by a reporter from the *Chicago Sun Times*, Duran Duran's Simon Le Bon said, 'He was a very, very close friend of mine. He was my closest friend in the music industry, outside of my own band. But I don't believe it was suicide. I know how much he had been dying to have that daughter for such a long time. He really wanted that kid. There's no way he would have knowingly done something where he would never see her again. Maybe he screwed up on drugs, but I don't think it was suicide. He would've left a note.'

Kylie Minogue, who had maintained her dignity through-out her break-up with Michael, remained generous to the end. 'It's difficult for me to put into words my personal feelings,' she wrote in a statement of condolence. 'Michael meant so much to me; he was a great inspiration. His charisma, intel-lect, talent and passion were boundless. He touched a great number of people and will be sadly missed.'

While U2's Bono was to send a large floral tribute to the funeral, band member Larry Mullen jr spoke about Michael to the media. 'Sometimes lead singers relate only to other lead singers,' he said. 'It's kind of this ego thing. But Michael wasn't like that at all. He was a really sweet guy, a very nice guy to everyone he met. He was the consummate pop star. And he had so much fun with it all. I love having people like that around, and there really aren't many like him, people with his kind of spunk.'

Michael's family, and members of the band and their rep-resentatives, started making arrangements for a funeral — but just as Michael's adult life had often been a tangle of obli-gations to family, loved ones, workmates and others, these final arrangements became ensnared in conflict. Everyone — the remaining members of INXS, Michael's father, Michael's mother and Paula Yates — had a different idea of what kind of funeral would form a fitting tribute. In their unimaginable grief, they found it impossible to resolve their conflicting opinions.

It was agreed that the funeral should be held in a large venue so that a number of Michael's most ardent fans could attend the ceremony. Within days, arrangements had been made to hold the funeral service in the largest Anglican church in Sydney, St Andrew's Cathedral. Before the band had a chance to become involved, a decision had been made to hold a traditional church funeral, complete with a choir, hymns, a sermon and prayers. This struck many as being out of step with Michael and the manner in which he lived his life and, as the funeral drew closer, a deal was struck that would allow some more appropriate elements into the service.

It was decided that two INXS songs should be played in the church: 'By My Side' for the opening of the service and 'Never Tear Us Apart' for the final procession. At Paula's request, Nick Cave was asked to perform a song ('Into My Arms') as a personal tribute. Richard Wilkins was asked to speak about Michael's life and lament his passing on behalf of the band's fans. It was decided that Andrew, representing the band, would deliver the eulogy, and it was also determined that Rhett and Tina would speak on behalf of the family.

'I was actually a little shocked when Kell asked me to deliver the eulogy,' recalls Wilkins, 'because I didn't regard myself as one of Michael's closest friends. But ultimately, I felt there were some good arguments for getting up there and reminding everyone of what Michael had achieved. The media coverage was focusing on all sorts of other stuff, like Paula saying she was going to wear a wedding dress dyed black, and I just thought it was important to restate the facts.'

Then Michael's mother Pat and his half-sister Tina surprised all parties by linking up with famed Sydney media negotiator Harry M. Miller. At various times an agent, theatrical producer, manager and entrepreneur, Miller was adept at brokering deals in the steamy world of chequebook journalism. Sure enough, within days, Miller emerged to announce that he had just signed a deal with the Seven Network, on behalf of Patricia Glassop, to broadcast the funeral. (The Nine Network had also shown some initial interest in screening the service but in a delicious irony, which would have amused Michael no end, they had to abandon any plans because of their commitment to televise a one-day cricket match.)

Kell Hutchence and the remaining members of INXS were horrified to learn of Patricia's deal with Channel 7 — and extremely concerned about the whole idea of a televised service. The world had recently been exposed to the lavish, televised funeral of Princess Diana in London, and even the band understood that it was neither appropriate nor desirable to have live TV cameras inside the church for Michael's funeral. But in their own profound grief — and the realisation that they were witnessing the final moments of the band they had worked in for all their adult lives — INXS felt powerless. Out of respect to Michael's mother, the band decided that they would not enter into a bitter dispute with Michael's family over the format of the funeral.

Matters became even more bizarre when a distraught Paula Yates arrived in Sydney two days before the funeral and attempted to place her stamp on the proceedings. Her suggestion that the service might accommodate Tom Jones singing 'What's New Pussycat?' (Jones was in Australia at the time and attended the funeral, in the official party, as Paula's guest) was overridden. Just when Michael's family and closest friends should have been united, the massive rifts were apparent. Whether it was justified or not, Paula Yates found herself battling hostilities from both of Michael's parents. It was a living nightmare for all concerned.

Only Nick Cave knew how to deal with the politics of the funeral with a degree of dignity: he informed Channel 7 that they had been denied permission to film his song. Cave delivered a sombre and moving rendition of 'Into My Arms' (during which a fan attempted to fling himself from an upstairs balcony — creating a brief moment of hysteria in the church) and the TV coverage was forced to resort to a hastily compiled package of Michael's career highlights. Ironically, the TV cameras were denied not only the most poignant moment in the service, but also the most dramatic.

Michael would have been pleased with the turnout at his own funeral. Everyone was there: Paula and Tiger, of course; Kylie, Helena, Michelle Bennett, Kym Wilson and at least 20 other women Michael had loved at one point or another in his eventful life. Chris Murphy was there, as was Gary Grant, Phillip Mortlock, Mark Opitz, Nick Launay and virtually everyone who had ever been a part of the INXS inner sanctum, as well as every person of note in the Australian music industry; a swathe of leading models and actors; and Australia's rich and famous. Because the archbishop insisted that the public have access to the service, St Andrew's overflowed with fans.

Michael's entire family were there. When the time came to carry out the coffin strewn with irises and a small arrangement of lilies, his younger brother Rhett — in an insanely striped suit that had once belonged to Michael — shouldered the load with the five remaining members of INXS and walked slowly down the aisle.

As the coffin was loaded into a black hearse for its final journey to the cemetery, an enormous clap of thunder erupted above the cathedral. After weeks of drought, and an almost unbearably hot and humid afternoon, huge, heavy raindrops began falling. By the time the mourners walked outside the church, it was pouring with rain.

As the cars carrying the official mourning party pulled away from the cathedral, the personal divisions between the mourners intensified. The familial bonds blew apart in a violent and unexpected fashion in the hours after Michael was laid to rest. As hundreds of his friends from the music industry gathered for a lively wake at popular Oxford Street nightclub the Grand Pacific Blue Room (complete with complimentary champagne, finger food and the services of DJ Andy Glitre), Paula and Michael's family traded insults and blows.

'Like a lot of people in the business, I thought the service was a lot more religious and formal than I would have liked,' says Wilkins. 'It wasn't what many of us would have wanted for our own funeral, or what we would have imagined Michael's to be like, but as someone pointed out to me, funerals aren't for the person who's gone, they're for those who are left behind. I guess if it was what Michael's parents wanted then it was fair enough.'

In the weeks that followed, the local and international media went into a frenzy of coverage and speculation on the likely causes of Michael Hutchence's death. Although the investigating police always remained adamant that the cause of death was suicide, lurid rumours began circulating. At the peak of the hysteria, there was a rumour — so voracious that it was reported on TV news bulletins — that Kym Wilson had been charged with manslaughter and had committed suicide. There was never any basis to these rumours, a point Wilson was able to make herself when she sold her side of the story (to tabloid magazines in Australia and the UK) for A$150,000. 'It was a night catching up with this very close friend,' she related, 'trying to find out the result of a court case about his family.'

If many were shocked at Wilson's haste to get her story into print, they soon forgot their disbelief as virtually everyone with any connection to Michael, including his father, his step-sister and his partner Paula, also sold their stories to various glossy magazines around the world. It was a damning reflection of the corruptive powers of the media that even Michael's own, beloved father had retained the services of an agent. The asking price for an exclusive TV interview was A$175,000. Kell Hutchence, Kym Wilson and others were quick to point out that some or all of this money would be donated to Paula and Tiger.

Away from the headlines, the talk in the bars of Sydney and Melbourne — and among INXS fans on the Internet — focused almost exclusively on the possible causes of death. Michael's friends had plenty of theories. Because he had expressed an interest in auto-eroticism more than once, many believed that at least some of the stories could be true. Others were convinced that Michael really had been depressed — and that he was perfectly capable of killing himself.

Richard Lowenstein thought that Michael's emotional vulnerability in the hours after Kym Wilson and Andrew Rayment left the hotel caused his death. 'Michael always had a problem being left alone at the end of the night —

especially if it was a couple leaving together,' he commented to *Juice*. 'I've been doing all-nighters with Michael and I've seen it happen when couples leave together and his face would just fall. That was the time when he'd reach for the phone and make the call to Helena or Paula or Michelle. Why couldn't the couple who were there that morning see that, especially when one of them claims to have known Michael so well? It would be right in front of your face.

'The thought that someone might stop loving Michael was terrible to him. Michael hated fighting, he never wanted anyone to dislike him, even after a relationship. That ties in with being a performer, too: you want your entire audience to love you.'

Kell Hutchence — and many other members of Michael's family and inner circle of friends — blamed Bob Geldof's overbearing behaviour. 'He made their lives miserable,' Kell reflected. 'It's like he was on a vendetta — to get them. And that's really the truth of it. He created extraordinary situations and I think contributed very much to what happened.'

Although there was mounting evidence that Michael had taken his own life — and that he had many reasons to be depressed and angry, Paula Yates herself found the explanation implausible. 'I don't believe he would have left Tiger deliberately,' she commented after his death. 'I truly don't believe that, and I'm not just saying it to make me feel better or try to make Tiger feel better in the future. I just know him.'

Acknowledging that 'I don't think there's anything on earth Michael wouldn't do', Paula felt it was almost less difficult to face the prospect that Michael had died by misadventure in the pursuit of sexual gratification: 'I suppose it would be easier to bear, in a weird way, easier than thinking of someone you loved that much being in such despair. I think he was beside himself. With anger and a loss of hope, and pain, and missing the girls. And I think he was drunk.'

When the members of INXS finally broke their silence — in an interview with respected TV journalist George Negus several weeks after Michael's death — they seemed to think that suicide was the most likely cause of his death. Tim Farriss confirmed that Michael had been depressed for some time, to the extent that he had sometimes doubted his ability to perform a show. The band revealed that Michael had occasionally informed them of the extent of his personal tribulations in London, and they had gained a sense of the immense pressure he was under. 'In the end, you know, I think that there were certain elements in his life that he couldn't get on top of,' speculated Tim.

Andrew was one member of the band who was concerned to point out that whatever problems might have been causing Michael pain, the band was not one of them. Jon spoke of INXS as Michael's 'sanctuary' from the other problems in his life. Andrew also addressed the question of why even Michael's own band hadn't realised the extent to which their singer was falling apart. Everyone had known a different Michael Hutchence. He had been whatever people wanted him to be, and it was with an increasing uneasiness that the band realised that they might not have known the real Michael at all. At the very least, the Michael they had once known had been replaced by a sadder, more confused version. It was profoundly disturbing.

'It doesn't matter how much you think you know someone,' said Andrew. 'There's always what you see and what you don't see, and there's things in there that I know ... little jigsaw pieces that I can never quite put into place. It doesn't mean we weren't getting on or didn't see eye to eye or he didn't talk or whatever. I just think he felt it was his own life.'

Tim parted with some words of warning about the consequences of mixing anti-depressant medication with alcohol. 'The world should be very careful about taking anti-depressants — that's all I think. I think the whole thing is a very grey area and people should respect when they're putting things like that into their bodies just exactly what they're doing. I know there's been a lot of recent things, things like anti-depressants and alcohol mixed together making people suicidal, and I think the world's got to take a deeper look at it and make sure that we're not giving these people who ... have a chemical imbalance in their brain ... the wrong things. It's a sickness, it's not a decision they make with a clear head. I can't be angry at Michael because if he did take his own life, I feel he was sick.'

What else could INXS say? They were now just five middle-aged men and, brutal as it may seem to state it, they were now missing the one magic ingredient that had made them whole. If they had never paused to realise their luck in having found Michael Hutchence at Davidson High more than 20 years ago, they must certainly have been reminded of it now.

Despite the media's contortion of his personality, Michael had lived in the spotlight, a rare and beautiful creature. He had burnt his wings against the flames of pleasure and desire. And now, perhaps selfishly, certainly in a moment of exquisitely poignant timing, he had gone through the exit door. It's a door that all of us have access to but few of us choose to use.

Postscript

As the new year dawned, it became apparent that the memory of Michael Hutchence was not going to be allowed to fade quietly into obscurity. Nor was it likely that posthumous coverage would give due acknowledgment to his professional achievements. While the members of INXS continued to maintain a dignified silence, Michael's warring family persisted in dragging their personal vendettas through the pages of the media.

The bickering was seemingly endless. Indeed, the parties couldn't even agree on a suitable resting place for Michael's remains. Paula Yates was insistent that Michael's ashes should be returned to London; Kell and Rhett Hutchence were equally adamant that a part of Michael should remain in Sydney; Michael's mother — said to be writing a book about her son's life and amassing a collection of his personal effects — wanted the ashes to remain at her home in Queensland. In music business circles, wags borrowed cricketing terminology to describe the dispute as 'the battle for the Ashes'. Finally, on what would have been Michael's thirty-eighth birthday, Kell took matters into his own hands. He took one third of the ashes and, in the company of Rhett and members of INXS, scattered them over the waters of Sydney Harbour. The remaining two-thirds were divided in half and delivered to Patricia and Paula respectively.

The pain was not confined to private wrangles; it spilt out onto the printed page with alarming regularity and astonishing viciousness. In one article, Michael's half-sister Tina blamed Paula for all Michael's unhappiness. 'It's fair to say that Michael was very unhappy with Paula at the time of his death,' she said. 'Michael had no intention of marrying Miss Yates. People in Michael's inner circle knew he had been trying to get out of the relationship. He felt trapped and boxed in. Paula could change from timid to intimidating. Michael told me he wished he could have the same Paula back that he had fallen in love with.'

Although Rhett Hutchence had remained relatively silent since his brother's death, he felt moved to respond, making a statement that would seal a new alliance between Rhett, Kell and Paula. 'I am deeply saddened and embarrassed by what my step-sister Tina has said publicly about Paula and Michael's relationship,' he announced in a prepared statement. 'I believe this will hurt Michael's daughter, Tiger, very much, as the woman being so cruelly discussed is her mother — her only surviving parent. I know Michael would be horrified by members of his family publicly speculating about his private life and hurting Tiger in this way. It seems he has become an easy target for gossip mongers.'

The cause of much of the bickering, of course, was the touchy subject of Michael's estate. While estimates of the singer's wealth ranged as high as A$40 million, Michael's will revealed no such fortune. Indeed, on paper, his total assets —

after subtracting liabilities — amounted to less than A$1 million. According to an exhaustive report conducted by the *Sydney Morning Herald*, the remainder of Hutchence's wealth — including houses in France, London and Hong Kong and a number of Australian investment properties — was tied up in a virtually impenetrable web of discretionary trusts and holding companies controlled by Colin Diamond and Andrew Paul. The only family member named in the trust structures was Kell Hutchence and, to the chagrin of Paula Yates and other members of Michael's family, the structures appeared to have been deliberately established to prevent claims being made on Michael's estate.

Kell and other members of Michael's family went on record to state that the main beneficiary of Michael's fortune should be — and would be — his daughter. Michael's will nominated Tiger Lily as the recipient of 50 per cent of his fortune, with the remainder to be split equally between Paula, Kell, Tina, Rhett and Patricia. The executors of the will were listed as Colin Diamond and Andrew Paul — an arrangement that made several family members feel distinctly uneasy. Although Diamond and Paul approached the beneficiaries privately to assure them that income would be forthcoming, they went to great lengths to deny that Michael was the legal owner of many of his supposed assets. According to correspondence sent to Patricia Glassop, none of the properties Michael thought of as his own — the houses in Hong Kong, London and France, the investment properties in Queensland — were his at all. As other members of his family prepared to lay claims against the estate, it was still far from clear who would receive the funds if and when the financial web was finally unravelled.

On February 6 1998, the speculation surrounding the circumstances and cause of Michael's death were officially laid to rest with the release of the official coroner's report. The three-page document was notably short on vital details (the only 'new', albeit hardly surprising, piece of information was that cocaine was found in Michael's bloodstream). While NSW Coroner Derrick Hand had decided not to proceed with a court hearing into the causes of death, he was emphatic that there were no suspicious circumstances to warrant further discussion or investigation. The report left many questions unanswered. (For example, exactly what drugs were found in the body? And in what concentration?) It completely neglected a number of issues that were of interest to Michael's friends and family — such as why his camera was never found, or what became of the CD copy of his new album, which he was known to have with him on the night before his death. But for all the loose ends the report failed to resolve, it was comforting to have some kind of resolution.

Of course, the story of Michael Hutchence and INXS was not to be so easily resolved. Over the past 20 years, INXS have amassed an enormous reserve of previously unreleased material as well as hours of rehearsal tapes, demos, band jams and rarities. As the months passed and Michael's death began to recede, the band started holding loose discussions about the possibility of releasing this material — perhaps over several albums. If INXS had been in a state of slow but dignified decline in the years leading up to Michael's death, it now appeared likely that they would become another profitable fossil of the rock 'n' roll era — preserved by radio playlists and endless re-issues.

In early 1998, Martha Troup — still managing the band's international affairs — announced that Michael's solo recordings were being collated and assembled for release. The question was not *whether* to release them — the songs were easily good enough to warrant public exposure — but *how* to release them with a semblance of dignity.

Fittingly, the real closure for many came in late February when Michael's old mates — and friendly INXS rivals — U2 arrived in Australia for a long-awaited national tour. U2 have always possessed a natural ability to strike the appropriate emotional chord, and this genius did not desert them as they acknowledged the loss of a fellow traveller. The band were aware that they were on the Australian soil INXS had once trodden so proudly, and in each of their five Australian concerts, U2 fashioned a touching tribute to their departed friend.

In the audience for all the U2 shows were tens of thousands of INXS fans — the two bands had shared a common constituency, after all. In Sydney, the five remaining members of INXS, as well as Richard Lowenstein, Gary Grant, Helena Christensen and Rhett Hutchence, watched U2's emotional tribute from the shelter of the mixing desk enclosure. They were arm in arm as they shared a public outpouring of grief and love that was infinitely more poignant and appropriate than Michael's funeral.

After delivering the standard PopMart show — a performance dense with riveting musical drama and a collage of post-modern imagery — U2 concluded the set with their uplifting internationalist anthem 'One' accompanied by a video montage of departed rock stars on the giant monitors. The montage gave way to the image of a beating heart, and then to a shot of Michael Hutchence that remained on screen throughout the final number, a haunting version of a song U2 had never previously performed live, 'Wake Up Dead Man'. As the band filed silently from the stage, eschewing any thought of an encore, the house remained in darkness and the PA resounded with the strains of INXS's 'Never Tear Us Apart'.

Few bands would have been selfless enough to turn the spotlight away from themselves and onto another act entirely at the very climax of their show — and perhaps even fewer would be brave enough to leave their audience in such a sombre and reflective state. And yet oddly, as bolts of lightning and cracks of thunder gave way to rain that steadily increased from a few light drops into a tropical downpour, the mood was one of strange and magical elation. It had been one of the hottest Australian summers on record. Week after week of scorching days had passed without even a sign of rain. For the many friends and fans of Michael's at the U2 concert, it suddenly seemed as if there had been no rain since the steamy afternoon of his funeral.

It was as though the same water that annointed his mourners was drenching the crowd as they filed quietly from U2's show. It was cleansing water, healing water, and as it soaked the parched ground, it felt as if Michael Hutchence was finally passing into a dignified place, safe from all that he had feared and dreaded, safe from the paparazzi and the tabloid journalists, safe from harm. With time and distance, his life — and indeed his death — were taking their proper place in history. He would not be forgotten.

'I still haven't figured out quite how I feel about it,' Bono told a reporter during the Australian tour. 'I don't know whether I'm angry or guilty ... You always think if it's a mate that there's something you could have done. I still find it hard to figure it all out, because I had a conversation with him not that long ago where we talked about something like this, and we both agreed how dumb and selfish it would be, and Hutch was not at all selfish. He was a nice guy to be around.'

At the time of their apparent demise, INXS appear to be finding new life within the global culture of the Internet. In a virtual universe devoid of geographical borders and unfettered by constraining elements like time, age or mortality, the band have their opportunity to live on in the hearts of fans from South Australia to North America — and all points in between.

For those of us living in real time outside the all-enveloping Web, it is apparent that INXS are already being relegated to their place in music history. Although the band made music in the seventies that reflected the colliding forces of disco and post-punk rock 'n' roll, they will never be associated with that era. And although they made some great music in the nineties — music that reflected the weariness and post-modern ennui of a confused society and an increasingly fractured musical landscape, they will never be seen as representatives of that decade either.

For better or worse, Michael Hutchence and INXS will remain forever entwined with that decade of greed and wild extravagance, the eighties. The era of cocaine and long white stretch limousines. The era of glamour and superstardom. The era in excess.

List Of Sources

As well as my numerous interviews with INXS between 1980 and late 1997 and the interviews I conducted especially for this book, I also referred to the following sources:

'Kick Start', Toby Creswell, *Rolling Stone* (Australia), November 1987
'Fatal Attraction', Adrian Deevoy, *Q*, September 1988
'It Just Happened', Katherine Tulich, *Sun-Herald*, 7 January 1989
'The Man Who Fell to Earth', Giles Smith, *Q*, October 1989
'Michael 2 The Max', Toby Creswell, *Rolling Stone* (Australia), December 1989
'Michael Hutchence', Jim Farber, *Seventeen*, February 1990
'Hutchence Hollywood Debut', Matt White, *Daily Telegraph*, 26 March 1990
'X-Aspirations', John O'Donnell, *Rolling Stone* (Australia), November 1990
'Wolf In Sheep's Clothing', Mandi James, *The Face*, September 1991
'Rockfest to Fix Hospital's Bills', Glennys Bell, *The Bulletin*, 17 March 1992
'Mr INXSible', Deborah Cameron, *Sydney Morning Herald*, 28 March 1992
'Sydney Celebrates', Brett Thomas, *Sun-Herald*, 29 March 1992
'The Day Rock Lost Its Bad Name', Mike Coleman, *Sunday Telegraph*, 29 March 1992
'Organisers Hope Park Concert Raised $1.5m', Mark Riley, *SMH*, 30 March 1992
'Concert of a Lifetime', John Bilic, *Eastern Express*, 2 April 1992
'That Concert: An Excess of Cost Revealed', Sian Powell and Jon Casimir, *SMH*, 23 May 1992
'Sex, Drugs and Kylie Minogue', Serge Simonaert, *Woman's Day*, June 1993
'Dirty Deeds', Glenn A. Baker, *Rolling Stone* (Australia), August 1993
'Welcome to INXS', John Ellis Thomson, *CD Plus*, June 1994
'Beautiful Guy', Dylan Jones, *Cleo*, April 1994
'A Whopping Great Bloody Big Rock Star', Dave Cavanagh, *The Guardian*, 19 November 1994
'Split Personalities', Sandra Parson, *Telegraph Mirror*, 29 April 1995
'INXS Manager C. M. Murphy Resigns', Glenn A. Baker, *Billboard*, June 1995
'Yates' Aussie Sex Sizzler', Simon Kent, *Sun-Herald*, 13 August 1995
'In Bed With Paula Yates', Susan Chenery, *SMH*, 28 October 1995
'New Sensation', Shelli-Anne Couch and Moira Bailey, *Who Weekly*, 27 May 1996
'It's Heavenly In Sydney', Maggie Alderson, *SMH*, 20 September 1996
'Disgraceful', Jane Withers, *Elle*, November 1996
'Mercury's INXS Elegantly Returns From Its Time Off', Chuck Taylor, *Billboard*, 15 March 1997
'Just Happy Playing Daddy', Brett Thomas, *Sun-Herald*, April 1997
'Mr Sexcess', Miranda Sawyer, *The Observer*, 4 April 1997
'Love Is All You Need', Howard Johnson, *Q*, May 1997
'Succeeding Like INXS', Miranda Sawyer, *Herald Sun*, 4 September 1997
INXS interview with George Negus, December 1997
'Michael's Final Hours', Leigh Reinhold, *Women's Day*, 15 December 1997
'Michael Hutchence 1960–1997', Andrew Mueller, *Vox*, January 1998
'Late INXS Singer Driven to Succeed on Solo Debut', Gil Kaufman, *Addicted to Noise*, 29 Jan. 1998
'Tina Hutchence Speaks', *New Weekly*, February 1998
'The Last Time I Saw My Son', Marcus Casey, *Daily Telegraph*, 3 February 1998
Coroner's Report: Inquest Into the Death of Michael Kelland Hutchence, D. W. Hand (State Coroner), 6 February 1998
'No Rest, No Peace', Marcus Casey, *Daily Telegraph*, 14 February 1998
On Tour with INXS, Donald Robertson, Music Sales, 1986
INXS: The Official Inside Story of a Band on the Road, INXS and Ed St John, Mandarin, 1992
Kylie: An Unauthorised Biography, Dino Scatena, Penguin, 1997

Index